W9-DIG-310

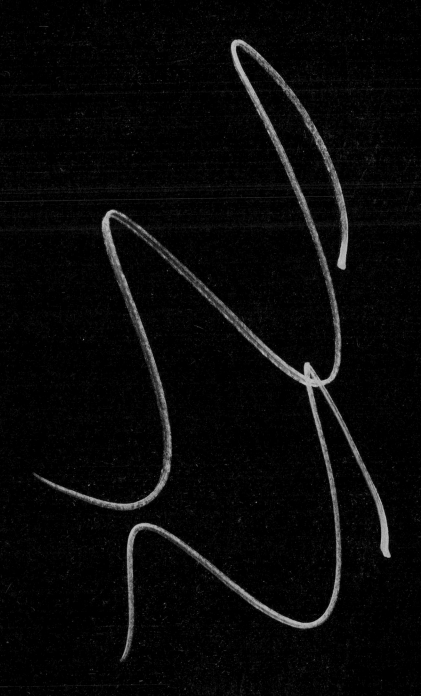

COLUMBIA HISTORY OF URBAN LIFE
Kenneth T. Jackson, GENERAL EDITOR

Adapting to Abundance

COLUMBIA HISTORY OF URBAN LIFE

Kenneth T. Jackson, GENERAL EDITOR

Adapting to Abundance

Jewish Immigrants, Mass Consumption, and the Search for American Identity

Andrew R. Heinze

Columbia University Press   New York

COLUMBIA UNIVERSITY PRESS

NEW YORK   OXFORD

Copyright © 1990 Columbia University Press

All rights reserved

Library of Congress Cataloging-in-Publication Data

Heinze, Andrew R.
Adapting to abundance : Jewish immigrants,
mass consumption, and the search for
American identity / Andrew R. Heinze.
p.   cm. — (The Columbia history of urban life)
Includes bibliographical references.
ISBN 0-231-06852-2 (alk. paper)
1. Jews, East European—United States—Cultural assimilation.
2. Jews—United States—Cultural assimilation.
3. Consumers—United States—Attitudes.
4. Jews—United States—Identity.
5. Immigrants—United States—Social life and customs.
6. United States—Ethnic relations.
I. Title.   II. Series.
E184.J5H535   1990
305.8'924073—dc20   89-70776
CIP

Casebound editions of Columbia University Press books are Smyth-sewn
and printed on permanent and durable acid-free paper

Printed in the United States of America

c 10 9 8 7 6 5 4 3 2 1

For Joanne

Contents

Contents

Acknowledgments

It gives me great pleasure to thank the people who supported me in the writing of this book. Their help was essential.

Gunther Barth at the University of California, Berkeley, was a consistent source of constructive criticism. I was deeply impressed by his standards of scholarship and writing. Disciplining my thinking without imposing on my thoughts, he approached the ideal expressed by Kahlil Gibran, who wrote of the true teacher: "If he is indeed wise he does not bid you enter the house of his wisdom, but rather leads you to the threshold of your own mind."

Moses Rischin of the San Francisco State University graciously agreed to read and comment on the study. True to his own high standards of scholarship, he made excellent criticisms and suggestions, which I tried to incorporate as much as possible in the book.

Virginia Herman was a loyal comrade, always willing to listen to my ideas, no matter how far-fetched, and always able to bring a sharp intelligence to bear on the reasonable ones. Michael Shiloh generously shared his equipment and technical skill so that I could work on a computer. Ron Zboray offered fine criticisms on various chapters of the manuscript, and Mary Saracino raised good questions about the conceptual framework of the study. Samuel Haber served not just as a reader but also as a friend, one who boosted my spirits at critical moments. Carolyn Porter gave kind reviews of an early draft.

The assistance of the inter-library borrowing office at Berkeley was key. Supervisor Jo Lynn Milardovich and staff-members Kathleen Messer, Leon Megrian, Rhio Barnhart, and Helen Ram were consistently helpful and cheerful in handling my many requests for documents from New York City and elsewhere. Daniel Soyer of the YIVO Institute for Jewish Research located some good articles on Jewish vacationing. The Eugene McCormac and Max Farrand Fellowships from the history department at the University of California, Berkeley allowed me to devote two semesters to research and writing. The helpfulness of the history department at the San José State University facilitated the revision of the manuscript. I would also like to thank the Lucius N. Littauer Foundation for a timely grant that helped me prepare the manuscript for publication.

My editor at the Columbia University Press, Kate Wittenberg, has been a source of encouragement and friendship. Her enthusiasm about the book inspired me more than she knows. I am grateful as well for the suggestions made by the reviewer of the manuscript at Columbia.

Many other friends, teachers, and librarians who are not named here helped me in one way or another as I worked on the study. They are all appreciated.

I view this book as being essentially a family affair, and the most gratifying part of these acknowledgments comes in expressing my sincere thanks for the moral support I was given by relatives. For their good words and thoughts, my appreciation goes out in alphabetical order to Helaine and Eric Freede, Karen Freede-Kuvach, Joan, Anthony, Cassie, Toni Marie, Michelle, and little Anthony Giardello, Peter and Eric Heinze, Marilyn Houpt, Scott Liebowitz, Leslie Oster, and John Williams.

It saddens me that two of my grandparents, Anne Houpt and Fred Heinze, saw the beginnings but not the end of this book; it thrills me that Hannah Heinze will see both.

The debt I owe my parents, Frank and Dolores Heinze, is too large to be either expressed or repaid. They gave everything a parent can give a child.

Justine and Aliyah Heinze-Giardello have given everything a child can give a father. The writing of this book was eased and improved by the delight of their company.

I cannot adequately acknowledge the support of Joanne Felicia Giardello. Her insight, humor, and devotion sustained me; the depth of her spirit has inspired me always.

This book is dedicated to her.

Adapting to Abundance

Introduction

Consumption: A Bridge Between Cultures

Material possessions are intrinsic to human identity. Garments, books, pictures, houses, and many other things are second only to physical attributes like limbs and hair, and to intimate relations with other people, in defining who we are. Possessions have thus been referred to as "extensions of self," objects with which people affirm their personalities and whose loss may be mourned or deeply regretted.[1] Long ago, G. W. F. Hegel recognized the potential vitality of material goods when he argued that to own something is to infuse it with one's character.[2]

The identity of a culture, too, depends upon the use and perception of things. "Culture" has been defined as a society's way of life and perspective on the world. In differentiating one society from another, a perspective is communicated through both language and nonverbal forms, which include not only art, architecture, music, and dance but also ordinary decorations and substances such as clothing and food. Thus, *culture* consists of the "accumulated resources, immaterial as well as material" which a people inherits, employs, modifies, and transmits from generation to generation.[3]

Because culture is broadly inclusive, the consumption of products and services plays a large part in defining it. One of the first scholars to focus

1

on the cultural role of consumption, the anthropologist Mary Douglas, has suggested that "the most general objective of the consumer can only be to construct an intelligible universe with the goods he chooses." As a result of the collective effort of a people to create meaning through these choices, material goods comprise "the visible part of culture."[4] Understood in this way, rather than as the flotsam and jetsam of day-to-day living, the seemingly trivial acts of acquiring new products assume a new importance.

In modern societies of large, often diverse, populations enjoying a wide range of products and conveniences, there will be less uniformity of consumption than in more closely knit traditional societies. A heterogenous nation like the United States would seem to lack a common perspective and mode of consumption. Yet, despite many differences of taste among many distinct groups of people, the majority of Americans have over time developed a uniquely high standard of living which has been identified and widely publicized as "the American standard of living." If there is any single factor of consumption that unifies Americans, it is the emphasis on consumption itself, the belief that individuals should expect an increasingly rich choice of products.[5] Characteristically American, this expectation has been based on the historical phenomenon of sustained material abundance.

The effect of abundance on American culture was addressed over thirty years ago by historian David Potter in a provocative analysis entitled *People of Plenty: Economic Abundance and the American Character.* Potter had been inspired by an earlier student of the national "character," Frederick Jackson Turner. In 1893, Turner transformed the study of American history by suggesting that the frontier experience had produced a unique American culture, differing fundamentally from that of Europe.[6]

Reconsidering the "Turner thesis," Potter argued that it was not the frontier per se, but the prospect of material abundance represented by the frontier, which made America different. Abundance, first in the form of land, and ultimately in the form of mass-produced consumer goods, paved the way for American democratic values by constantly enlarging the proverbial "American pie" which individuals sought a piece of. Belief in the value of individual attainment, personal mobility, and equal opportunity, according to Potter, rested on an extraordinarily expansive economy that allowed the great majority of people to improve their material condition, if not always their occupational position. Even though opportunities for moving from common labor to self-employment may have decreased over time, the steady growth of mass consumption sustained a comparatively high standard of living. As a result, Americans upheld their expectation and conviction that every individual should aspire to comfort and security.[7]

Although a few distinguished historians have linked American identity to the phenomenal rise of mass consumption in the nineteenth and early twentieth centuries, Potter's thesis has lain dormant for a generation, often cited but rarely extended or adapted by scholars.[8] One reason for this has been a great reluctance to speak of American identity. In the 1960s and 1970s, the persistence of distinct ethnic groups within the United States seemed to destroy permanently the mythic image of the nation as a vast "melting pot." Since then, scholars have hesitated to describe a national identity that would embrace the vast majority of citizens. Yet, as Philip Gleason, a noted historian of American Catholicism, has observed, Americans of all backgrounds have been united by a commitment to the democratic ideas that were established in the Declaration of Independence and the Constitution.[9]

It should be recognized, too, that the nation has been united by another goal, one that is both more tangible and more accessible than lofty political values—the American standard of living, which Potter felt was so basic to the maintenance of democracy in the United States. Whereas the commitment to individual liberty and social equality has wavered, Americans have been steadfastly unanimous in their pursuit of an affluent lifestyle. Almost certainly, the millions of immigrants from abroad have understood American identity to imply not only the freedom to vote and speak freely but also the ability to enjoy the fruits of the economic system in which they labored, the ability, in effect, to live as an affluent person would have lived in their native lands.

If the American people has been characterized by a peculiar faith in the principle of a rising standard of living, then the adaptation of immigrants to the "perspective of abundance" must be considered an essential part of Americanization. Most newcomers to the United States underwent a virtual revolution in material conditions and expectations, and their specific response to the American standard of living was determined by the culture in which they were raised.

For eastern European Jews, who immigrated in large numbers during the decades before World War I, adapting to abundance proved to be a complex experience. Suddenly, poor newcomers from backwater *shtetls**

---

*With the exception of words such as *shofar* and *challah*, which are common in English, and of newspaper titles, whose spelling has been standardized in the historical literature, Yiddish words in this book have been transliterated according to the guidelines of Uriel Weinreich's *Modern English-Yiddish Yiddish-English Dictionary* (New York, 1968).

3

and overcrowded ghettos found themselves in a world where spending rather than saving money was promoted; where the rising standard of living had to be reconciled with religious customs that had been fitted to the fact of ongoing scarcity; where a new suit of clothes was understood to be an instrument of cultural transformation; where women, as rulers of domestic consumption, assumed a new power over the social adjustment of their families; where such symbols of affluence as the vacation, the parlor, and the piano were put at the disposal of wage earners; where modern corporations, instead of local shopkeepers, solicited business through sophisticated advertising, instead of countertop chatter; where sellers of consumer goods had a mecca of consumers before them and could thus become magnates in the province of mass consumption.

As consumers, Jews sought important elements of American identity more quickly and thoroughly than other groups of newcomers. As entrepreneurs in consumer-oriented trade, they, more than others, enriched the potent environment of urban consumption which had become such a distinctive feature of American society. Although a few social scientists have tentatively proposed that American Jews are innovative consumers, the idea has remained inchoate and without historical foundation.[10] In building that foundation, this study will attempt to show that consumption was central to American acculturation.

Impoverished newcomers of all backgrounds relished the symbolic as well as the physical properties of the American standard of living. As if to prove the axiom that "clothes make the man," almost all immigrants sought a new suit of clothes as an emblem of their desire to move up in the world. The unusual interest of Jews in American dress, however, signaled a particularly keen awareness that items of consumption in general constituted important building blocks of American identity.

Whereas most other newcomers initially retained solid bonds to their native lands, eastern European Jews were fleeing a particularly insidious persecution, and they immigrated with an intense desire, as well as a distinct ability, to fit quickly into American society. This predisposition, in addition to the special role of the Jewish woman as the manager of domestic consumption, sensitized the group to the American creed of the rising standard of living.

These aspiring people identified several components of the American urban lifestyle, beyond fashionable dress, as especially meaningful: the vacation, the parlor, the piano, and nationally advertised products. Compared to immigrants in general, their pursuit of these ends was vigorous. More than simply commodities, these things were evocative aspects of American culture. The vacation in the mountains or by the sea embodied

4

the Jewish vision of an earthly paradise, a haven from persecution; the well-furnished parlor, crowned with a piano, supported American democratic ideals by upholding the inherent dignity of the ordinary family, despite the unsettling conditions of immigrant life in the city; the famous brand-named product testified to the superiority of the American system of mass production and distribution, which was viewed patriotically as a pacesetter of Western civilization. Thus, for immigrants, these consumer goods had more than practical and social functions. They were culturally effective as well. Easier to comprehend than the English language or the vote, they served as the most accessible tools with which Jewish newcomers could forge an American Jewish identity.

The making of this new identity depended on the fusion of Jewish habits from eastern Europe with urban American ways. A fundamental part of traditional Jewish culture was engaged, both positively and negatively, by the immigrants' pursuit of the American standard of living. For centuries, Jews had used items of luxury in the celebration of the Sabbath and holidays in order to deepen their distinction between the holy and the mundane spheres of life. During those special times, the humblest Jew was thought to be blessed with a foretaste of God's splendor, which was signified by prized things reserved exclusively for the occasion. The distinction between the holy and the mundane was bound to collapse in the American city, where luxuries were routinely converted into necessities. Not only did the holy days lose the support of material luxury, but, signaling the eminent decline of traditional Judaism in America, the Sabbath, the proverbial "queen" of pious Jews, became a shopping day.

Yet, newcomers also found that American abundance added a dimension to the holidays that anchored Jewish identity in the new world. By the turn of the century, when the great migration from eastern Europe was in full swing, they were expressing their dual loyalties as Jews and Americans by integrating mass-marketed luxuries into major celebrations. On Sukkot, they acknowledged as part of God's bounty not just the agricultural harvest referred to in scripture but also the feat of American manufactured abundance; Chanukah was elevated in the hierarchy of festivals and infused with the spirit of shopping that characterized the American Christmas; Passover was reoriented, so that this festival of festivals came to reflect the anticipation of higher living standards as well as the remembrance of spiritual captivity and liberation.

If the religious traditions of the shtetl had accustomed Jews to think of luxuries as a type of instrument for dignifying the individual on holy days, the secular American environment refocused the awareness. Finding themselves in a society that seemed to worship the principle of social equality, newcomers were quick to detect the democratic symbolism of mass-marketed luxuries in America. Their traditional culture thus helped them realize that Americans sought, in the realm of consumption, a parity with each other that was unattainable in the world of capital and labor. By recognizing and utilizing American merchandise as democratic symbols, Jewish newcomers found a way to express social aspirations that had smoldered in Europe.

The Jewish response to American advertising exemplified the merger of old and new habits bearing on consumption. By virtue of its distinctive characteristics, the Yiddish press attracted national advertisers and assimilated the prevailing American style of promotion. Recognizing eastern European Jews as a potential market, consumer-oriented corporations stressed the capacity of the latest brand-named products to meet the special needs of these newcomers. In return, the comparatively cosmopolitan outlook, the old appreciation for festive luxury, and the unique dietary concerns of Jews impelled them to find these modern products acceptable. The relatively quick response of eastern European Jews to modern American advertising illustrated the cultural flexibility of these newcomers, who applied some inherited attitudes of the shtetl to the novel conditions of "mass society."

Transplanted in an urban terrain that thrived on mass consumption, the traditional Jewish talent for marketing consumer goods attained full blossom. By expanding the prospects of the urban consumer, Jewish entrepreneurs left the mark of the immigrant generation on American culture. Although eastern European Jews entered and flourished in a number of consumer businesses, they actually changed the face of two commercial occupations, street marketing and movie marketing. In New York City, Jewish peddlers turned street marketing from a simple form of retailing into an important forum for mass consumption. In cities across the country, Jewish merchants changed the form and content of the American cinema by devising a new method of marketing films. They transformed a crude type of entertainment into the monument of mass leisure within the short span of a decade. Jewish innovation in street marketing illustrated, in a local context, what Jewish innovation in film marketing had writ large—that immigrants could refashion those aspects of the American environment which their traditional culture had prepared them to understand.

As the twentieth century progressed, Jews of eastern European origin would assume increasing importance in the development of the newest media of mass consumption. The guiding spirit of the Radio Corporation of America (RCA) and the National Broadcasting Company (NBC) was

Consumption: Bridge Between Cultures

David Sarnoff, who left a shtetl in the Russian province of Minsk at the age of nine; that of the Columbia Broadcasting System (CBS) was William Paley, the son of a Russian Jew who became a successful cigar manufacturer in Philadelphia. A keen sense of what American consumers expected from radio, and, later, television, fueled the rise not only of these businessmen but of a host of producers, writers, and performers whose names have become almost synonymous with urban entertainment over the past six decades. The organic connection of mass entertainment to American identity can be illustrated simply by citing "God Bless America," "White Christmas," and "Easter Parade," a few of the songs composed by Irving Berlin, who came to America by way of Siberia in 1893 as four-year-old Izzy Baline. Amounting to a revolution in the world of American consumers, the contributions of famous individuals rested on the broad foundation of cultural exchange that marked the adaptation of eastern European Jews to American society between 1880 and 1914.

Because American abundance affected many areas of Jewish culture, from the celebration of holidays to the relation of the sexes, attitudes toward leisure and social status, and methods of selling merchandise, a study of Jewish consumption in urban America is a study of profound cultural change. It is a study of intense *acculturation*, because the meeting of two different cultures left a deep impression on each, turning old world Jews into urban Americans and turning the American city into a more sophisticated place. While the study of consumption as a means of adaptation is vital to an understanding of American immigration in general, it is indispensable to the story of the Jewish response to modern society.

It has become common over the last few decades for historians to try to reconstruct the way of life of ordinary people who left behind few written documents. Yet, scholars have overlooked a virtual goldmine of evidence about habits of consumption that would broaden our understanding of how immigrants adapted to American society.

Stirred by the struggle of newcomers with adversity, historians have naturally been attracted by its tragic and noble aspects, which embrace so much of American history. The shock of alienation from all that had been familiar in the lands of origin, the exploitation of human beings for the sake of their labor, the degradation of souls unsuited to the new environment—these disturbing elements of American immigration have been clearly identified. Inspiring expressions of collective determination on the part of newcomers have also been studied. The formation of religious bodies, labor unions, and benevolent institutions, the growth of political awareness and power, the achievement of economic success, the adaptation of families, the rise of artists and intellectuals—all these events have been appropriately depicted to show the resilience of the human spirit.

The quest for what is noble in the heritage of American immigration has yielded a *production-oriented* history, in which people appear as vital producers of labor, and producers, as well, of money, families, religion, politics, art, and intellectual life. As consumers, however, immigrants have been rendered almost faceless.

The neglect of consumption as a historical factor reflects a general tendency among scholars to consider production, the use of capital and labor, as the basis of social relationships.[11] Not what a person buys and uses, but what a person does for a living, has been perceived as the key to his or her social identity. This bias, in turn, reflects a subtle moral attitude toward production and consumption that is rooted in language itself. Whereas "producing" suggests the positive act of creation, "consuming" implies destruction and waste. The profoundly negative meaning of *consumption* is conveyed dramatically by its application to a dreadful disease, one which, incidentally, plagued Jewish immigrants in American cities.

Mesmerized by the positive aura of production, historians have missed an abundance of evidence that will shed light on the role of consumption in the adaptation of immigrants.[12] The stigma of consumption has even led some to perceive the desire for more and better things as an obstacle, instead of an aid, to the healthy adjustment of foreigners in America.[13] Yet, far from being an engine of degeneration, the activity of consumption, in general, is an act by which people convert the stagnant inventory of factories and stores into personal possessions capable of signifying one's attitude toward and place within society.[14] In the context of immigration, the consumption of American products becomes a viable way to express a change in identity, as newcomers transfer themselves psychologically from the old world to the new. The role of material goods in bridging the gap between cultures, in forging a meaningful cultural identity, has thus far been poorly understood by social scientists.[15]

Students of assimilation have long recognized that the adoption of certain American products and styles was one of the first steps taken by immigrants in order to fit into a strange society, but this aspect of cultural change has been subject to interpretation that is often cursory or ambiguous. In 1915, Horace Kallen, one of the early defenders of cultural pluralism in American life, contended that "Americanization" seemed to mean the adoption of American clothes and manners, in addition to American speech and political attitudes.[16] Of these three keys to the new society, "clothes and manners" were evidently the most readily under-

8

stood and easily acquired. That they could be attained easily, however, seemed to diminish their significance. In a 1921 study of newcomers adjusting to American society, sociologists Robert Park and Herbert Miller argued that the initial changes made by the immigrant, those "relating to dress, manners, and the other signs which will betray him as a 'greenhorn,' " were "more or less superficial."[17]

The idea that consumption was relatively superficial to the adaptation of immigrants gained strength from sociologist Milton Gordon's influential analysis of *Assimilation in American Life*, which appeared in 1964. Gordon divided the cultural traits of an ethnic group into two categories, "intrinsic" and extrinsic." Prominent among the intrinsic traits were religious beliefs and practices, ethical values, musical tastes, folk recreational patterns, and literature, all of which Gordon deemed to be "essential and vital ingredients of the group's cultural heritage." Like Kallen, and like Park and Miller, Gordon referred specifically to dress and manners, which he identified as extrinsic traits, those features that were "external" to the "core" of the group's ethnic identity.[18]

The variety of activities comprising consumption was not closely considered in the theory of intrinsic and extrinsic traits, which Gordon admitted to be a tentative concept. In the highly commercialized society of the United States, some elements of consumption, such as popular entertainment, would influence the "folk recreational patterns," musical tastes, and literature that were categorized as intrinsic to ethnic identity. Yet others, such as modes of clothing and household furnishing, would clearly seem to belong to that group of external features that comprised "the first of the types of cultural assimilation to occur when a minority group arrives on the scene."[19] When it has not been dismissed as an uneventful force in the making of Americans, the complex activity of consumption has defied clear-cut analysis.

The significance of consumption has been further obscured by the belief that integration into American society had to be gradual. Mastery of English has usually been considered the essential first step in the process, if only because this mastery was often necessary for economic advancement.[20] In addition to learning American speech, participation in American institutions appeared to be the essential way to develop a new cultural identity. Labor unions, social clubs, churches, schools, and political bodies furnished newcomers with a sense of those attitudes that were approved by the native-born. Containing the structure of American thought and custom, the language and the institutions of the United States offered the passwords of the society to everyone who spent the time and energy necessary to understand them.

Consumption: Bridge Between Cultures

Supporting the idea that American identity had to be methodically earned, scholars have often interpreted the American standard of living primarily as a reward for economic success. According to a recent evaluation of the immigrant experience in urban America, the pursuit of comfort and status through the American lifestyle was generally restricted to families that had attained relative affluence. The proverbial "promise" of American life, the prospect of material improvement, was supposedly lost on the majority of immigrants, who failed to make a lot of money.[21]

A tendency to portray immigrants as ascetic has also strengthened the notion that the advantages of mass consumption came to be appreciated only after economic improvement had been secured. Accustomed in their native lands to material standards that were far lower than those enjoyed by city people in America, the multitude of newcomers from eastern and southern Europe allegedly maintained a depressed condition of daily life as they saved money in the hope of moving up the economic ladder. By focusing on long-term economic gains, some of the most important studies of "upward mobility" among American immigrants have inadvertently perpetuated the mythic idea that newcomers practiced "ruthless underconsumption" in order to achieve a more secure economic position.[22] The outstanding record of Jewish economic success appeared to substantiate the belief that these immigrants came to America endowed with the so-called "middle class" traits that were supposed to win wealth: foresight, sobriety, and the willingness to save money by deferring gratification in the present for the sake of future rewards.[23]

The rich documentation of Jewish immigrant life in urban America, however, undermines the stereotype of the deliberately ascetic newcomer. Embedded in the vivid chronicles of the Yiddish press, outlined in the accounts of American journalists, and articulated in the prolific, sharply realistic fiction of Abraham Cahan, the saga of urban consumption among the majority of eastern European Jews was one of swift and radical change in the style of life. Acquiring American speech, participating in American institutions, and making economic advances were important to the search for a new cultural identity, but vast numbers of people with little sense of the language and limited exposure to institutions were engaging, virtually from the moment they entered the streets of the city, in a new cycle of consumption that defined a uniquely American approach to life. With the exception of the slim minority of individuals who were alienated from the economic and social activities on which American society was based, immigrants explored a whole range of products and

10

services that pulled them into the new culture and uprooted them from the old.

In order to introduce a study of consumption among eastern European Jews in America, several points about the time period, 1880–1914, and about the nature of the analysis must be made.

The reputation of the 1920s as the dawn of the "age of mass consumption" has obscured the importance of the decades between the Civil War and World War I. In the aftermath of the Great War and prior to the Great Depression, American consumers were suddenly deluged by a host of flamboyant products. Electrical appliances transformed the home; the automobile appeared at popular prices, instantly endowing people with another dimension of personal freedom; and huge institutions of credit arose to minister to the demand for such expensive products. The appearance of these items, of the credit necessary to afford them, and of the advertising used to sell then, has prompted historians to speculate that Americans suddenly acquired a consumption-oriented frame of mind that nullified the old-fashioned, Protestant value of frugality.[24]

Yet, the technologically flamboyant products of the 1920s can more profitably be viewed as an extension of patterns of consumption that were established during the nineteenth century. By the 1880s, Americans had already effected a major shift in the proportion of their budgets devoted to expensive durable items, expanding this allowance from 2 percent at mid-century to 11 percent, a level that remained static until the period after World War II.[25] Underpinning the purchase of luxuries like the piano and the gas stove, the installment plan had become a staple of American consumers long before the rise of large credit companies in the late 1910s and 1920s.[26]

Based on the mechanization of industry and on the extension of railroads, a mass market of products supported the rise of the commercialized and mechanized home between 1870 and 1900. As early as 1830, a number of household furnishings had been transformed from homemade into store-bought goods in the industrial regions of the United States. During the late nineteenth century, however, the change in domestic life was phenomenal. By 1880, the laborious making of men's and boys' clothing at home had virtually ended, and, within the next two decades, women's and girls' garments also appeared on the shelves of the department store. At the same time, the marketing of canned and bottled condiments, preserves, soups, beans and vegetables, and baby foods freed women from much of the tedious preparation of foods. Stoves fueled by oil and gas, better washing machines and wringers, set tubs, running water, and lighter irons and kitchen utensils reduced the hauling, lifting, and handling that made housework so onerous and time-consuming.[27] The multiplication of domestic devices prompted *Good Housekeeping* to comment in 1887 that "housekeeping is getting to be ready made, as well as clothing."[28] Durable goods for the living room and the bathroom also came into their own during the final decades of the century. In Grand Rapids and other midwestern cities, large furniture factories mass-produced attractive wooden tables, chairs, sofas, cabinets, sideboards, and bureaus for the average home. Glistening porcelain bathtubs and toilets emerged to sanitize and refine the bathroom of modern apartments.[29]

The search for a fuller standard of material life was aided by a long decline of prices from the the 1870s through the 1890s, but it was the inflationary period of the early twentieth century that witnessed the signs of a boom in the spending of consumers. A rising cacophony of complaints about the "high cost of living" testified amply to the fact that city people, having emerged from the depression of 1893–1897, were increasingly impatient to enjoy life once again, but in higher style.[30] Though punctuated by several recessions, the Progressive Era was a time of prosperity. Whereas the subsequent inflation of 1917 to 1929 battened off the shortages of wartime and presaged a great economic collapse, the modest increase of retail prices during the first decade and half of the century reflected the rising aspirations of urban consumers. As a government report stated in 1910, one of the most potent causes of the inflation was "the general advance of the standard of living throughout all the ranks of the population, from the highest to the lowest."[31]

Thus, Jewish newcomers from eastern Europe arrived in the United States at a moment of great expectations on the part of urban consumers. The abundance of land that had originally lured immigrants and sustained a distinctly American faith in the future was now accompanied, and partly replaced, by the abundance of commodities and leisure pursuits in the city. As dramatic as this evolution was to Americans, it was an even more potent stimulus to the imagination of newcomers from impoverished homelands abroad. The psychological dimension of American abundance, the subtle yet salient attitude that had turned a disparate populace of hopeful immigrants and migrants into a "people of plenty," infused the experience of eastern European Jews, shaping the overall pattern of their response to urban America.

Like any analytical tool, the concept of consumption as the vital point of Jewish adaptation to American society accentuates one aspect of the human experience as it relegates others to the background. In reality, the responses of eastern European Jews to the American city formed a complex whole. The "stress of life," as psychologist Hans Selye has referred to the creative and exhausting tasks that people set for themselves, permeated every sphere of the immigrant experience. At the workplace and the synagogue, in the classroom and the meeting hall, Jews conducted the exhilarating yet troublesome search for an American identity. In countless areas of endeavor and forms of expression, the task was pursued. That I have chosen to dwell on the fashionably dressed crowds of the city streets, on the carefully decorated parlors of the tenement dwellers, on the curbside of the pushcart peddler, and on the advertising section of the daily newspaper, does not mean that the stage of Jewish life in the city had no other sets.

For the purposes of analysis, I have focused on the mass of documentary evidence suggesting the largely untold story of the immigrant as a consumer. To flesh out this story in a way that illuminates the powerful influence of material abundance on American attitudes and on the Jewish response to American culture, some rough edges have inevitably been smoothed out. Whereas the experience of human beings is full of contradiction and ambiguity, the task of historical analysis demands passionate and almost singleminded attention to one focal point of life. In arguing that Jewish newcomers fairly rapidly adopted and extended urban habits of consumption, this study will have to pass over some of the impulses that pulled Jews back from the new society. There were numbers of people, particularly among the Hasidic Jews and the elderly, who found it undesirable or impossible to conform to the pattern of American Jewish consumption, who diverged from the path of the majority. The presence of counter tendencies, however, does not invalidate a concept. Consequently, it is my hope that the rendering of historical evidence here will persuade the reader that an overlooked region of the immigrant experience in America, the region of getting and spending, is a fruitful topic of our history.

By focusing on a particular group of people undergoing the specific historical experience of immigration and acculturation, this study is able to examine consumption more comprehensively than usual. Because consumption covers such a range of activities, it has been difficult to interpret as a general phenomenon. Recently, a few imaginative and perceptive scholars have made generalizations about the role of consumption in human societies, but the immensity of the subject has defied the creation of unified theories.[32] Historians have normally approached the topic of consumption indirectly, by breaking it down into specific elements such as food, drink, clothing, home furnishings, housing, and activities such as shopping, driving, and leisure-seeking, which includes observing sporting events, vacationing, attending vaudeville, theater, concerts, movies, and nightclubs, reading books, magazines, and newspapers, listening to radio and records, and watching television. Each of these has been studied as a distinct subject, often by scholars with specific interests in the fields of biological science, technology, museum studies, architecture, mass communications, city planning and public policy, women's history, urban history, and business history. Rich information has been garnered about each subject in isolation.

Yet, because these studies focus on objects and activities, rather than on people, they are incapable of addressing the large question of how people use a range of products and services simultaneously, so as to shape their world. In order to gain this type of insight, the unit of study must be human, not material—an individual, a family, a social or ethnic group, a community, a city, or a nation.

Although this study does not attempt to encompass all aspects of consumption, and deliberately avoids some which might merit books in themselves, such as drinking, housing, and reading, its scope allows us to reflect broadly on the meaning of consumption for people in a state of change. In this context, activities as disparate as clothing, home furnishing, vacationing, and advertising are integrated, each one interpreted as part of a concerted effort by immigrants to acquire a new cultural identity.

By focusing on the shared meaning of these commodities within a specific group of people, I hope to illuminate the unclear concept of "symbolic consumption."[33] One of the most productive methods for studying the symbolic importance of products is to isolate a group of consumers who would be likely to have a common perception of certain objects. In the world of Jewish newcomers, the new suit of clothes, the piano and the parlor, the vacation, and the nationally advertised product became *symbolic* luxuries, luxuries because they were previously unattainable to most eastern European Jews, and symbolic because they stood for something other than what they were.

Wealthy Americans who could afford custom-made clothing and furniture tended to view the mass-marketed merchandise of the American factory as cheap and tawdry. But, to poor newcomers, and to the majority of Americans as well, the new staples of mass consumption that emerged in the late nineteenth century were luxuries—they represented a great improvement over the things they had grown up with. Furthermore, the American system of mass-marketing could even define an item with little intrinsic value as a luxury by applying to it a well-respected brand name, as was the case with Crisco vegetable shortening or Borden's condensed milk. By virtue of this capacity, Metropolitan life insurance could plausibly be categorized as a luxury in the world of immigrants, because it carried an impressive *American* title that contrasted with the "generic" product of the mutual aid society.

The mass-marketed products composing the bulk of the American standard of living may be defined as luxuries not simply because they contrasted with the more modest commodities of the eastern European shtetl but also because they had communicative power. Social scientists have pointed out that luxury items tend to have a "rhetorical" capacity in addition to a practical use.[34] The most conspicuous goals of many Jewish immigrants as consumers—fashionable clothing, a piano in a parlor, a summer vacation, nationally advertised brands—comprised a symbolic "package" with a distinct message.[35] Whether or not these luxury items were linked in the minds of consumers, possession of most or all of them proclaimed silently that the newcomer was a prospective citizen, and not the "wretched refuse" of Europe's "teeming shore," to cite the inscription on the Statue of Liberty penned by Emma Lazarus, a member of New York City's Sephardic Jewish elite. As a badge of the desire for citizenship, such a package was easier to obtain than the intellectual "possessions" that symbolized American identity: knowledge of the Constitution and the great presidents.

To facilitate the analysis of a phenomenon as broad and unwieldy as urban consumption, the Lower East Side of New York City has been used as a geographical anchor. The dominant habits of urban consumers appeared throughout the cities of the United States, and the adoption of those habits by eastern European Jews occurred wherever that populace settled in numbers. By no coincidence, these immigrants were attracted overwhelmingly to New York, a city of unparalleled vistas for consumers seeking Jewish as well as American luxuries, and for entrepreneurs looking to satisfy the unquenchable thirst of the American people for better products. One of the primary Jewish products to emerge from the Lower East Side of New York City, the Yiddish newspaper, provided accounts of immigrant life on which much of my interpretation rests. This downtown beehive of social, cultural, economic, and political activity also captured the imagination of American reporters who left an impressive body of descriptions about Jewish life in the American city.

Although the Lower East Side dominated the chronicles of the period before World War I, this neighborhood, as a unique enclave of Jewish newcomers, disintegrated as quickly as it had appeared. By the early 1890s, Jews were spreading out to Brooklyn and to the Upper East Side of Manhattan. The development of new transit facilities in the early 1900s encouraged the flow to the north and east, opening up the Bronx and Harlem to Jewish residents and expanding the settlements in Brooklyn. In 1892, seventy-five percent of New York's Jews lived on the Lower East Side, but the proportion shrank steadily, to 50 percent in 1903 and to 23 percent in 1916, by which time the approximate Jewish population of 1,400,000 constituted well over one-fourth of the city's people.[36]

Despite the exodus of residents from the district, the Lower East Side continued to be the staging ground for the Jewish newcomer's initial contacts with American society. Moreover, because the pattern of consumption that emerged there was replicated in other districts and in other big cities, this neighborhood gives a comforting sense of geography to the vaguely bounded evolution of popular habits.

A final point of explanation about the interpretation of consumption is in order, as the behavior of consumers has been subjected to an element of moral scrutiny that is not applied to the activity of people as producers. Social critics have tended to distrust the human impulses to acquire luxuries and to engage in unproductive leisure. At the turn of the century, numbers of American intellectuals and social workers began to applaud the spread of goods and services to the majority of urban people, but their praise was mixed with fear that the comparatively uneducated masses would drift toward the lowest common denominator of pleasure rather than seek the more refined products of art and leisure.[37]

During the twentieth century, criticism of popular consumption in Europe and America has taken on a more overtly political tone. One of the most subtle critiques of modern society to question the growing power of ordinary consumers was *The Revolt of the Masses*, a commentary by the Spanish philosopher José Ortega y Gasset that appeared in 1930. Reflecting on the social levelling that had enabled the mass movements of syndicalism and fascism to challenge the parliamentary democracies of Europe in the 1920s, Ortega y Gasset linked the rising material and social position of the multitude to the predominance of mediocrity in modern culture. Arguing that civilized society is based on the ability of individuals to confront and master a difficult physical and social environment, the philosopher saw a dark side to the spread of comfort among the masses of people. Endowed by modern industry with a variety of conveniences and luxuries, ordinary people became like the children of self-made aristocrats, who inherited a wealth of things without appreciating the ingenuity and effort that had produced them. When the "señorito satisfecho," the little self-satisfied man, emerges as the dominant character of society, Ortega y Gasset warned, "it is necessary to sound the alarm and to announce that humanity finds itself threatened with degeneration."[38]

Consumption: Bridge Between Cultures

The spectacle of crowds of people flocking behind the banner of fascism also caused Marxist intellectuals to look for moral implications in mass consumption. During the 1940s and 1950s, with the stimulus of German Marxists who had fled to the United States, the Marxist critique of American popular literature and broadcasting tended to depict the consumer as being victimized by shallow entertainment that lowered artistic tastes, promoted individual isolation and passivity, and maintained an inequitable status quo. There were differences of tone as to the moral gravity of mass consumption, but, within this framework, it was possible to charge that the mass media had the capacity to "brutalize" the senses "while paving the way for totalitarianism." [39]

Although Marx himself had paid little attention to the subject, his notion of "the fetishism of commodities" has proven to be a source of inspiration for contemporary observers of Western culture. Marx felt that the value of products derived essentially from the labor invested in their production. In the marketplace, however, these objects acquired a "mystical character"—they came to be seen not as the reflection of human labor but as valuable in themselves, being worth a certain amount of money or being equivalent to a certain amount of another commodity. Inclined to focus on the physical qualities of products, consumers failed to recognize the exploitative social relationship of capitalist to laborer upon which the production of goods was based. [40] Marx's "labor theory of value" has fallen into disregard, but the argument that the sphere of consumption obscures the inequitable mode of production has continued to be the focus for Marxist students of Western culture. Perceiving the conduct of modern consumers as excessively self-indulgent and at odds with the creation of a truly egalitarian society, this critique has retained the moralistic tone in the interpretation of popular consumption. [41]

The present study takes no moral position in regard to the adoption of American ways by Jewish consumers. To be sure, the socialists and anarchists who abounded within the great immigration of eastern European Jews criticised, even as they shared, the so-called "bourgeois" tendencies of the majority of newcomers. Together with radical politics, orthodox religion stamped the conscience of American Jews with a brand of nonconformity that would challenge the group's precocious acceptance of American manners. In *The Old Bunch*, Meyer Levin's novel about second-generation Jews growing up in Chicago after World War I, young people who outwardly resented the traditional culture of their parents were nonetheless capable of objecting to the "new breed of rabbis who looked like dentists." [42]

While recognizing that the radically changed lifestyle of eastern European Jews in America fostered spiritual unrest, I want to avoid the prejudices with which the American standard of consumption is often confronted. The material abundance that generations of Americans have created and renewed through their struggle with hardship and discontent has been as often a source of envious resentment as of generous admiration. In a world of great and enduring inequalities, the material successes of America have been difficult to fathom, and they have occasioned the stereotype of Americans as a greedy people.

Addressing this misinterpretation of the American courtship with abundance, the French philosopher Jacques Maritain wrote in 1958 that the American people, unlike Europeans, were "neither sqeamish nor hypocritical about the importance of money in the modern world." Money was openly cared for in America, Maritain went on to say, because it was not considered an end in itself. Instead, it was viewed as a means for improving one's own life, for increasing one's freedom of action, and, in addition, "for improving the lives and freedom of others."[43] In other words, Americans have adapted to their own material wealth by using it to alter the quality of their daily life, expand their realm of choices and prospects for personal development, and envision the spread of material comforts across the world. This is not to suggest that affluence has no suspicious companions, but simply to emphasize that in America it has become a cornerstone of culture.

As such, material abundance inevitably affected newcomers to the United States. In the case of Jews from eastern Europe, the domain of buying and selling accommodated the ample energies of a people zealous for freedom, and made for a rich and subtle interweaving of old world traits and new world ways. These newcomers were determined to establish themselves in America, and their buoyant attitude led them to sense something more than matter in the products of the urban consumer.

18

PART I

The Promise of Abundance

ᢙᢀᡒ 1 ᢙᢁᢗᡒ

The Perspective of Abundance

The majority of European immigrants to America in the late nineteenth century had been exposed, if only slightly, to the momentous changes in the mode of production wrought by the factory system. Some of them had been liberated from real or virtual serfdom on the land only to find a new master in the machine. Familiarity with the other conspicuous feature of modern industrial society, mass consumption, escaped most of these people until they arrived in the United States, where the trend had developed more fully than anywhere else in the world. What they found there was a way of living and a point of view that had been shaped by the fact of material abundance.

The decades of the 1880s and 1890s marked a turning point in American history in regard to both immigration and consumption. For the first time, the bulk of newcomers to the United States came from the most impoverished regions of Europe, and they settled overwhelmingly in cities, rather than dispersing to the countryside, as many immigrants had done during the early and mid-nineteenth century. Standing in stark contrast to the economic scarcity of the European homelands, the material conditions of urban America had improved to the extent that the average city person enjoyed a range of comforts and conveniences still unavailable to the mass of people in the most industrialized areas of Europe. During the late nineteenth and early twentieth centuries, the United States attained a state of being in which an abundance of products for the consumer, rather than shortages, became the chronic feature of daily life. The dynamic growth of advertising for prepared foods, soaps, dentifrices, skin powders, cigarettes, ready-made clothes, silverware, watches, gas appliances, and bathroom fixtures in the 1880s and 1890s mirrored the entry of America into an age of surplus.[1]

Nineteenth-century America was not the first historical locale in which consumers enjoyed the fruits of abundance. Some historians have speculated that the early stirrings of a modern "consumer society" may be found in the diffusion of luxuries during the Renaissance in Italy. Yet appreciable and regular improvement in the material standards not just of affluent groups but of society as a whole has been more surely dated to seventeenth-century Europe. In that period, peasants and workers started to give up a work ethic aimed at subsistence and to enter the market economy as consumers of luxuries, both those imported from Asia and America and those made by small-scale, local industry.[2] The rising aspirations of commoners were enough to justify the wry comment of an English court that, in 1661, it was becoming difficult to distinguish English masters and servants "except it be because the servant wears better clothes than his master."[3]

Although the phenomenon of converting luxuries into necessities appeared in Europe, in America it would be pervasive. By the late nineteenth century, the Industrial Revolution had assured urban Europeans of higher material standards, but the chief consumers of new luxuries were the business and professional people of the middle classes, whose style of living differed radically from that of laborers.[4] In the cities of the United States, however, the vast majority of people steadily gained access to better merchandise. Throughout the nineteenth century and into the twentieth, American workers enjoyed consistently high real wages, and the material standard of living of the poorest groups of urban laborers rose in proportion to the productivity of the dynamic American economy.[5] By 1870, the urban poor had acquired domestic refinements—beds, bedding, chairs, tables, kitchen utensils, dishes, knives and forks, clocks, mirrors, sideboards, china closets, carpets—that consumers of modest affluence had first incorporated into their lives only forty years earlier. By 1910, working girls and women could own silk petticoats and skirts, and it was not unusual for their families to have pianos.[6]

Thus, although the number of poor people in urban America rose, so did their material standards. By the early 1900s, social workers and reformers formulated a new definition of poverty that revolved around the ability of a family to maintain an "American standard of living" rather than around the ability to stay off the charity rolls. This standard was high, based on modern social work's concept of a well-rounded and plentiful diet, spacious living quarters and sanitary fixtures, and recreational time that included a summer vacation—preferably outside the city.[7] Many urban people failing to meet the official standard nonetheless enjoyed a great variety of consumer products and services. A report of the United States Bureau of Labor, published in 1888 to inform young working women about the conditions they could anticipate in large cities, stated that in New York City "the comforts of life are found in the vilest tenements" which contained carpets and clean beds, lace curtains, upholstered furniture, pictures, and pianos and organs.[8]

The American redefinition of poverty according to the demand for greater comfort and convenience reflected a triumph over the struggle for subsistence. The comparative affluence of American workers during the last decades of the nineteenth century stemmed considerably from the great decline in the cost of food, which freed more income for the purchase of luxuries. In 1900, the French political economist Pierre Emile Levasseur remarked upon the fact that American workers spent less than half of their income on food, while the French parted with three-fifths. Furthermore, as late as 1910, the British Board of Trade found that among the middle range of the working classes in England and the United States, the former spent between 61 and 66 percent of their income on food, whereas Americans fed themselves on 37 to 47 percent of their earnings.[9]

American workers seem to have gained this comparative advantage after 1880. The pioneering budget studies of wage earners in Massachusetts carried out in 1875 by Carroll D. Wright, later the United States Commissioner of Labor, recorded nearly two-thirds of the average income devoted to food.[10] Subsequent investigations by the state of Massachusetts in 1884 and by the United States Senate in 1891 charted a significant decline in this percentage. By the turn of the century, statisticians could agree that typical working families were spending approximately 43 percent of their income on food. Young single men and women, who ate more haphazardly, sometimes spent as little as one-fourth of their earnings on food. In what amounted to a victory over the age-old need to work mainly in order to eat, urban Americans had acquired a larger share of "discretionary income," that which could be spent on luxuries.[11]

The diet of urban American workers was itself comparatively luxurious. With some variation due to ethnic differences, the average family's diet revolved around certain basic foods that were high in protein and vitamins.[12] In 1910, a Northern, native household of five people would typically consume in one week approximately thirteen pounds of meat, primarily beef, eight pounds of bread, almost two dozen eggs, six quarts of milk, five-and-a-half pounds of sugar, two pounds of butter, twenty pounds of potatoes, ten pounds of wheat flour, a half-pound of cheese, a pound of coffee, in addition to a less regular quantity of vegetables and fruit. Such a diet, as the British Board of Trade noted in a comparative examination of workers' budgets, was conspicuously high in protein. A bracket of American workers consumed 95 percent more meat and fish, 116 percent more eggs, and 383 percent more vegetables and fruit than an English group of similar economic status, and even the poorest group of Americans ate more of these foods than did a group of much higher status in England.[13] One survey devoted to the poor of New York City in 1906 found that families with a weekly income of nine dollars or less normally ate a pound and a half of meat each day, in addition to four or five pounds for Sunday dinner.[14] Social workers commented also on the tendency of the urban poor to indulge in the luxury of delicatessen and packaged foods.[15]

Accustomed to a comparatively high standard of living, Americans developed a uniquely optimistic attitude about the future that supported their upward spiral of consumption. In *Recent Economic Changes*, a study published in 1889 by the respected economist David A. Wells, the peculiar outlook of American consumers evoked special comment. When the price of sugar declined sharply in 1883, Wells explained, American workers surprised the nation's sugar refiners by switching to more expensive, refined sugar rather than increasing their consumption of the lower grades they usually purchased. Wells remarked that the European worker, by contrast, would have responded to the decline in price by buying a greater quantity of the usual grade or by saving the difference in cash. "When the American people find their pecuniary ability is abundantly sufficient to enable them to satisfy their desire for certain commodities or services," the economist concluded, "they will disdain to economize."[16] The trend observed by Wells would be documented and explained by later generations of economists: accustomed to relatively constant economic improvement, Americans apparently viewed their material destiny with an optimism that led them to raise their level of consumption at times when Europeans would save in preparation for an economic slump.[17] Abundance shaped the mind as well as the marketplace.

Early in the history of the nation, the tendency to emphasize eye-catching consumption over quiet saving had been recognized as an American trait. In 1831, Alexis de Tocqueville made a visit to the United States that formed the basis of the classic social commentary *Democracy in America*. Tocqueville observed that the lack of well-defined class divisions in the young nation had induced the majority of people to strive for an appearance of affluence. "In the confusion of all ranks, every one hopes to appear what he is not," he stated, as he added that "the hypocrisy of virtue" applied to every age, whereas the "hypocrisy of luxury" belonged specifically to the age of social democracy that had evidently arrived in America.[18]

Strengthened by the flexibility of the American social order, the perspective of abundance blossomed in the city. During the late eighteenth and early nineteenth centuries, the legacy of Puritan belief in the potential dangers of luxury fit well into the predominantly rural setting of the United States, where material abundance was tied closely to productive labor on the land. As a companion to industriousness, frugality held a high place in the American hierarchy of values. In his autobiography, written between 1771 and 1790, Benjamin Franklin named frugality as one of the thirteen virtues by which a good life should be led.[19] Although Americans would not disavow the value of frugality, the urban setting that had emerged by the late nineteenth century demanded the rejection of this trait as an ideal. Comparing the meagerness of domestic and personal adornment in 1840 to the attractiveness of furnishings in 1880, a writer for *Harper's Bazaar* affirmed the "falsehood of that old, strict idea that one could not be good and be comfortable" and the truth "that enjoyment of fine colors and fine contours does not belong exclusively to the Scarlet Lady."[20]

Intensifying American irreverence for tradition, the pace and style of city life encouraged the practice of acquiring new things. From the beginning of the colonial period, the British settlers of America had virtually abandoned primogeniture and entail, the feudal customs that preserved the landed estates on which the economy and social order of England had continued to depend. In the new world, the prosperity and position of a family hinged not on the preservation of hereditary estates but on the continuous acquistion of new properties and the frequent fragmentation and sale of existing ones.[21] The view of real estate as a transient source of profit, rather than a monolithic source of veneration, guided the development of the American city. Whereas the landscape of the great cities of Europe was planned, in varying degrees, to satisfy royal and aristocratic visions of social harmony, the cities of the United States were divided into small rectangular lots conducive to the whims of speculators. As homage to the substance of the past buckled under the pressure for profits in the future, old buildings were constantly replaced by new ones. Upholding the rule of change, the American city provided fertile ground for the idea that "newer" meant "better."[22]

The same ethic that governed urban real estate shaped urban consumption. In the 1890s, an English visitor to New York City noticed two peculiarities of the popular attitude toward housing: people preferred to move frequently, and they spent a large percentage of their income on furnishings, often going into debt to buy them.[23] The mobility of urban Americans, which was as considerable within cities as it was between them, inevitably promoted the ethic of change in relation to personal possessions. Particularly when the decision to find another apartment was motivated by aspirations for a better standard of living, a new home seemed to demand a different set of furnishings.

The constant revision of material standards intertwined with the belief in progressive change on which much of urban American life was based. In a report of 1880 that advocated the enlargement of foreign markets for American products, the *New York Times* emphasized the flexibility of attitude that differentiated American from European consumers. Paraphrasing the remarks of the United States Minister at Brussels, the newspaper claimed that "while an American will promptly discard any article he has in use for something he considers better adapted to his requirements, it is a very grave mistake to suppose that a Belgian is equally progressive."[24] Thirty years later, an official report on the standard of living in the United States reached the same conclusion, stating that the American population had a strong tendency to accept products, from automobiles to breakfast foods, according to the principle that "the newest is the best."[25]

The old ideal of frugality withered, as spending, instead of saving, became the standard of social behavior in the city. Authors on domestic economy frequently expressed regrets about urban American disregard for the once revered quality of frugality. In the view of these social critics, the conduct of Europeans, who criticized the extravagant consumer, was superior to that of Americans, who considered a thrifty person stingy and and frugal one a miser.[26] The attachment of city people to a standard of acquisition was mirrored in American literature, which contained no paragon of parsimony like Ebenezer Scrooge, provided for England by Charles Dickens, or the father of Eugenie Grandet, given to France by Honoré de Balzac.

Moreover, the habits of urban American consumers inspired the first theoretical explanation of modern consumption, Thorstein Veblen's *The Theory of the Leisure Class*, which appeared in 1899. Although Veblen devoted much of his interpretation to the habits of the wealthy, whom he called "the leisure class," he observed that the continual acquisition of luxuries had become an imperative for virtually all city people in America. "The standard of expenditure which commonly guides our efforts is not the average, ordinary expenditure already achieved," the scholar argued, "it is an ideal of consumption that lies just beyond our reach, or to reach which requires some strain."[27]

In the first decade of the twentieth century, studies of the household budgets of wage-earners documented the tendency of urban Americans to emphasize spending over saving. Two major surveys, by Louise Bolard More and Robert Coit Chapin, found that relatively few New York City households with annual incomes under $1,000 reported savings. Only when income reached about $1,200 did one-half of the households claim to have saved any money. Yet, barring unusual expenses due to sickness or other emergencies, this amount of income would have permitted families to reserve money after paying for their necessities. The possibility of saving in spite of relatively limited earnings was illustrated by two families from the Lower West Side of New York investigated by Louise More. With an annual income of $797, an Italian barber's household of four kept a comparatively expensive apartment and spent $110 on "sundries," which usually comprised miscellaneous luxuries and conveniences, yet still managed to save $100. A Jewish-American upholsterer's family of five with the same earnings put away $123 in order to prepare for its preadolescent sons' eventual enrollment in Columbia University.[28]

The nature of saving itself had changed in the environment of the city. In one sense, the bank account served as a kind of commodity denoting social status, particularly for people looking to marry. Walter Weyl, the Progressive reformer whose writing focused on the impact of American affluence, explained in 1909 that "a bank account to-day is what a log cabin and a hundred-acre lot were a hundred years ago."[29] Savings accounts were also used to hold money intended for consumption in the immediate future. Of the New York City households studied by social workers, those with savings usually intended to purchase special durable items, such as a gas stove, a sewing machine, or a piano.[30] Deposits for holiday shopping had also become common. According to a 1906 report on the Penny Provident Fund of New York City, which had tens of thousands of financially limited depositors, the majority withdrew money during holidays in order to buy presents.[31]

The use of a bank account as a conduit for consumption was apparent as well among the roughly 350,000 young women who expanded the white-collar work force in the 1880s and 1890s.[32] According to an 1894 report in the *New York Herald*, several of the city's banks estimated that one-half of their savings accounts were in women's names. An employee of a bank on Chambers Street explained that clerks and secretaries, the depositors most likely to save in "spurts," tended to "deposit money until they have $50 or $75, then they draw it out and spend it for clothes, presents and such things."[33]

The well-rooted urban custom of buying luxuries on credit undermined the position of frugality as an American ideal. Although the quickening demand of American consumers has often been associated with the unprecedented use of credit in the mass-marketing of automobiles after 1915, the automobile actually culminated a long developing trend toward the acquisition of expensive durable goods on the installment plan. The systematic marketing of domestic furnishings on the principle of deferred payment appears to have originated in the first decade of the nineteenth century, when Connecticut clockmaker Eli Terry designed an installment plan for the sale of his $25 clocks. As the production and distribution of domestic furnishings that could be repossessed grew in the second half of the century, so did the application of credit. Sewing machines had been customarily sold on installment since the 1850s, and furniture and pianos were commonly marketed in this way since the 1870s. By the end of the century, the intensity of retail competition in many American cities yielded installment terms that were accessible to most consumers, who often bought furnishings with a down payment of several dollars and subsequent payments of from twenty-five cents to one dollar each week.[34]

Practiced by wage earners and salaried workers alike, the widespread use of credit for the acquisition of luxuries reflected the perspective of abundance that urged urban Americans to raise their material aspirations above their incomes. In a commentary on American domestic life published in 1910, Katherine Busbey recorded that among the lower middle classes, a category meant to include many manual workers as well as lower echelon white-collar employees, the "failure to make ends meet is not regarded as ominous."[35] The following year, a scholar discussing the "enormous growth" of installment selling in the clothing, furniture, jewelry, and book businesses, commented on "the almost universal use" of this form of credit among city people of limited means, many of whom made it "an invariable rule" to supplement necessities with luxuries bought on time.[36]

Once people in white-collar occupations began to accept debt as a means of obtaining what they considered necessary luxuries, the old ideal of frugality perished. The ability to defer the desire for the unaffordable had long been regarded as a commendable form of self-restraint expected

28

of people who stood securely within the middle classes. But, by the beginning of the twentieth century, the use of credit for the acquisition of luxuries had become common enough to be cited as a cause of the inflation that was disturbing the pursuit of higher standards of living by white-collar workers.[37] Describing the difference between the method of the credit customer and that of the burglar as being "merely one of politeness," a writer for *Cosmopolitan* in 1899 observed, with an outmoded tone of moral outrage, how normal it had become for people who regarded themselves "as upholders of the law and pillars of the church" to buy expensive luxuries on credit.[38]

The growth of lending institutions testified to the new emphasis on immediate acquisition among the middle classes. In a path breaking study that helped to bring about the Uniform Small Loan Law of 1916, the first federal law relating to personal loans, the reform-minded scholar Clarence Wassam found that, by 1908, there were thirty known salary-loan offices in New York City, with the likelihood of many more operating inconspicuously. These institutions made small loans to workers receiving regular salaries, which served as a guarantee of repayment. Wassam estimated conservatively that thirty thousand New Yorkers were making daily payments on loans with an average principal of $20, a sum equivalent to the earnings of a week or a week and a half for many people. Regarding the nature of these loans, he noted the frequency of borrowing not from hardship but for the purpose of "a suit of clothes or anything which requires an unusual expenditure."[39]

During the relatively prosperous decades following the depression of 1893–1897, the expanding business of New York's Provident Loan Society also illustrated the new importance of rising material standards as a motive for borrowing. A principal provider of low interest loans, the Society's volume of lending sky-rocketed from the depressed year of 1895, when 20,804 loans totaling $229,155 were made, to the more buoyant years of 1905, when 205,683 loans totaling $7,202,916 were awarded, and 1915, when the volume of nearly 600,000 loans totaled almost $20,000,000. During these decades, the character of borrowers underwent a remarkable shift, from the unskilled worker faced with a medical or other emergency to salaried and professional people who needed extra money to "bridge the gap between income and cost of living necessitated by existing standards."[40]

Refusing to hold their aspirations within the boundaries of income, urban Americans ultimately interpreted the desire for luxuries to be an imperative. By the turn of the century, the tendency of young wage earners to buy elaborate parlor furniture on the installment plan was applauded by social workers, whose profession had always emphasized thrift and solvency. Instead of representing a sad lack of self-restraint, this method of consumption had come to be seen as a sign of healthy "ambition" for a higher standard of living. In the age of mass consumption, an attitude of resignation to a limited material existence appeared to be a problem.[41]

As a result of this perspective, the conspicuous thrift of immigrants accustomed to scarcity posed a conflict with American ways. To the surprise of an Italian traveler who visited the United States in the first decade of the twentieth century, some of his countrymen who had prospered and adopted many American customs were nonetheless scorned by "real" Americans for their habit of meticulous saving.[42] Signifying the general absence of material aspirations, frugality seemed to threaten the foundations of urban life.

In the urban communities of African-Americans, the importance of liberal spending as a sign of cultural identity was particularly evident. In the 1880s, Jacob A. Riis, the influential reporter of living conditions in New York City, noted the role of consumption among the city's growing population of blacks, many of whom had migrated from the South in the hope of entering American society more fully than had yet been possible. "Even where the wolf howls at the door," observed Riis in reference to the financial hardships accompanying racial discrimination, African-Americans made a "bold and gorgeous front" of luxury with Sunday promenades, in fine dress, down the avenues of the city and with a flare for "good living."[43] Despite their nativity, blacks felt an urgent need to demonstrate their membership in American society, which had long maintained the fiction that they could not fit in. Visible habits of consumption provided the perfect vehicle for doing so. Consequently, while black leaders criticized the activity of many consumers, invoking Booker T. Washington's dictum that racial uplift would depend on sober economy, the majority of people perceived spending to be as vital for social identification as was saving for economic improvement.[44]

Although blacks had less cause than others for optimism about the future, their adoption of the spending habit illustrated how deeply the awareness of abundance had extended into American urban society. Surrounded by desirable products, Americans naturally expressed their hopes for advancement through the consumption of things that suggested a more secure social position. Poor people were no less driven by that impulse. On the contrary, the prospect of poverty often made the appearance of comfort all the more important. Acceptance of the outward signs of destitution reflected the end of hope, an attitude that contradicted the American approach to consumption, which was rooted in aspiration. The inseparable connection between the American psyche and the material standard of living was observed by Albert Einstein, whose first impressions of the United States were published in a Berlin newspaper in 1921. "Great importance attaches to the material comforts of life," the scientist remarked, adding that "the American lives even more for his goals, for the future than the European. Life for him is always becoming, never being."[45]

The progressive perspective of the material world seemed to be rooted in the original statement of American distinctiveness, the Declaration of Independence. As Thomas Jefferson considered the words with which to articulate the inalienable rights of his people, he decided to alter "life, liberty, and property," the conventional phrase of republican rights. Although the word "property" conveyed the economic aspirations that people wanted to secure, it was a static term that failed to express the sense of dynamic movement, the yearning for vast improvements, that Jefferson captured with his eloquent substitute, "the pursuit of happiness."

Jefferson conceived of the grand pursuit within the predominantly rural setting of the early United States, but the quest for a sophisticated standard of living ended up as a preoccupation of the city. When Theodore Roosevelt rearticulated the "promise" of American life during his 1912 campaign for the presidency, he addressed the special concern of urban consumers about the impact of inflation on their pursuit of a higher standard of living. "The main purpose of the Progressive movement," Roosevelt explained, was "to place the American people in possession of their birthright," which meant securing "unobstructed access to the fountains of measureless prosperity" which God had ordained for them.[46]

In one sense, Americans viewed their standard of living as symbolic of life in general. Many of the arts and artifacts invented in America, from the musical idiom of jazz to the architectural wonder of skyscrapers to the mundane item of chewing gum, embodied the quality of endlessness, as if to reflect the preoccupation with "becoming" that intrigued Albert Einstein.[47] What artists and inventors expressed in a moment of creation, the multitude of urban Americans experienced continually through the elevation of material existence. They made the rising standard of living an integral part of American culture because it addressed so concretely their belief that history was progressive and that the world was a place of inextinguishable promise.

The Promise of Abundance

When eastern European Jews arrived in America, they encountered not only a host of new products but a new perspective that was intimately related to the fact of material abundance. In adopting the American standard of living, they would inevitably be adapting to a characteristically American attitude. As consumers, then, they would lay the foundation of an American identity.

⚜ 2 ⚜

From Scarcity to Abundance: The Immigrant as Consumer

The chasm between a past of inveterate want and a future of potential comfort profoundly shaped the perspective of immigrants to the United States between the 1870s and 1914, when the First World War ended the great migration of over 20 million Europeans to America. Louis Borgenicht, a Galician Jew who came to New York City in 1888 and shortly afterward launched a successful career in the garment industry, expressed clearly the revolutionary change of condition that was inherent in immigration to the United States. "Even at his wealthiest, my father lived in very much the same fashion as his tenth-generation grandfather," Borgenicht observed—"I have shifted my mode of living more in fifty years than my ancestors [had] in a thousand."[1]

No transition was more dramatic than the movement from a material life that was nearly medieval to one that thrived on modern mass production. The psychological adaptation of the immigrant to American society was defined largely by this enormous leap in material circumstances and possibilities. Because of an overriding desire to become established in the United States, eastern European Jews responded especially quickly to the condition of mass consumption. They recognized that, as consumers, they could begin to move toward the goal of fitting into American society.

The Promise of Abundance

In the sphere of consumption, virtually all newcomers to America discovered an opportunity for social advancement that often eluded them in the domain of production. By contrasting the status of urban immigrants as consumers to their position as laborers, a comprehensive study of industrial workers in the United States published by the British Board of Trade in 1911 emphasized this fact. In the workplace, the differences between newcomers and citizens were often accentuated, as immigrants typically were pushed into, and congregated in, the least tolerable kinds of labor. Through the marketplace, however, newcomers had the opportunity almost immediately to adopt basic forms of American life. The report explained that "the industrial status" of most southern and eastern Europeans was "different from and lower than" that of most Americans. But, the position of immigrants "as measured by the command of material comforts" began "at once to be relatively 'American' in standard." Consequently, even among the poorest groups of urban workers the term "American" was found to have a meaning that was "definable and real."[2]

The significance of emulating the American consumer was highlighted by the impoverishment of those millions who had come from eastern and southern Europe between 1880 and 1914. The shifting source of immigration to the United States directly reflected economic changes across the Atlantic. As the German economy expanded in the last decades of the nineteenth century, the number of German immigrants to the United States, which neared one-and-a-half million between 1881 and 1890, dropped to one-half million, at the most, between 1891 and 1900. At the same time, the deterioration of economic opportunities in the largely agricultural societies of eastern and southern Europe stimulated a titanic increase of people from Italy, Austria-Hungary, Russia, and from Poland, which had been divided and annexed by Russia, Austria-Hungary, and Prussia in the late eighteenth century. Between 1881 and 1890, approximately 926,116 people arrived from these lands; between 1891 and 1900, the number jumped to about 1,846,610; between 1901 and 1910, roughly 5,788,449 flooded into the United States.[3] In all, about ten million had left for the United States between 1880 and 1914. The one characteristic unifying these diverse peoples was poverty. Not only did they arrive, on the average, with virtually no capital, but they had known a meagerness of material existence that was fast becoming outmoded in the more industrial regions to the north and west of Europe.

The regions that supplied so many emigrants had an aspect that contrasted sharply with the setting of urban consumption in the United States. The people of southern Italy conceived of their society as having two major groups—those who ate white bread and those who ate black bread. This point of view clarified the deep division between the gentry and the peasantry, for whom white bread symbolized an unattainable style of life. The peasants of southern Italy lived in abysmal homes that were often no more than hovels made of interwoven sticks or straw and daub. Some inhabited caves. In the cities, particularly Naples, several families of impoverished workers typically cohabited in underground apartments that made the tenements of New York City seem luxurious. The average diet was as poor as the water supply, consisting mainly of corn meal, pasta, rice, beans, and bread. Meat was esteemed a "rich man's food."[4]

The impoverishment of eastern Europe was accentuated by the fact that, until 1863, masses of Russian peasants were serfs. Designed to turn peasants into urban factory workers, the abolition of serfdom actually provided little relief from the unrelenting pressure of poverty. Many laborers continued to be tied to land that they did not own, and factory operatives ended up with extremely low wages. In Lithuania and Poland, the regions of northwestern Russia that provided a large proportion of immigrants to America, life on the land had become increasingly untenable after the breakdown of the traditional agricultural order. Descriptions of Lithuanian life prior to World War I were portraits of drabness and want. The average diet revolved around cottage cheese and sour cream, beet soup, onions, cabbage, potatoes, and rye or raisin bread. Rolls and pastries were unusual, as were most vegetables and fruits. Fresh milk was rarely enjoyed, and butter, considered a luxury, was made to sell rather than to eat. Tea and coffee were rare, the main drink thus being water. As forks were used only by the rich, peasants relied on handmade wooden spoons and other small utensils. Their clothing and interior furnishings were simple and nondescript.[5]

Estranged from the land, the Jews of eastern Europe endured material conditions that differed somewhat from those of the surrounding peasantry. Working primarily as artisans and merchants, Jews had much greater familiarity with urban refinements, and their autonomous, communal institutions helped the poorest among them to enjoy the special foods of the Sabbath and holidays. Dispersed throughout the Russian Pale of Settlement—the stretch of land between the Baltic and Black Seas that confined most Jews—the eastern edges of Austria-Hungary, and Rumania, they varied in their customs and tastes. Yet, their culture was remarkably uniform, and their experience of material scarcity was quite consistent.

Despite the effort of Jews to punctuate the year with religious celebrations that included luxurious foods, gabardine, cashmere, or silk garments, and handcrafted silverware, the want of daily life in eastern Europe was ineluctable, often demanding that the holiday diet be hedged, the clothes be well-worn, and the tableware inherited. In fact, the Jewish perception of luxuries as an important part of regular celebrations made for a trying tension between expectation and reality. Echoing the impact of deprivation, some Jewish immigrants recalled in detail the most minute elements of the daily diet—a piece of bread, an apple, or a cookie that persisted in memory despite the passage of years.[6]

The cities of eastern Europe often lacked the most basic commodities and conveniences enjoyed by the poor in American cities. In the 1880s and 1890s, the women of Minsk chopped their own wood for the oven, walked distances to draw well water, and washed the family's clothes in the river with the aid of a wooden hammer and board. In the winter, washing had to be done through a hole in the ice.[7] Lacking domestic appliances, the vast majority of urban families were also burdened by a limited selection of garments. Until 1912, residents of the Galician city of Shniatyn had neither shoe stores nor retailers of ready-made clothes.[8] The confinement of the consumer in the largest cities of the Pale was conveyed by a description of a Jewish marketplace in Warsaw in 1898: "All kinds of old clothes, and some new ones of the worst quality are sold by auction in the wooden shanties . . . sometimes a pair of high-boots constitutes the whole of their stock-in-trade, and a whole day is sometimes uselessly devoted to getting rid of them."[9]

The embrace of material scarcity on the consciousness of Jews extended to their attitude toward living space. Disproportionately urban, the Jews of eastern Europe suffered acutely from the miasma of over-crowded housing. In 1900, a traveling correspondent for the New York *Yiddishes Tageblatt*, America's first successful daily newspaper printed in Yiddish, described as indescribable "the want, the misery, the wretched-ness" of the poor in Kazmierz, the Jewish suburb of Cracow, "where half-a-dozen families . . . live together in one cellar with bad food and scanty light."[10]

The journalist's impassioned chronicle was well corroborated by de-tailed reports of living conditions in the Jewish Pale of Settlement during the first decade of the twentieth century. The majority of artisans' homes was described by one investigator as being "small, crowded, and poverty-stricken."[11] This terse description was amplified by an inspector of the United States Immigration Service who visited the homes of urban Jews in the Pale during the summer of 1906. In one cellar room, twelve feet underground, three families totaling seventeen people were found living together. For several families to cohabit one room was "a common sight."[12]

These city residents were so conditioned by the fact of material scarcity that they calculated joint "ownership" of a single room in terms of fractions as minute as one thirty-second. In one case, three families claimed twenty-eight thirty-seconds ownership of a room, one individual with a one thirty-second share had to live elsewhere, and the remaining parts were viewed by their "owner" as an investment.[13]

Even families that were comparatively comfortable lacked the stimulation provided by a variety of domestic furnishings and personal possessions. Marc Chagall, the most renowned of the Jewish artists to emerge from the Pale, recalled what to his eyes was a painful lack of adornment in his childhood home of Vitebsk, where "there wasn't a single painting, not a single engraving on the walls of the rooms." Until the age of nineteen, Chagall had "never seen drawings or paintings."[14] The painter's recollection was significant partly because, by prevailing standards, his family was not poor. In the homes of comparatively comfortable Jewish families, the dearth of possessions was often relieved only by the presence of religious and ceremonial objects, such as pictures of great rabbis, Jewish shrines, and Jewish philanthropists, a *yortsayt*, or memorial tablet for relatives, a charity box, brass candlesticks, a finely wrought spice box, a wine beaker, a menorah, a silver-plated ornamental box to hold etrog, the Mediterranean citrus fruit used for the celebration of Sukkot, and perhaps a set of silver goblets and a special snuff box for use on Sabbath and holidays.[15] The lack of secular commodities in the homes of all but the affluent bred monotony. "No dolls, no books, no games," recalled Mary Antin of her childhood in a moderately well-off family in Polotsk—"the days drew themselves out too long sometimes, so that I sat at the window thinking what should happen next."[16]

The desire to escape a world of deprivation figured prominently in the constellation of motives that moved people from Europe to America after 1880. In 1911, a report of the United States Immigration Commission stated that "the chief motive behind the movement" to the new world was "a laudable ambition for better things" than the emigrants possessed at home.[17] As had been the case throughout the nineteenth century, letters brimming with optimism about American prosperity passed from the recently arrived to their relatives back in the old country, and this personal correspondence constituted one of the most powerful catalysts of immigration.[18]

In the era of exodus from eastern and southern Europe, however, the content and impact of letters home changed in a subtle way. During the middle of the nineteenth century, the rhetorical enthusiasm of land-hungry newcomers from central and northern Europe dwelled on the agricultural dimension of American prosperity—the abundance of inexpensive land, superfluous crops, and light taxation of the farmer.[19] At the end of the century, the factory-bound arrivals from eastern and southern Europe focused more on the scale of wages and the urban refinements of the new society. Moreover, the formidable gap in material condition separating the impoverished newcomer from the American at this time made for many analogies between the status of the average worker in the United States and the nobleman in Poland or Italy. An American consular official reported in 1904 that "the greatest influence in promoting emigration" came from relatives and friends in the United States who wrote "glowing accounts of the enormous wages received, food such as the nobility [ate] at home, and houses grandly furnished."[20] Historians of the immigration of Italian and Slavic peasants have found these newcomers to have been motivated by a fierce commitment to the pragmatic goal of accumulating money and material possessions, both of which served as tangible signs that they had transcended the degradation of their material and social condition in Europe.[21]

The vision of America as a place of bounty had a unique significance for Jews because of the circumstances behind their immigration. Although the eastern European Jews responded to similar pressures of population growth, economic disruption, and political persecution that had motivated most immigrants to the United States, they contended as well with special, and potentially catastrophic, problems. Since the beginning of the nineteenth century, the dramatic growth of Europe's population had aggravated the economic frustration of multitudes of peasants who had lost the ability to make a living from farmlands that were quickly being consolidated by powerful landlords.

By the second half of the century, the Jews of eastern Europe were also unsettled by the joint pressure of overpopulation and economic dislocation. Around 1800, Russian Jews numbered approximately one million. Fifty years later, they were three and a quarter million. By 1900, nearly five and a half million Jews lived in the Russian Empire. As the Jewish population grew, economic opportunities dwindled. Since the abolition of serfdom in 1863, the customarily Jewish occupations of provisioning and administering the estates of noblemen were subverted, and the role of Jews as small-scale moneylenders and merchants was further undercut after 1880 by the growth of large-scale industry, which relied on major banks for credit and on the railroads for the shipment of goods.

Throughout the nineteenth century, the burgeoning number of Russian Jews had migrated within the Empire in search of new opportunities, but this alternative had inherent limits that would eventually make emigration inevitable. Flowing out of the densely populated provinces of Lithuania and Poland into the areas of "New Russia" around the Black Sea, the migrants rapidly achieved roughly the same ratio to the Gentile population that existed in the older regions of settlement. Further expansion was precluded by the boundaries of the Pale of Settlement.[22]

Physically cramped to the point of frustration, many Jews needed only an upsurge of anti-Semitism to convince them that the future in Russia would be increasingly dismal. The decline in the security of the eastern European Jews accompanied the decline in the eighteenth century of the Kingdom of Poland, most of which came into the possession of Russia. Under the Tsars, the insecurity of the Jews was accentuated by policies that both inadvertently and deliberately undermined their political autonomy and economic privileges. After the assassination of Tsar Alexander II in 1881, the group's position turned from a state of insecurity to one of virtual siege. Led by high ranking, anti-Semitic officials and sustained by deeply rooted suspicions and animosities among the Russian folk, the government began systematically to bar Jews from customary occupations, to limit sharply their enrollment in universities, and to incite pogroms that destroyed millions of dollars worth of Jewish property as well as thousands of lives. Although other ethnic and religious minorities in the Empire, notably the Lithuanians and Poles, suffered persecution that helped produce waves of emigration, the plight of Russian Jews between 1881 and 1914 was unparalleled in scope and intensity.[23]

The two million Jews who left eastern Europe for the United States in this period—nearly one-quarter of whom fled deteriorating conditions in Rumania and Austria-Hungary—held a deep desire for freedom that lent special importance to the vision of abundance inspiring the majority of impoverished newcomers. More than for other groups of immigrants, America represented for Jews a promised land, a mysterious place of redemption from the accumulated iniquities of the past. As a form of relief from the harrowing conditions of scarcity, the anticipation and experience of material abundance in the United States enriched the perception of the new world as a source of liberation and promise.

Since the publication in 1817 of a Yiddish edition of Joachim Heinrich Campe's *The Discovery of America*, which attained great popularity in eastern Europe, the United States had acquired a mystique among Jews.[24] As larger numbers of Polish Jews started to emigrate to America in the 1870s, the images of American prosperity conveyed through letters and return visits to the homeland took on greater clarity, deepening the country's appeal. In the summer of 1880, a thirty-eight-year-old Polish Jew living on East Houston Street was interviewed by a reporter for the

New York Tribune about the conditions and attitude of the small community of immigrants. In answer to the question of whether the Polish Jews sought to return to Jerusalem, the man stated, "we are satisfied here; indeed, among us America is known as 'the new Jerusalem.' "[25]

The vision of American abundance intertwined with the vision of America as a haven. Interpreting American life in intensely spiritual terms, Jewish newcomers tended to view their new material existence as an integral part of the New Jerusalem. While acknowledging that the life of the Jewish garment worker was difficult, Abraham Cahan, the socialist editor of the New York *Forward* and the conscience of the city's Yiddish-speaking community, recalled that most Jewish newcomers perceived their new living conditions as justification for the claim that "America was paradise."[26]

The cultural heritage of the newcomers had prepared the ground for such an attitude. Although Judaism had not systematically formulated a description of Paradise, a conception arose among eastern Europeans that the sublime world of redemption might be full of milk and honey, a splendid banquet for the sake of the righteous. The tradition of Hasidism that flourished in eastern Europe in the eighteenth and nineteenth centuries encouraged the idea of a mystical union of the act of eating and spiritual liberation. One older version of Paradise was contained in an Aramaic poem pertaining to the holiday of Shavuoth. In the time of the Messiah, the poem foretold, meat, fish, and wine would be enjoyed at a special banquet, and God would set forth jars of wine that were made during the six days of Creation and sealed until the occasion of redemption.[27]

The concept of the afterlife that prevailed among the Jewish folk of eastern Europe, and that influenced the vision of American abundance, was articulated by Isaac Loeb Peretz, the brilliant writer of Yiddish short stories whose simplicity of style managed to evoke the popular imagination of Polish and Russian Jewry. One of Peretz's best stories, first published in 1894 in the New York *Arbeter Tsaytung*, was "Bontshe the Silent," the tale of a physically and spiritually downtrodden Jew who finds himself transported to the Other World.

The story of Bontshe played on the profound tension between the impoverishment of the Jews and their grand vision of redemption. Having endured in apparently noble silence a life of constant abuse and poverty, Bontshe arrives in the divine kingdom to receive his final Judgment. Surrounded by little angels with gold-filigreed wings and silver slippers, the subdued "hero" is received with a gold easychair and a gold crown with inlaid gems, and he is escorted into the Court of Virtue, the floor of which (Bontshe is too awestruck to lift up his head) is composed of alabaster and diamonds. A review by the divine court ends so favorably that Bontshe is offered everything he desires from the glorious realm of the Afterlife. In Peretz's satirical conclusion, the hero turns out to be an anti-hero, his lifelong silence having reflected not noble forbearance but an utter lack of spirit. Bontshe answers the court meekly that he would like every morning to have a hot baked roll with fresh butter![28]

Although written as a commentary on the degrading aspects of Jewish life in eastern Europe, "Bontshe the Silent" gave form to the evocative sense of Paradise harbored by impoverished Jewish immigrants. Unlike Bontshe, these people had not been beaten down into passivity by deprivation—they were able not only to envision the splendor of redemption but also to imagine and pursue the prospect of a satisfying standard of material existence. A more realistic, poignant expression of the yearning for a worldly paradise was given by Kate Simon, in her recollection of immigration to New York from Warsaw just after World War I. "My life was filled with images of raisins and chocolate, cookies and dolls, white slippers and pink hair bows, all waiting for me in a big box called America," she wrote of her last days in Poland. Her rich mental image of a promised land had been formed from the stories of comfort and luxury told by adults expecting to emigrate.[29]

If the new potential for consumption completed the Jews' notion of America as a promised land, it served also as a starting point toward a goal that was more immediate for them than for other newcomers—the goal of fitting into American society. There was a strong desire among the peasants of eastern and southern Europe to make money quickly in the United States in order to buy land and raise their social position in the old country. Consequently, most groups of immigrants included a greatly disproportionate number of young males who originally viewed America as a means to an end rather than as an end in itself. Of the most populous groups of newcomers, the Italians exemplified the tendency to return home. More than two million Italians arrived in the United States between 1899 and 1910, over three-fourths of them males, largely "birds of passage" aiming to return home with American wages. During the period 1897–1906, more than one-half of the immigrants repatriated, and, from 1907–1911, almost three-fourths returned to Italy.[30]

By contrast, few Jews returned to Russia, Poland, Galicia, or Rumania. Statistics for the period 1908–1914 showed only 7 percent re-emigrating, compared to 31 percent of immigrants in general. Furthermore, Jewish immigration consisted of families rather than single men, including almost twice as many women as the groups from southern and eastern Europe contained. The reason for these striking differences was clear: Jews intended to stay.[31]

The unique attitude of Jews toward America motivated them to view items of consumption as foundation stones of American identity. A study of the cultural adjustment of American immigrants conducted by sociologists Robert Park and Herbert Miller in 1921 described six personality "types" that characterized the majority of immigrants. Of the six, two were formulated by immigrants themselves and thus arose directly from the milieu of urban communities rather than from the observation of social scientists. These two stereotypes were the "allrightnik" and the "cafone," deriving from the Jewish and the Italian immigrants respectively. In the contrast between the "allrightnik" and the "cafone," the significance of being a consumer in the American way emerged most clearly.

Reflecting the old-world orientation of many non-Jewish immigrants, the "cafone" represented the Italian who sought only to make money in America in order to gain a higher position in the native community in Italy. As a result of his singleminded focus on a future in the old world, the "cafone" cared neither about adopting American ways nor about fitting into the settled group of Italians in the United States. Standing in diametrical opposition to the "cafone," the "allrightnik" reflected the deep tendency of Jewish immigrants to view themselves in the light of potential roles and social position in America, rather than in the European birthplace. The "allrightnik" stood for the successful Jewish immigrant who adopted American habits, particularly habits of consumption, so thoroughly as to blend into the group of cosmopolitan Jews who had attained a high degree of cultural assimilation.[32]

The cultural flexibility and cosmopolitan outlook of Jewish newcomers made it easier to understand and adopt American habits of consumption. Unlike the majority of immigrants, who had been raised within the narrow confines of village life, Jews had an almost proverbial versatility stemming from a history of migration within and beyond national borders. Mendele Moykher-Sforim, the "grandfather" of modern Yiddish literature, evinced the breadth, as he satirized the depth, of perspective of the most ignorant shtetl Jews of the mid-nineteenth century, whose conversation behind the old stove of the synagogue ranged beyond domestic secrets to "the politics of Istanbul, the Sultan, the Austrian Kaiser, high finance, Rothschild's fortune compared with the wealth of the great aristocrats and the other magnates . . . and so on and so forth."[33] The cultural flexibility of the Jews was characterized by a traveler who had spent enough time in Russia to recognize that the Russian had "great facility in language" but that the Russian Jew was "the most versatile man in the empire."[34]

In the American setting, viewed overwhelmingly as the best available to Jews, the cultural adaptability of Jewish newcomers made for the rapid adoption of American ways. Perhaps the surest sign of quick cultural change was the commitment to learning English. David Blaustein, a Russian immigrant who gained a reputation as a social worker on the Lower East Side, where he served as a director of the Educational Alliance, noted that, in Russia, the vast majority of Jews made no effort to learn the dominant language, whereas in America "they feel they are welcome, and with high hopes" they set at once to learning English with the aim of lessening "as far as possible the gulf between them and native-born Americans."[35]

The intensity of Jewish motivation to fit into American society by learning English underlay the success of Alexander Harkavy's "briefen-shteller," handbooks written by the Yiddish lexicographer to instruct newcomers in the forms of American correspondence. The popularity of the first two "letter writers" in the 1890s prompted the issue of an expanded third edition in 1902. Although the English model in the handbook was at times rigid and melodramatic, the volume guided the newcomer through virtually every social situation that would warrant a verbal exchange, from complaints to a wholesaler about defective merchandise, to apologies for late payment of rent, from greetings and invitations relating to holidays, rites of passage, concerts, meetings, and telegrams to letters containing passionate expressions of love as well as delicate phrases of distaste. Harkavy's letter-writer also included extensive lessons on English pronunciation—with a special section of words most likely to be mispronounced by the speaker of Yiddish—as well as exercises in spelling, punctuation, diction, and penmanship.[36]

As a result of such efforts to master the language, many eastern Europeans gained access to the thoroughfare of urban American society. A survey of readers of the Yiddish press in New York City, which was undertaken after 1914 but probably reflected tendencies among Jews in earlier years as well, found that almost two-thirds of the randomly sampled readers could and did read English-language newspapers. They patronized the Yiddish press out of desire, rather than from necessity.[37]

The English language was an essential avenue into American culture, but it was time-consuming and often difficult to adopt. In contrast, habits of consumption constituted the most easily accessible element of the new society. New clothes, foods, and furnishings were as tangible as syntax was abstract and as obtainable as idioms were elusive.

In responding to the environment of consumption in urban America, Jewish newcomers shared with other immigrants a general sense of wonder and enthusiasm. The simplest changes in lifestyle, such as increasing the size of meals, were accepted with little hesitation by virtually all newcomers. The prevalence of high-protein foods, like meat, milk, and eggs, and the abundance of food in general made for a sharp and immediate change in daily life, not only for newcomers from the poverty-stricken regions of eastern and southern Europe but even for western Europeans like the Germans.[38] In good part, the craving for old world dishes reflected the fact that these foods could suddenly be afforded in America.[39]

First impressions of mass-marketed products like clothes and furniture were also universal. Many newcomers must have experienced the amazement of David Levinsky, the protagonist of Abraham Cahan's novel *The Rise of David Levinsky*, which first appeared in 1917. Newly arrived in New York City from a Lithuanian shtetl, Levinsky sees an evicted family sitting on the sidewalk with its belongings. He is shocked to discover that the furniture of these poor people would have properly belonged to a prosperous family in Russia. "But then," Levinsky reminded himself, "anything was to be expected of a country where the poorest devil wore a hat and a starched coller."[40]

Although the prospect of consumption in America attracted people of various origins, Jews adopted the ways of the American consumer more quickly, largely because of their dedication to the new society. One of the surest signs of the comparative sophisitication of Jewish consumption was the flourishing retail business established in the neighborhoods of these eastern Europeans. The Jewish districts of the American city prior to 1914 offered immigrants a range of products that would have been inconceivable in the ramshackle shtetls and urban ghettos of the eastern European Jews. The streets of the Lower East Side of New York inspired Henry James to speak of the "new style of poverty" in the American city, a social phenomenon of the first order that eluded most observers who were preoccupied with the environmental problems of the Lower East Side. As the great novelist walked through the area in 1904, after a twenty-two-year sojourn in Europe, he was surprised and impressed by "the blaze of the shops addressed to the New Jerusalem wants and the splendor with which these were taken for granted." Not oblivious to the sordid aspects of the crowded Jewish neighborhoods, James nonetheless considered the massive striving of the people for a more refined existence to be "the larger harmony" that united the energies of immigrants who had become urban consumers in America.[41]

The development of the Lower East Side as an emporium for immigrants betrayed the mythic image of the area as a monument to poverty. The dense Jewish section of lower Manhattan has been perceived as a prototype of urban poverty in the United States, and the Jewish population that lived there continues to be broadly described as impoverished.[42] Notorious for its crowded housing, the Lower East Side did have residents who lived in a deplorable condition. Nonetheless, the rapid flowering of retail commerce in the district would have been impossible without a population that upheld standards of consumption.

The ability to cultivate such standards had everything to do with the bustling activity of eastern European Jews. By the late 1880s, when the number of Jewish newcomers in the area approached 100,000, the influence of the Jews' traditional familiarity with commerce began to be felt. The saloons and rundown shops that had marked the Lower East Side as a slum gave way steadily to groceries, cafés, and restaurants, and to clothing, jewelry, and furniture stores.[43] Particularly after the depression of 1893–1897 had ended, the signs of material sophisitication came clearly to the surface of the community. Reviewing the retail boom of 1901, the *Yiddishes Tageblatt* concluded that the flourishing of business provided "the best proof of the great buying power of the people."[44] Visitors to the Lower East Side frequently commented on the quality of the food sold on the streets as well as in groceries and butcher stores, on the fine appearance of Jewish children, and on Jewish standards of domestic furnishing.[45] In 1902, the *Tageblatt* justifiably boasted about the regenerative power of Jewish consumers and merchants on the downtown community.

> In clothing the East Side beats all other worker neighborhoods and it does not stand behind the most beautiful business areas. The Jewish quarter is the best customer for silk and velvet, and also for gold and diamonds. . . . Furniture stores have multiplied and grown big and beautiful. The most beautiful furniture is sold on the East Side, and pianos have become a fashion in Jewish homes.[46]

The newspaper went further, suggesting that Jews were becoming more definitely American by raising their material standards. This point was made by linking the popular concept of "greening oneself out" ("oysgrinen zich"), which meant becoming more like an American, to sophistication in the area of consumption. Purporting to give "Clear Evidence How Jews Green Themselves Out Very Quickly in this Land," the paper dwelled on the change in attitudes toward housing that had occurred over the previous decade. In the early 1890s, many Jewish newcomers lived in small "room and bed-room" apartments rented for eight or ten dollars a month. A three-room place in a modern building was a distinct luxury. But, within a few years, many of the old tenements had been demolished, and the newcomers became accustomed to four- and five-room apartments with more conveniences. As the pace of modernization quickened, rents rose, but the supply was met by demand as newcomers entered the cycle of heightening tastes. By 1902, there had been a burst of construction of buildings with five- and six-room apartments and the latest conveniences. Bathrooms had become a commonplace, and electricity and elevators were not unusual. "The same people who had earlier been proud of living in three rooms," the *Tageblatt* stated, "began to be ashamed of their living situation and they opted for the new houses."[47]

The phenomenon of continually rising expectations was officially documented by the New York City Tenement House Department, which reported that, by 1914, the city housed around 1,500,000 tenants in over 22,000 buildings constructed since the passage of the New York Tenement House Law in 1901, which required much better lighting and ventilation, and a bathroom inside each apartment. As the pressing demand of consumers for better housing suggested, the standards of 1900 were well outmoded by the end of the decade.[48] A changing sense of desirable housing inevitably spurred desires for newer furnishings as well. Recalling her childhood in New York City around the turn of the century, a Jewish immigrant from Serbia explained that belongings that had been "perfectly acceptable" in one apartment became "impossible" in a different dwelling.[49]

Adjusting to the idea that luxuries could regularly be converted into necessities, newcomers found themselves involved in what appeared to be an endless cycle of acquisition. A Jewish version of the American notion of "keeping up with the Joneses" gave expression to the new view of material standards. "If the Browns next door hang up expensive lace curtains," a social commentator declared, replacing "Jones" with a name more common to American Jews, "we are discontented until lace curtains have gone up to our windows, no matter how much smaller our income may be than that of the Browns."[50] In eastern Europe, the concept of a continually rising standard of material life would have had little foundation. In urban America, however, it found sustenance.

With subtle yet irresistible force, new habits of consumption triggered a profound change in perspective among the majority of newcomers. Acquiring the American perspective of abundance, Jews learned that aspirations need not be tailored to means. By the start of the twentieth century, the Yiddish press could focus on the topic of "Families That Live Better than They Earn." Although many Jews saved money fastidiously, an equal number apparently lived well beyond their means as a result of credit, particularly the installment plan. Exemplifying this phenomenon was a family that had a combined income of twenty-three dollars a week from three wage-earning members, but that spent twice that amount in order to have a new suit "every two months" and diamonds "as big as icicles."[51] Although most Jews were not spendthrifts, they had to balance the pressure to save money against the imperative of increasing their standard of living.

The installment plan relieved the potential conflict between saving and spending. Despite the desire to identify with urban Americans through consumption, Jews shouldered a double burden of saving. They needed to accumulate money for the sake of relatives in Europe, most of whom required financial aid, and many of whom also wanted to emigrate to the United States. In addition, they needed savings for investment in business and real estate, two important avenues of economic success, and for education, a prerequisite for the social advance of the young in America. The economic and educational success of the newcomers and their children demonstrated the ability to save money in the hope of achieving long-term goals.[52] Saving money for investment in the future, however, did not preclude American habits of consumption.

The practice of installment buying initiated newcomers into the possibilities of immediate acquisition and familiarized them with the impatient optimism that characterized the American consumer. One immigrant suggested the impact of installment buying upon Jews by entitling a chapter of her memoirs "Buy Now, Pay Later—Mama Discovers an American Custom."[53] On the Lower East Side, items as various as children's treats, wedding dresses, and cemetery plots were available on the installment plan in the 1880s and 1890s.[54] Musician Samuel Chotzinoff remembered how luxuries bought on credit relieved the tense existence of his mother, who had to run a large household with small earnings. A percentage of the family's income was regularly devoted to "the never-ending succession" of domestic furnishings and personal possessions that his mother "could not resist buying" on installment.[55]

Encouraged by the activity of installment peddlers, young couples and families were particularly impressed by the possibility of instantly furnishing a new apartment with elegant-looking parlor sets and with dining room and bedroom pieces that contained the promise of a comfortable life. Abraham Cahan recalled that, when he married in 1885, he and his wife moved into an apartment furnished on the installment plan. The "three new rooms with brand-new furniture" passed even the stern scrutiny of the Russian intellectuals who composed Cahan's circle of friends. They gave the home high approval, judging the furniture to be "just fine."[56]

Tha availability of consumer credit was viewed not only in pragmatic terms, as a means of expediting consumption, but also as the outward sign of the dynamic state of demand that seemed to animate American society. Thomas Eyges, a Russian Jewish anarchist who immigrated from England to America in 1902, was prompted by his first law class—on the topic of contracts—to comprehend intellectually the general sense of wonder about American abundance which he had held for over a decade in the new society. Once his law professor made the opening comment that the underlying principle of American economic life was the assumption that everybody is honest, Eyges felt that he suddenly understood how such a young nation could become the richest in the world. "The extension of credit to everybody," he reflected, on the practice of selling luxuries on installment, was "the key to success," enabling virtually everyone to imagine material abundance and to realize that spending could be a legitimate way to confront the future.[57]

In 1914, as Europe verged on a war that would both assure the economic superiority of the United States in the world and herald the end of free immigration for Jews, an editorial in the *Yiddishes Tageblatt* made it clear that Jewish immigrants had developed the American perception of material abundance as a precious legacy. "Who can deny that [America] is more fruitful," began the argument under the title "A Great America—the Land of Tomorrow," which continued, "that her inhabitants eat better, dress more beautifully and live more comfortably than does the average population of other lands?"[58] Capping a generation of feverish immigration, this patriotic message reflected the psychological adaptation of eastern European Jews to the phenomenon of American abundance.

Though critical to the adaptation of immigrants, acceptance of the ever-rising American standard of living conflicted with traditional Jewish culture. In the old world, Jewish identity depended upon a venerable distinction between the holy and the mundane spheres of existence. To augment that distinction, Jews had cultivated a unique concept of material luxury, one that would be undermined by American abundance.

PART II

The Divinity of Luxury

ᨢᨵ 3 ᨢᨵ

The Holy and the Mundane

Of the various contrasts between life in eastern Europe and life in urban America, Marcus Ravage was most intrigued by the difference in attitude about luxuries. Having immigrated from the small city of Vaslui, Rumania, in 1900, Ravage spent his first days in New York City with relatives whose nonchalance about luxurious products seemed strange in light of the old Jewish ways that were still fresh in the newcomer's mind.

Boarding with his cousins, the Segals, he first marveled at the soap used by Mrs. Segal to clean the kitchen. Wrapped in a neatly printed package, it would have seemed to the women of Vaslui, who scrubbed their kitchens with sand, too good even for the washing of garments. After finishing the housework, Mrs. Segal went out shopping dressed in a way that Jews in eastern Europe considered appropriate for the Sabbath and holidays. She wore a taffeta gown kept from her wedding, jewelry that had once been reserved for visits to the synagogue, and a new pair of patent leather shoes. The first lunch and dinner eaten by Ravage with his New York cousins included meat, which was rarely eaten twice in one day back home, in addition to challah, the braided white bread prepared only for the Sabbath, and rice and raisins, which was customarily a dish served for the holiday of Purim.[1] Pondering the effect of this lifestyle upon the religious sensibility of Jewish newcomers in the United States, Ravage commented that "in a land where every day was some kind of a denatured holiday—where you could eat Sabbath twists on Wednesday, matzohs on New Year's—the holidays themselves became meaningless and dull."[2]

Although the regular enjoyment of luxuries did not necessarily conflict with Jewish law, it undermined the contrast of "holy" and "mundane" things that inhered in the Sabbath, which was the focal point of Jewish identity in the old world. That distinction could not be sustained in urban America, where luxuries were routinely converted into necessities. Not only did the Sabbath and other festive holidays lose the richness that traditional luxury items had added in the old world of material scarcity, but the lure of mass consumption combined with other conditions of the American city that eroded traditional Judaism. Culminating the decline of old-world religion, the Sabbath ended up as a shopping day.

The traditional Jewish attitude toward consumption was shaped by the pervasive spirit of religious devotion in eastern Europe. Morris Raphael Cohen, a Russian Jew who became a distinguished professor of philosophy at the City College of New York, remembered the contrast between the dismal surroundings and the vibrant spirituality of the Jewish Pale, where he lived from birth, in 1880, to emigration in 1892. "Anyone accustomed to the American standard of living who might have come to Neshwies in those days and walked through its unpaved and unlighted streets, looked into its small, unventilated and often overcrowded wooden houses, devoid of all plumbing . . . would have wondered how its six to eight thousand inhabitants managed to live at all," Cohen said of his shtetl in the province of Minsk. "But while outwardly correct," he continued, "he would thus have reckoned without its inner life and religious devotion which ennobled its joys and sorrows and provided strength and dignity for meeting the tasks and perplexities of the day."[3] The "inner life" of eastern European Jews would be nourished by the incorporation of material things into religious celebrations.

Judaism had always used objects to consecrate activities. Some ceremonial items, such as the tallis, a fringed prayer shawl, and the tephillin, or phylacteries, originated in the Torah. Others developed long after the Biblical age. The candle holders, wine cups, and spice box used for the Sabbath and for the Havdalah ceremony concluding the Sabbath appear to have derived from changes in custom that occurred in the first century B.C.E. and the first century C.E. The power of this category of objects to symbolize the Jewish relationship to God derived from the religious

distinctiveness of the things themselves. Specific to Judaism, these ceremonial articles differed clearly from ordinary possessions.

Perhaps the most fundamental division of material things into categories of holy and profane arose from the Jewish dietary code. Based on
scriptural passages and on Talmudic interpretations of those passages, the
concept of *kashruth*, or ritual fitness, generated an elaborate system of
prohibited and permitted foods. The dietary code was considered a principal means of differentiating Jews from Gentiles. In the perspective of
traditional Judaism, an indiscriminate diet constituted a flagrant disregard
of the exacting code of behavior designed by God to epitomize the
uniqueness of the Jews. The effectiveness of dietary distinctions as a
hedge of Jewish identity was recognized explicitly in the early Christians'
rejection of kashruth, which they deemed an obstacle to the conversion of
pagans.

Whereas ceremonial objects and kosher foods served as the material
cornerstones of Judaism, items of luxury acted in a less obvious way to
sustain the Jewish relationship to the Almighty. The interpretation of
luxuries also originated in the Torah. In Exodus (25:3–8), God commands
Moses to have the Israelites build a holy sanctuary out of "gold, and
silver, and brass; and blue, and purple, and scarlet, and fine linen,"
precious materials that the people would give up in order to consecrate
the physical structure of the divine Covenant. To enhance the sacred
aspect of the sanctuary, priests were required to wear fine garments in
the performance of their duties, and they were enjoined to sacrifice only
those animals that were "perfect," free from injury and disfigurement. In
contrast to ceremonial objects and kosher foods, which gained symbolic
power from being distinctly Jewish, the potential of luxuries to exalt the
Jewish covenant with God came from their physical superiority.

Originally, the religious sense of luxuries was confined to places of
worship. Between the reign of King Solomon in the tenth century B.C.E.
and the Roman defeat of the Jews in 70 C.E., the first and second temples
of Jerusalem contained the objects of finery with which the people honored the Lord. During this period, the Temple provided a focal point for
the separation of the holy from the mundane. Within its walls sacred
objects were kept, and consecrative meals, like that of the Passover, were
served. As the house of God, the Temple of Jerusalem embodied the
realm of holy acts and holy things, standing in physical opposition to the
outer world of ordinary activities and possessions. Only in the age of
exile that followed the destruction of the Second Temple in 70 C.E. would
the burden of separating the holy from the mundane shift from the high

priests to the Jewish people at large. Then, the use of luxuries to reinforce the aura of holiness would begin to evolve into a popular custom.

After the destruction of the Second Temple, Jews would sustain the division of the holy and the mundane through the meticulous preservation of holidays in their synagogues and homes. Jewish holidays punctuated the year with sacred moments of joy and sadness that commemorated events of the ancient past, events as momentous as the exodus from Egypt and the destruction of the Temple. These holidays kept people in touch with a basic principle of Judaism, the historically unique relationship to God that distinguished Jews from other nations. The eastern Europeans, who, by the nineteenth century, comprised the largest group of Jews in the world, maintained a private sanctuary by observing holidays in the homes and synagogues of disparate communities. As Joseph H. Hertz, the Chief Rabbi of the British Empire (1913–1946), explained in his edition of the Daily Prayer Book for Orthodox Jews, the celebration of Sabbath and festivals "diffused in the humblest Jewish home" a feeling of "holy joy" that was "impossible to convey to those who have not experienced it." Both the home and those who dwelled in it became, in Rabbi Hertz's words, "hallowed by their observance."[4]

The Jewish calendar focused on the Sabbath, which routinized the use of luxuries to substantiate the division between holy and mundane spheres. The only religious observance to have been mentioned in the Ten Commandments, the Sabbath has been described by rabbis as "the supreme example of the hallowing of life under the sanctifying influence of the Law" and as "the focus of Jewish belief."[5] Across the generations, rabbinic authorities elaborated the definition of the Sabbath as a day of rest from mundane labor and activities. No other holiday was marked by the detailed and strict prohibitions that assured the Sabbath a unique place in Jewish life. To divorce this day as completely as possible from the other days of the week, thirty-nine types of activity were explicitly prohibited: carrying, burning, extinguishing, building, demolishing, cooking, washing, writing, erasing, finishing, tearing, knotting, untying, shaping, in addition to a number of tasks required for agriculture, animal husbandry, and domestic production. In emulation of the seventh day of Creation, the Sabbath was stripped of the possibility of labor. It was perceived as a "foretaste" of Paradise, filled with *menukhe*—tranquillity, repose, serenity, peacefulness.[6]

The paradisiacal aspect of the Sabbath came to be experienced partly through the enjoyment of fine things. Although the concept of the Sabbath as a "delight" was first articulated by the prophet Isaiah (58:13) in the eighth century B.C.E., the day of rest appears originally to have been

viewed as a time for serene prayer and study. Between the first century B.C.E. and the third century C.E., however, the rabbis tended increasingly to emphasize the physical preparations required for a proper Sabbath. To the already established customs of cleaning clothes and houses, and of preparing substantial meals, the sages added the drinking of wine for the ceremony of kiddush, or sanctification, the notion of having at least three meals instead of the usual two, the emphasis on wearing fine clothes, the centrality of the attractively set dinner table, the obligation of lighting candles, and the custom of attending the bathhouse prior to the Sabbath. By the third century, the essential features of the luxuriant Sabbath had been established.[7]

With the added emphasis on joyous celebration that was inspired by the spread of Hasidism through most of eastern Europe in the eighteenth and nineteenth centuries, Jews in the era of immigration thrived on the use of luxuries in celebrating the Sabbath and other holidays. Delicious meals, fine garments, and choice tableware all contributed to the spiritual transformation of the household. The notion of the *neshome yeseyre*, the "additional soul" that was presumed to inhabit the Jew during the Sabbath, was fleshed out by the tangible presence of luxuries. "Often, my father would tell me about the *neshome yeseyre*," Abraham Cahan recalled in his reminiscences of childhood in Vilna—"I would feel it in the service and afterward at home" where "the white tablecloth and the shining candlesticks with their glowing candles" were surrounded by "a holy aura."[8]

The contrast between the deprivation of daily life and the luxury of holidays fortified the distinction between the holy and mundane spheres of Jewish life. Whereas the weekday fare of most Jews was plain and often lacking in meat, the advent of Sabbath meant a feast of gefilte fish, chicken noodle soup, stewed meat with carrots or potatoes, stuffed chicken parts, pudding with raisins and nuts, cakes filled with chopped almonds, raisins, and cinnamon, and large loaves of challah, the rich, white, braided bread that was placed next to the kiddush cups of wine to create an elegant setting for the imminent celebration. Morris Raphael Cohen described the foods of Sabbath as the "green oases in the desert of our early life."[9]

The participants in the celebration gave as much attention to their own appearance as they did to that of the festive table. For the Sabbath and holidays, they kept fine garments of silk and velvet, cashmere and gabardine, clothes embroidered with gold and silver. Some women wore their wedding dresses on these occasions. After emerging from the bathhouse clean and refreshed, the men often greeted "the Sabbath bride" or "the Sabbath queen," as the day had come to be known, by wearing white clothes. Luxuries such as these transformed the presence of the humblest Jew. The artist Marc Chagall remembered how his father, who hauled barrels of herring for a living, used to don a special white outfit for attending synagogue on the Sabbath. Dressed in this fashion, he caused his young son to imagine the prophet Elijah.[10]

Although items of luxury were not essential to the observance of the Sabbath, they gave substance to the vision of divine plenitude. While a few of the devout may have been able to achieve spiritual transcendence solely through the liturgy of celebration, the verses and prayers exalting the holy, most people needed a more tangible format for rising above the ordinary world. The enjoyment of luxuries in a setting of scarcity provided this essential bit of material support, rendering visible and tactile the contrast between the foretaste of paradise and the dull taste of daily life. The opposition between special and common things dramatized the state of mind that ebbed and flowed with the Jewish calendar. As symbols of spiritual wealth, luxuries entered into the very definition of Jewish identity in eastern Europe.

Under the pressure of life in the American city, where the distinction between the holy and the mundane appeared suddenly tenuous and unstable, the old symbolism of luxuries dissolved. The most obvious sign of this momentous change was the decline of the Jewish Sabbath in America.

The Sabbath appears to have been neglected throughout the nineteenth century. In an address honoring the foundation of New York City's Hebrew Orphan Asylum on May 16, 1883, Charles Patrick Daly, the Chief Justice of the New York City Court of Common Pleas, recalled that, as a boy in the early 1820s, he often would peek in at the Sabbath services of congregation Shearith Israel, whose synagogue was the oldest in the United States and, until 1825, the only one in New York City. Although the small structure on Mill Street could not hold many people, Daly observed that it was usually not crowded.[11] In a chronicle of New York City published in 1877, Matthew Hale Smith remarked that the Jews of the Lower East Side "know no Sabbath," keeping their stores open on Saturday "because they live in a Christian country" and doing the same on Sunday "because they are Jews."[12] By 1913, despite the great influx of Jews raised in the traditional world of eastern Europe, a survey of nearly three thousand stores located in the heart of the Lower East Side found that almost 60 percent stayed open on the Sabbath.[13]

Of the explanations for the decline of traditional Judaism in the United States, one of the most important has focused on the character of the immigrants themselves. Sociologist Charles Liebman has set forth the thesis that most Jewish newcomers were willing to abandon traditional laws, in part because they failed to understand the difference between habits that were rooted in Jewish law and those that were not. They retained secondary customs, as they gave up integral rituals.[14]

This interpretation hinged on the questionable claim that Jewish newcomers neglected to establish the *mikves*, or ritual baths, required for the "purification" of women after menstruation and of men prior to the Sabbath and holidays.[15] Although it is difficult to assess the state of ritual bathing in the late nineteenth and early twentieth centuries, observers of the Lower East Side did not fail to notice the presence of mikves. In December 1884, a reporter for the *New York Tribune* pointed out that Russian Jews commonly made use of the free mikves belonging to the synagogues of the area, a practice that he felt would check the potential for an outbreak of cholera in the city.[16] Several years later, in 1892, a writer for the *Century* magazine confirmed that orthodox synagogues often had ritual baths in their basements or annexes.[17] Shortly before the turn of the century, the *Yiddishes Tageblatt* criticized a plan to resettle newcomers in the suburbs of New York City, on the grounds that the traditional people who were targeted by the proposal wanted to remain near the downtown hub of religious activities, which included visits to the mikve.[18]

During the first decade of the twentieth century, ritual baths dotted many square blocks of the Lower East Side. According to insurance maps covering most of this region for the years 1903 and 1905, there were at least thirty-two baths at the disposal of newcomers, with the probability of others existing uncharted. Sixteen were connected to synagogues, one to a Hebrew school, and fifteen stood by themselves among the dwellings and stores of Jewish neighborhoods.[19] By 1908 and 1909, when journalist Ray Stannard Baker investigated conditions on the Lower East Side, enough contruction had taken place to justify the observation that municipal baths faced competition from the "innumerable little Jewish bath houses" of the area.[20]

Although some of the baths to which Baker referred probably were steam baths as opposed to mikves, which had highly specific requirements of construction and maintenance, it would appear that Jewish newcomers made an effort to transplant this vital institution on American soil. If, as the *Tribune* report of 1884 claimed, there were at least fifteen ritual baths housed in the synagogues of downtown New York, the ratio of people to baths was sufficient. At that time, the population of eastern European Jews in New York City probably did not exceed fifty thousand, which would have produced a ratio of one mikve to approximately three thousand people, many of whom were too young to require the rite of purification. In the typical shtetl, one bathhouse served thousands of people, and in small cities such as Shniatyn in Galicia, a population of over ten thousand Jews relied on a single mikve.[21] If the mikves of New York were not ritually up to par, a question that remains unaddressed, this would have reflected the ineffectiveness of leaders in the immigrant community. The construction of the baths, however, represented an initial attempt by the multitude of newcomers to preserve Judaism in urban America.

Not only did most Jews originally expect to perpetuate traditional ways, but when in the face of new pressures and temptations they began to cross some of the boundaries of Jewish law, they remained fully conscious of the transgression. In a deft portrayal of Jewish life on the Lower East Side at the turn of the century, the writer Hutchins Hapgood captured the ambivalence of newcomers breaking the Sabbath in order to attend the Yiddish theater. "The orthodox Jews who go to the theatre on Friday night, the beginning of Sabbath, are commonly somewhat ashamed of themselves and try to quiet their consciences by a vociferous condemnation of the actions on the stage," Hapgood observed, as he pointed out that actors whose roles required that they appear with a cigarette in their mouths were "frequently greeted with hisses and strenuous cries of 'Shame, shame, smoke on the Sabbath!' from the proletarian hypocrites in the gallery."[22]

The self-consciousness of traditional Jews in the modern city was as plainly manifested in an incident recorded by a regular columnist of the *Tageblatt*. On a Sabbath day in early December 1901, the journalist watched a sweatshop contractor strolling with his son down Park Row. As the pair passed a street peddler selling hot roasted chestnuts, the father stopped, looked around, and proceeded to whisper into the boy's ear. The youth then took a coin out of his father's pocket and looked up. Having thus pretended to comply with the prohibition of making a purchase on the Sabbath—even though the act of carrying money was itself forbidden—the man nodded to his son, who bought a bag of chestnuts.[23] Encouraged by the relative anonymity and freedom of city life, newcomers relaxed the standards that had continued to bind the majority of Jews in the old world. Their gradual departure from traditional law was characterized more by unsettling choice than by ignorant dereliction.

The argument that the people who chose to emigrate were prone to abandon traditional Judaism has a measure of validity, but it fails to comprehend the coercive conditions of city life in America. Particularly during the 1880s and 1890s, those who left eastern Europe were probably among the poorest and least educated of Jews. The wealthy, the learned, and the prestigious had good reasons to remain within the old social order. Furthermore, a distinct minority of immigrants, primarily intellectuals like Abraham Cahan, had already abandoned tradition in favor of the more secular lifestyle available in the largest cities of the Pale. Nonetheless, the majority of newcomers, while possibly seeking a more flexible mode of living, wanted to maintain traditional ways.[24] The thesis put forth by Charles Liebman has encouraged healthy speculation about the intensity of religious sentiment among the Jewish immigrants, but it must be tempered by the awareness that newcomers were sucked into the maelstrom of urban American life, which upset all customs and shattered the foundation of former beliefs.[25]

The chronicles of immigration testified fully to the shock of new conditions on the piety of incoming Jews. Commenting upon the numbers of young adults who had once observed the Law but, after a short time in New York City, had given up "old-fashioned things" such as matzoh, the *Tageblatt* called this phenomenon a "remarkable transformation."[26] Typically, newcomers arrived with well-ingrained religious convictions and immediately criticized their already settled relatives for failing to uphold the time-honored rites of Judaism. Yet, within three or six months, having found a job, saved some money, acquired the basic commodities of city life, and "plunged into the social whirl," they began to moderate their dedication to the old ways, which often came to be honored more in the breach than in the practice.[27]

The saga of Rose Soskin, who came from Poland in 1923, illustrated the contrast between the old and new worlds. Although her father had emigrated to America in 1914, the First World War delayed the departure of Rose's family. In spite of the devastation endured by Poles during the war, Rose and her family refused to eat nonkosher food even when they were hungry enough to eat grass. Once they had settled in Chicago, the Soskins maintained a "very religious" style of life for a short while, but the decision of one family member to work on Saturdays ended up ushering in a general relaxation of Sabbath observance.[28]

The unique conditions of the modern city shaped the outcome of traditional Judaism in the United States. In order to underscore the conflict between the fast pace of city life in America and the stolid piety of eastern Europe, journalist Ray Stannard Baker dwelled on a street scene that conveyed the pathetic fate of Judaism in its new setting at the turn of the century. Baker had visited many synagogues in which congregants waited in vain for a minyen, the quorum of ten men required for the conduct of community prayer, the recital of the mourner's prayer, and the reading of the Torah. At times, driven by a sense of spiritual desperation, a devout Jew would leave the building and try to hail a participant from the traffic of pedestrians outside. "I never shall forget one of these old Jews," the writer said, "his wistful eyes, his gentle, ineffectual movements . . . stepping out like some patriarch from his fifteenth century synagogue and seeking to stop with a call to prayer, the tide of the twentieth century as it rushed through the streets."[29]

The anxious encounter with unexpected social pressures made the American immigrant experience one of moral complexity. Abraham Cahan clarified this fact in "Rabbi Eliezer's Christmas," a short story published by *Scribner's Magazine* in 1899.[30] Rabbi Eliezer is a pious Jew who sells cigarettes, Yiddish newspapers, cheap novels, and candy from a stand on the Lower East Side. Approached on Christmas day by two Gentile women who work in a nearby settlement house and who are sentimentally interested in the story of the old man's life and aspirations, Eliezer soon finds himself the recipient of a check for twenty dollars, charitably intended for the purchase of a better stock of goods. As soon as the women leave, Jewish onlookers interrogate the peddler about the amount of the gift and needle him about accepting what appeared to be a Christmas present.

Conflicting with the desire to refurbish his business and to buy some personal luxuries, Rabbi Eliezer's feeling of guilt compels him to visit his benefactors and to inquire if the check was meant to be a Christmas present, which he would have to reject. To allay the old man's fears, one of the settlement workers offers to hold the money until the next day. Momentarily relieved, he attends the evening services at his synagogue, but his devotion is now interrupted by the nagging thought of the gift that he hopes to receive as promised. In this vignette, Cahan managed to condense the circumstances that tested the Jewish newcomer in the American city: the relaxation of relations between Gentiles and Jews, the emphasis on economic success, and the lure of material luxury.

Although this pattern of circumstances was distinct to the United States, the contest between traditional Judaism and urban ways had been anticipated within the Russian Pale of Settlement. During the middle and late nineteenth century, Jews responded to the cosmopolitan and tolerant atmosphere of Odessa, the port city on the Black Sea, by abandoning some old ways. They altered the rituals of prayer in favor of the popular German format, attended the opera, abandoned Jewish modes of dress, and learned to speak Russian, a tongue for which the Jews of the shtetl had little use. In addition, Odessan Jews took up the habit of smoking on the Sabbath. Most migrants to Odessa adopted popular customs not because of the ideology of "modernization" promoted by intellectuals but because the city itself permitted a greater degree of individualism than they had known before.[31]

It was, then, not simply urban living, but the environment of individual cities that molded the fate of traditional Judaism. The experience of Odessa was unique within the Pale of Settlement. In the densely populated Jewish provinces of Poland, sacrilegious behavior belonged more exclusively to young intellectuals. During the first three decades of the twentieth century, the large cities of Poland, which contained roughly 40 percent of Polish Jews, were able to boast a high degree of adherence to the laws of Sabbath and the other holidays. One account of Jewish life in urban Poland claimed that Jewish merchants evaded the Sabbath prohibition of money-handling by taking cash "through a piece of stuff, paper, or a corner of [their] *halat* [caftan coat]," but the covertness of this alleged technique contrasted with the Sabbatical piety of most Polish Jews.[32] As late as the 1920s, of the three million Jews of Poland, the number of laborers who worked, and shopkeepers who opened, on the Sabbath was negligible.[33] The cloistered religious spirit of Polish cities combatted the secular attitudes that managed to thrive in cosmopolitan Odessa.

If the nature of a city and a region shaped the course of Jewish observance, the setting of the American city, particularly that of New York, could only aggravate the corrosive tendencies that had appeared in Odessa. The establishment of a centrally powerful religious structure in the United States had long been difficult because of the physical mobility and the antiauthoritarian attitude of the American people. Characteristic of American Protestantism, the spirit of defiant impatience with constituted authority came to characterize American Judaism as well by the nineteenth century. In Continental Europe, Orthodoxy was normal and Radical Reform was isolated to an enclave of Berlin. In the United States, however, Orthodox Judaism failed to gain a foothold and Reform Judaism expanded dramatically, in tune with the demand of the German-Jewish laity for greater freedom from traditional forms. The absence of a strong, traditional leadership in America would pose a critical problem for the newcomers from eastern Europe.[34]

By 1898, when the Orthodox Jewish Congregational Union of America was founded as the first official organization to speak for traditional Judaism in the United States, the rabbinate had already been doomed to suffer an institutional system based on the tendency of congregations to splinter and multiply as a response to discontent. This tendency was intensified by the eastern Europeans, who initiated the "*landsmanshaft* principle" in regard to the formation of synagogues. Rather than try to adapt to the congregations that existed on their arrival in the United States, these newcomers preferred to start new groups, no matter how miniscule, based on a common locality in the old world. By 1854, the immigration of Jews from central and eastern Europe into New York City had brought into being seventeen synagogues to serve the city that, until 1825, had relied only on Shearith Israel. By 1888, the influx of Jews was predominantly from eastern Europe, and the number of synagogues had risen to one hundred and thirty. Within another thirty years, the industrious congregation-builders from Russia, Galicia, and Rumania had endowed Greater New York with nearly eight hundred permanent—and over three hundred temporary—synagogues.[35]

Disoriented by the institutional anarchy that they had helped to promote, newcomers from eastern Europe looked in vain for the familiar moorings provided by the rabbinate. "You can imagine the confusion in the immigrant's mind when he reaches America," social worker David Blaustein told an interviewer for the *Tribune* in 1903, "he finds his church of no account whatever." Blaustein explained further that "in place of finding the congregation all powerful and all embracing, he finds when he joins a congregation that he has simply joined a liberal society."[36] To impose religious order on a sprawling locale of autonomous synagogues was a task that overwhelmed the few masterful rabbis who had immigrated to America from eastern Europe in the 1880s and 1890s. Consequently, newcomers stumbled into a world virtually devoid of the leadership that they needed to insure the quality of kosher meat and to impose the sense of urgency about maintaining critical institutions—the Jewish school and the mikve.

Abetting the reckless spirit of antiauthoritarianism in the American city, the drive for economic success and cultural assimilation defied the Jewish calendar. In the shtetl, time was structured by decrees embedded in the scripture and the history of the Jews. By divine commandment, the Sabbath gave order to the week, and by a combination of biblical and historical injunction, the major holidays—Rosh Hoshanah, Yom Kippur, Sukkot, Simchat Torah, Chanukah, Purim, Passover, Shavuoth, and Tisha B'Av—as well as a host of minor festivities and fasts defined the course of the year in terms of the monumental events of the past.

In urban America, to the contrary, time adhered to the rhythm of work, and this derived from the gospel of economic success. A popular guidebook for immigrants in circulation at the end of the nineteenth century sermonized that "the wheel of fortune turns quickly . . . do not take a moment's rest. Run, do, work, and keep your own good in mind."[37] The American view of success as the Prime Mover was best expressed in the aphorism "Time Is Money" that was chanted to newcomers almost as soon as they put down their baggage in the homes of relatives.[38]

The unremitting cycle of hard work and hectic recreation nullified the devotional atmosphere of old-world Judaism. Instead of holidays dictating the mood of people, popular striving affected the spirit of celebration. Whereas the streets of a Russian shtetl on Yom Kippur (the Day of Atonement) were marked by a "dead stillness, a sadness," in America Jewish streets were "alive and brimming with liveliness."[39] The tense and restrained mood of New Yorkers dampened the joyousness of festivals and contrasted sharply with the attitude of the Jews in Russia, who "knew how to be merry when one was supposed to be merry."[40]

David Blaustein pinpointed the subversive effect of the work-oriented week on the Jewish sense of holy and mundane time as he characterized the ceremony of the *brith* (pronounced "bris" by the eastern Europeans), or circumcision, as it was often conducted in America. Customarily an occasion of joy, the brith, if it fell on a weekday, was often postponed on account of work until the following Sunday. But, then the hosts and the guests "know that it is not the right day, their consciences smite them, and the occasion is one of secret sadness rather than rejoicing."[41]

Defying the atmosphere of devotion and coercing immigrants to violate the Sabbath's prohibition of labor, the gospel of success infiltrated the leadership of American Jewish congregations. As the Jewish Communal Register indicated in 1917, a large proportion of synagogue presidents comprised men who were relatively young and successful in business.[42] In his autobiography, *Bleter Fun Mayn Leben* (Leaves from My Life), which was published in 1926, Abraham Cahan ruefully depicted the subordination of the truly learned rabbi to the uneducated young synagogue president whose only claim to prestige was that he had "worked his way up." Recalling the first appearance in synagogue of Rabbi Jacob Joseph, the sage imported from Vilna in 1888 to take the unenviable position of Chief Rabbi of New York, Cahan vilified "the greened-out orthodox Jews" of the congregation. "Dressed up in the American style" with "beautiful, pressed suits, with white, starched collars, with neckties and cuffs," these prosperous men "viewed their imported Rabbi as a greenhorn, and he felt this."[43] The new breed of leaders infused secular American standards into the primary Jewish institution, the synagogue.

In the American city, the spirit of antiauthoritarianism, the drive for economic success and cultural assimilation, and the lack of pervasive anti-Semitism all worked to counteract the cohesiveness that sustained the

Jewish sensibility of eastern Europe. Another quality of the urban setting in the United States, the presence of material abundance, directly challenged the role of luxuries as an underpinning of the Jewish distinction between the holy and the mundane.

The vast majority of eastern Europeans, Christians as well as Jews, had inherited a spiritual attitude toward the material world that was challenged by conditions in the American city, but the new potential for consumption collided directly with traditional Jewish culture. Peasants from eastern Europe had been used to living in close touch with nature. In a world where animals and trees, and even lumps of soil, acquired personalities, traits, and powers, people had defined themselves in relation to animated beings and things. Yet, in the cities of the United States, the moorings of nature vanished, and the immigrant floundered in an impersonal habitat of tenements, sidewalks, and machines.[44]

Much more tenuously connected with the land and with agriculture, the Jews of eastern Europe had developed a different, though no less spiritual, view of the material world. Against the monotonous background of scarcity, Jews had separated items of luxury from those of daily use and had woven these things into the fabric of their religious life. As a means of clarifying and deepening the distinction between holy and mundane spheres, the enjoyment of luxuries helped to sustain Jewish identity in eastern Europe. The Jews' symbolic approach to material things was subverted not by the physical environment of urban America but by the influence of abundance upon the lives of city people.

In a society that continually turned luxuries into necessities, the vivid contrast between regular and special products disappeared, leaving the spiritual distinction between the holy and the mundane without a complement in the material world. Marketed throughout the year, holiday treats lost the almost mystical aura recalled by immigrants from eastern Europe. Subjected to the fashion cycle, holiday garments appeared suddenly humble and ungainly. Juxtaposed with everyday silver-plated tableware that looked like the genuine item, holiday utensils no longer stood out as a reflection of divinity. The banality of luxury in America was inescapable, and it closed an avenue of spiritual expression even for newcomers who were determined to uphold traditional Judaism.

The rigorously pious Hasidic Jews continued to divide the realm of objects into superior and inferior categories, but their distinctions reflected the competitive loyalty of sects rather than the separation of the holy from the mundane. Prior to World War I, Hasidism transplanted itself with difficulty in America. Few *tzaddikim*, the "righteous men" who headed Hasidic sects, had immigrated to the United States, and many of the Russian Hasidim, as opposed to the Poles and Galicians, had apparently become "quickly Americanized" in their style of living.[45] Among those who immigrated in subsequent decades, however, many maintained a strict code of behavior that affected consumption. In the same way that traditional Jews approved some brands and some vendors of kosher food and rejected others that they felt to be insufficiently supervised, the Hadisim judged some merchants, usually those affiliated with their own tzaddik, to be acceptable and others unacceptable. By association, the products of retailers were considered either "sanctified" or impure.[46]

Though continuing to view the world according to an elaborate code of purity, the strictly religious Jew in America could not revive the declining significance of the luxury whose symbolic effect had come from its trait of material superiority in a setting of poverty. As the awareness of people in the Middle Ages had been molded by the physical extremes of heat and cold, darkness and light, silence and sound, so the inhabitants of eastern Europe had been keenly sensitive to the difference between sheer silk and rough wool, stuffed fish and thin soup, silver goblets and clay vessels. The gap between things of substance seemed analogous to the gap between things of spirit. This kind of awareness vanished in the new world.[47]

Moreover, the relationship between holidays and luxuries was inverted in the American city, as a result of the popularity of shopping. Whereas consumption had formerly bolstered the concept of holiness, holidays now promoted the cause of consumption. As the *New York Times* noted in 1905, the Jewish holidays had evidently become "a great time for the peddlers."[48]

The gradual acceptance of work as the organizing principle of time was accompanied by the evolution of the Sabbath into a day for shopping. The many stores on the Lower East Side whose doors stood open on Saturday offered silent testimony to the new importance of the American shopping schedule in the Jewish calendar. During the first decade of the twentieth century, the embarrassment attaching to this kind of sacrilege had diminished enough to encourage some merchants to advertise Sabbath sales in the Yiddish press. The large clothing store of Pursch and Greenthal on Canal Street used the New York *Forward* to advertise in bold print the commencement of their "giant" reduction sale on a Saturday morning in the middle of December 1907, which coincided nicely with the upswing in shopping for Christmas and Chanukah presents.[49] The *Yiddishes Tageblatt*, which catered to more traditional Jews, was no more resistant than the socialist *Forward* to the promotion of sales on the Sabbath. At the turn of the century, Lord and Taylor's store on the corner of Grand and Chrystie Streets, which advertised regularly in the *Tageblatt*, headlined its advertisements with the Yiddish banner "Special Bargains for Sabbath."[50]

By exploiting the Jewish concept of honoring a holiday, merchants and consumers turned the religious occasion into a pretext for shopping. Traditionally associated with the purchase and preparation of special items, holidays were inevitably wound into the spiral of American urban consumption. In a setting that placed more emphasis on the activity of shopping than on the veneration of religious events, the latter increasingly appeared as a rationale for the former. In April 1889, the East Broadway firm of Schlang Brothers conveyed this relationship in a way that would become typical during the next two decades, by claiming that its bargains on fine clothing provided consumers with the "opportunity to have a delightful Passover."[51]

During the numerous holidays of the Jewish calendar, all types of products won prestige. Cast as principal players in the performance of Passover, Purim, Chanukah, and the High Holidays, the clothing of the prosperous Siegel-Cooper Company, the footwear of the nationally known Regal Shoe Company, and the luxuries marketed by an array of lesser known firms sought the mantle of religious legitimacy.[52] In April 1906, an advertisement for the Co-operative Store, located on Grand Street, baldly exposed the exaggerated emphasis on merchandise as a component of the Jewish holiday. Alluding to the Four Questions of Passover that spelled out the characteristics distinguishing that holiday from all other days, the headline of the advertisement trumpeted: "The Four Questions Answered!" The follow-up line read, "When you see the beautiful stock for spring—suits and overcoats, hats, shoes, and men's furnishings."[53]

By the late 1890s, the promotional use of the Jewish attitude toward holidays had assumed its most explicit form, as products were marketed "in Honor of" a particular holiday. This phrase, "le-koved" in Yiddish, derived from the Hebrew words "le" meaning "to" and "kavode" meaning "honor." Usually reserved for special religious occasions, it possessed a corresponding dignity. In the bustling marketplace of the Lower East Side, the term became a promotional cliché. "Now is the time to adorn your house, In Honor of Passover, with the most beautiful and best oil cloth," "special presents in Honor of the Holiday," "premiums of glassware sets . . . in Honor of Purim," "the finest wares . . . in the greatest selection In Honor of the Splendid Holiday [the High Holidays]"—the venerable phrase was sounded throughout the city like staccato blows of the shofar, the ram's horn used to honor Rosh Hoshanah and Yom Kippur.[54]

Like all clichés, the honorary phrase ultimately lost contact with its original source. In an advertisement that appeared soon after the American New Year of 1914, the F. Saks Furniture Store on Second Avenue at 106th Street announced "Rare Furniture Bargains, in Honor of the New Year 1914."[55] Once the concept of "le-koved" embraced non-Jewish holidays, the priority of consumption over devotion became unmistakable. Sanctification of Jewish events was no longer pertinent—any secular holiday could furnish an excuse for acquiring new things.

As a pretext for shopping, Jewish holidays merged subtly with the fashion cycle. Although a chasm separated the religious festivity from the shopping spree, proximity in time was enough to bring about a superficial merging of the two. Almost imperceptibly, the promotion of "fall and winter styles" mingled with pleas to buy new clothes "in Honor of" the High Holidays that took place in September and October.[56] The unalterable differences between Passover and Easter were subordinated to the fact that they both occurred during the spring shopping season. By virtue of this tenuous bond, products for Easter and Passover could be advertised together.[57] The "white" sales of January also found a place within the Jewish calendar, even though no major holiday came between Chanukah in December and Purim in March or April. On the second day of 1913, Pursch and Greenthal promoted their apparel for men and boys as a "half year reduction sale."[58] At best, January fell in the fourth month of the Jewish year, but in order to attract newcomers to the custom of the winter sale, the Jewish calendar was squeezed into alignment with the American cycle of consumption.

Although the old role of luxuries as a symbol of earthly holiness collapsed under the pressure of city life, objects of beauty and expense would acquire new meaning in the American environment. In the celebration of three major holidays that involved special forms of consumption—Sukkot, Chanukah, and Passover—newcomers would articulate their dual identity as Jews and Americans. The appreciation of luxuries would help to establish Jewish identity in the new world as it had in the old.

᭡᭡᭡ 4 ᭡᭡᭡

Luxuries, Holidays, and
Jewish Identity

Jews relied on the holidays of Sukkot, Chanukah, and Passover to
express an American Jewish identity and, by the 1890s, they were altering each one in response to the condition of American abundance. As a
celebration of the earth's bounty, Sukkot naturally expanded to include
the new awareness of mass-marketed plenty in America. By proximity to
the secularized American Christmas, Chanukah rose to importance in the
United States, where it allowed Jewish newcomers to integrate themselves more fully into the larger society through the ritual of holiday
shopping and gift giving. In the cause of spiritual purification, Passover
raised the concept of festive luxury to a high point, where it would blend
with the American emphasis on a rising standard of living. This premier
festival became an occasion not just to commemorate the liberation from
Egypt but also to overhaul household and personal possessions. As Chanukah allowed Jews to share in American festivities while nominally
respecting tradition, Passover watched the old command for purity give
way to the new quest for a higher standard of living.

Respect for Jewish tradition and appreciation of American life were
suitably mixed in the celebration of Sukkot (pronounced "Sukkos" in
Yiddish), the Feast of Booths. This holiday combined a harvest festival

68

with the commemoration of the forty years wandering in the wilderness, the period after the exodus from Egypt in which the Israelites dwelled in *sukkot*, or booths. Sukkot was venerated in scripture as the time appointed by Moses for the public reading of the Torah that he had committed to writing.[1] The occasion of great pilgrimages to the ancient Temple, the festival gained additional esteem from the prophecy of Zechariah (14:16) that all nations would one day come to Jerusalem to celebrate Sukkot with the Jews. After the destruction of the Temple, Jews were supposed to construct their own loosely roofed sukkahs. These temporary dwellings were customarily well furnished and, if the weather permitted, primary domestic activities took place within the structure for the seven days of early autumn when the holiday occurred. Sukkot recalled and celebrated both the protection given by God in the aftermath of liberation from Egypt and the bounty that awaited Jews in the promised land. Reverence for a sacred past and hope for a secure and satisfying future found a home in the sukkah.[2]

Against the inhospitable background of the modern city, the effort of Jewish immigrants to perpetuate Sukkot showed a deep respect for tradition. Describing the holiday as a bulwark of Jewish identity, the New York *Yiddishes Tageblatt* declared that Judaism did not use weapons of destruction in the struggle of the great religions—it fought instead with "weapons of the spirit," of which a vital one was the observance of Sukkot.[3] Under the harsh conditions of American life, Sukkot may have been, as Abraham Cahan expressed it, a time of "tortured joy," but newcomers considered the festival well worth preserving.[4] In the court-yards and on the rooftops of tenements, they erected booths in the urban wilderness, using planks of wood and imported boughs of fir trees, as well as boxes, sheets, shawls, quilts, wicker, green-painted cane, and any other materials fit for the task. "Each back yard of the East Side these last six days . . . with hardly an exception," the *New York Tribune* stated on September 24, 1899, "has possessed one of these houses of boughs, the tents of the Judeans in the wilderness modernized, yet of the spirit of centuries bygone."[5]

The effect of the modern sukkah as a haven of traditional Judaism in strange surroundings was evoked by a reporter covering the Lower East Side for the *Tribune* in October 1895. "Down in the street, far below, the noise of traffic and the tumult of the city made a deafening roar," the journalist recorded, "but up by the tabernacles on the reddened roofs all was peace and quiet, except for the children who were enjoying the novelty of the occasion, and the voices of the householders as they spoke of the festival and its meaning." Welcomed into an unusually elaborate sukkah by a matron who spoke little English, the writer was struck by the interior, which was illuminated by three "walls" of orange, crimson, and purple stained glass, and covered by a tentlike roof of plaited wicker. On a side table, there were prayer books and candles in burnished candlesticks, and over the substantial rear wall of the booth the customary inscription for Sukkot was emblazoned in Hebrew letters: "Seven Days Shalt Thou Sit in the Tabernacle." Set against the chilling depression of 1895, the impression of domestic warmth was completed by a host of delicious foods — "golden pears, ruddy-cheeked peaches, apples and clusters of grapes hung from the matter roof, and decanters of wine, plates of fruit and fancy cake stood ready to be served on the hospitable table."[6]

Described so vividly in the *New York Tribune*, the elegant sukkah carried its own message about the changing nature of this holiday in urban America. The tabernacle stood as a visible reminder of the contrast between Jewish life in the United States and Jewish life in the "wilderness," which referred not only to the desert of ancient Palestine but also to contemporary regions of persecution, most notably Russia. Delicate and vulnerable to the elements, the sukkah served as a perfect symbol of Jewish life among the nations of the world, and it gave newcomers to America a vehicle through which to express their appreciation of the relative security they had found. In 1912, the *Tageblatt* considered "Our American Sukkah" symbolically, stating that the Jews "have never had in any place such a comfortable, such a solid Sukkah" as that which they had in America.[7]

As a time of thanksgiving for both plenty and security, Sukkot gained a new dimension not only from the political character of the United States but also from the influence of material abundance. Formerly an acknowledgment of nature's bounty, the festival accommodated the keen awareness of manufactured plenty as an element of American society. After the depression of the 1890s, renewed optimism about the future generated a new lavishness in the holiday. As the commodities of city life entered into the sukkah, mingling with the fruits of nature, the two forms of abundance struck a balance that was mirrored in the title of a Yiddish feature story of 1904, "The Green Horn of Plenty: The Piano in the Sukkah."[8] Mandated by the Torah to be an occasion of great feasting, Sukkot seemed a good occasion for the appreciation of luxuries acquired by newcomers in the American city. Posed to reinforce the contrast between the hardships of a nomadic existence and the comforts of a settled life, the holiday, in one sense, culminated in America.

Whereas Sukkot achieved a measure of harmony between the traditional Jewish and the modern American identity, Chanukah plunged into the complexity of Jewish adaptation to American society. In contrast to Sukkot, which was rooted in the Bible, this holiday derived not from scripture but from a historical conflict between Judaism and paganism.

In the period 175–164 B.C.E., when Antiochus IV assumed the leadership of the Seleucid dynasty that controlled Palestine, the Jews of Jerusalem and surrounding areas were confronted with a nemesis who would provoke the Maccabean rebellion commemorated on Chanukah. Abetted by the willingness of some Jews, particularly those in prominent positions, to accept Greek customs as a way of increasing their political power and social prestige, Antiochus IV encouraged the growth of paganism in Jerusalem and turned the venerable position of the High Priest into an object of barter. The assault on Jewish tradition climaxed in 167 B.C.E., when the king outlawed Jewish worship and instituted pagan rites in the Temple. While some Jews deferred to royal decree, many pietists rebelled, and the struggle against the Seleucid forces began, at first with little success.

The prospects of the religious rebels turned upon an uprising against royal officials and soldiers in the town of Modin to the northwest of Jerusalem. There, a Jewish priest named Mattathias appears to have incited a riot against the authorities who had demanded that the Jews make sacrifices to idols. After the slaughter of the king's agents and soldiers, groups of Jews fled to the nearby mountains, from which they waged guerrilla warfare against troops dispatched from Syria, the base of the Antiochene empire. After two years of war under the command of one of Mattathias's sons, Judah, who was given the honorary surname Maccabeus, which may have derived from the Hebrew word for "hammer," the Jews defeated the ostensibly more powerful Syrians. Jerusalem was reclaimed and, in the autumn of 164 B.C.E., the Temple was rededicated. Sustaining the legendary miracle of the cruse of oil that was sufficient only to light the Temple for one day yet lasted for eight, the Festival of Lights, as Chanukah quickly came to be known, focused on the ritual of lighting candles for eight days.[9]

Illuminating the problem of cultural assimilation, Chanukah found new relevance and popularity among Jewish newcomers to America. With the rise of Zionism as a response to European persecution at the end of the nineteenth century, the heroism of the Macabean struggle was emphasized by ideologically minded Jews who envisioned the creation of a Jewish nation based on a tough-minded attitude of self-determination. But, among the multitude of American Jews, the popularity of Chanukah had little to do with ideology. It stemmed instead from the powerful presence of Christmas as the American rite of consumption.

The approximation of Chanukah to Christmas was based on the desire of Jewish newcomers to adopt secular American holidays. Labor Day harmonized with the socialist leanings and organizational flare of Jewish workers, and it fit well into the rhythmic alteration of working and vacationing that would define Jewish life under the American calendar. The holiday called for the end of summer relaxation and the renewal of hard work during the colder seasons of autumn and winter.[10] The Fourth of July was a jubilee for Jewish immigrants, who had a visceral respect for American pluralism. Unlike their native countries of eastern Europe, where citizenship was often defined in opposition to Judaism, the United States seemed to welcome the participation of those newcomers whose politics were not disturbingly radical. Consequently, as the *Tageblatt* editorialized in 1904, the Jews felt they had "a place in America" and celebrated "the great holiday of July 4th."[11]

The gradual acceptance of Thanksgiving showed a willingness to fuse Jewish and American rituals. Elizabeth Stern, a social worker whose family had immigrated from Russia to New York City in 1892 when she was two years old, remembered how Thanksgiving was adopted in her home. As the children grew up and began to speak English at home, their parents tried to adapt to some American ways. One Thanksgiving, Stern's father brought home a turkey, which her mother repeatedly compared to a duck and a chicken, the poultry that Jews had traditionally enjoyed on holidays and festive occasions. In a further blending of American and Jewish features, the table was set with a white cloth, "as if it were a holy day," and her father, who made a meager living teaching Hebrew, recited tales from the Talmud. Afterward, the young Stern explained the meaning of Thanksgiving. Her mother responded with approval but managed to give Judaism the last word by reminding the inquisitive daughter that "one must not give thanks only on one day and for one bird!"[12]

With the rise of Christmas as the primary secular holiday of urban Americans, the preconditions for an American Chanukah were established. Originally, the predominantly Protestant populace of America did not consider Christmas to be an occasion worth honoring. In 1659, the Puritan colony of Massachusetts made the celebration of Christmas, through abstention from work or feasting, an offense punishable by a fine of five shillings. Although this law was ultimately repealed, people continued to work on Christmas Day at least until the end of the seventeenth century, and the holiday had minimal effect until the second half of the nineteenth century.[13] By that time, the great immigration of Germans had begun to boost the nation's interest in Christmas. After the Civil War, department stores began to stay open late on the days before

Christmas, ornaments for trees became popular, and the first American Christmas cards appeared, following the example set by German immigrant Louis Prang, a leading maker of color lithographs, who started the trade in Christmas cards in 1874. Within a few years, Prang was producing millions of cards each season.[14] The stirrings of a great interest in the holiday were prompted by entrepreneurs rather than ministers.

By the late 1880s, Christmas appears to have asserted itself as the primary holiday of the United States. In 1888, *Good Housekeeping* lamented the fact that the simplicity of Thanksgiving, which commemorated a time of material hardship, had been overcome by the extravagance of the American urban Christmas.[15] Although Thanksgiving was distinctive to America, Christmas bore seeds—in the ritual of gift-giving—that would be nourished in the uniquely American climate of consumption. The increasing sophistication of retail displays, the growing mythology of Santa Claus as a grand dispenser of merchandise, the ornamentation of the home and the tree, the development of card sending as a social obligation, all of these qualities of the secular Christmas insured the superiority of the day in the hierarchy of festivals. One week after the Christmas of 1897, the *New York Tribune* indicted the intriguing commercial atmosphere of "the modern Christmas," which was fast becoming "a time for barter, for display, for acquisitiveness."[16]

The drama of Christmas exerted a strong influence on Jewish newcomers, as the spectacle of the Christmas tree and the rite of gift giving altered the celebration of Chanukah. In December 1900, the *Tageblatt* contended that the ancient struggle of the Jews against the "turbulent forces of Antiochus" found no better parallel than "the struggle between the poor, quiet, little Chanukah lights and the brightly illuminated, dressed-up and decorated Christmas tree."[17] On the awareness of Jewish children, the impact of the splendid tree was inestimable. The ritual of decorating Christmas trees established itself in the public schools and settlement houses. In 1906, Abraham Stern, a member of the New York City Board of Education, noted that most of the kindergratens in Jewish neighborhoods had trees. Jewish youngsters apparently enjoyed the festivity of decoration and, Stern added, "in many cases the Jewish mothers helped in trimming the trees."[18]

The charm of the Christmas tree was best reflected in the introduction of trees into some Jewish homes. Reformed Jews in the United States, like the affluent and cosmopolitan Jews of Odessa, St. Petersburg, and Moscow, had already adopted certain features of Christmas. Yet, when Rabbi Judah Magnes of New York City's prestigious Temple Emanu-El denounced the "cringing" behavior of those who brought Christmas trees into their homes, an action that constituted, in his opinion, "one more step in their gradual disappearance as Jews," the respected leader may well have been referring to newcomers from eastern Europe as well as to the affluent congregants of his Reformed synagogue.[19] Addressing the influence of Christmas upon immigrants, a reporter for the *Tageblatt* claimed at the start of 1899 that it was not necessary to travel uptown to witness the holiday's effect, because "East Broadway and Henry Street showed quite a number of Christmas trees in Jewish houses."[20] Four years later, the Yiddish press regretted to report that "the Christmas-tree parade in Jewish homes" was growing, and, if the tree itself were not present, it was likely that "the holly and the mistletoe" would be.[21]

Yet, despite the appearance of the emblems of a Christian holiday in the tenements of the Lower East Side, Jews had no intention of adopting Christmas. As the festival had become secular in nature, its symbols posed a minimal threat to Judaism. The impact of Christmas could be measured most effectively in terms of changes in the celebration of Chanukah. Largely as a result of the popularity of the secular Christmas in America, the Jews developed a new enthusiasm for the Festival of Lights.

A view of the Lower East Side in the 1890s showed that Chanukah had survived the shocks of immigration. During that time, passengers on the Second Avenue "El" train heading down toward 1st Street in the darkness of a December evening were struck by the rows of burning candles that illuminated the windows of tenement house after tenement house.[22] In the Chanukah season of 1897, the downtown press made reference to the upsurge of interest in the holiday among eastern European Jews. "The tendency has been of late years to celebrate the festival quite generally, only it is given over for the most part to the little ones," a newspaper explained, suggesting the resemblance to the child-centered day of Christmas, and advocating the new emphasis on festivities with the declaration that "the Jews, too, even in our day, must have an occasion for merry-making, and here it is."[23]

Traditionally, Jews had not suffered from a lack of "merry-making," but the focus of fun-filled celebration apparently shifted in America. Although the eastern Europeans rejoiced on a variety of occasions, the leading time for unrestrained fun was Purim. Celebrated a month before Passover, Purim commemorated the legendary rescue of Persian Jews from annihilation at the whim of an evil prime minister, by virtue of the intervention of the Jewish Queen Esther. Marked by an enthusiastic reading of the Book of Esther in synagogue, by *spiels*, or plays, rendering the cataclysmic events of the story, by the generous exchange of delicious treats, and by parading in masks and costumes, this special day was the only time in which transvestism, a violation of biblical law, was permitted, and in which the normally sober Jews were enjoined to become drunk to the point that they were unable to tell the difference between the phrases "cursed be Haman," referring to the legendary hater of the Jews, and "blessed be Mordecai," referring to the heroic cousin of Esther. Recalling the celebration of Purim in the Russian shtetl of Lida in the 1870s, David Blaustein explained that the fun-filled occasion was the climactic point of the year for children. Although the holiday continued to be observed with the accustomed enthusiasm in eastern Europe, in the United States it had become "a lost day."[24]

Had Christmas been in March, Purim would undoubtedly have held a high position in the calendar of American Jews. Although it included activities that paralleled those of Christmas—the exchange of gifts, the entertainment of children, the production of plays—Purim failed to synchronize with the American calendar of festive consumption. If this day of merriment waned in the face of an insurgent Chanukah, it was not for lack of substance.

In contrast to Purim, Chanukah did not originally include the custom of gift giving that had become so prominent a part of the American Christmas. The giving of coins, or "Chanukah gelt," to children in honor of the holiday had gained popularity in eastern Europe, having derived from the seventeenth-century Polish practice of sending a sum of money with children for the benefit of local teachers.[25] And, although Chanukah was not a particularly important holiday, it was anticipated by children. The excitement of visiting relatives to receive small sums of money provided the motif for Sholom Aleichem's short story "Chanukah Gelt," in which two brothers endure the bothersome conversation, the gratuitous squeezes, the peculiar personalities, and the worthless pieces of old Russian money inevitably donated by their Uncle Moishe-Aaron, in their pursuit of coins for the holiday.[26] Possessing some of the excitement that Christian children associated with Christmas, Chanukah nonetheless lacked the emphasis on presents that made the Gentile festival a rite of consumption. The introduction of retail products into the Jewish holiday was spurred by the exotic commercial atmosphere of the secular Christmas.

The mystique and the drama of Christmas shopping exerted tremendous pressure on Jewish newcomers in the city. In 1898, a "large proportion" of the Jewish population of New York was observed shopping in the major retail stores during December. These shoppers apparently considered Christmas to be a holiday in which they were "to an appreciable degree interested."[27]

Not restricted to retail stores, the commercial attractions of the holiday season pervaded the city's street markets as well. During the weeks before Christmas, peddlers competed intensely for spaces on the street. Many camped out overnight in their desired locations and made fires to keep themselves warm. Some alternated nights with fellow merchants, watching each other's wares in turn. Still others hired proxies who, for fifteen cents per night, agreed to guard merchandise while the vendors went home to sleep.[28] Often garnished with wreaths of holly and evergreen boughs, the displays of pushcarts were carefully and colorfully designed to attract urban customers. Jewish wholesalers on the Lower East Side distributed large stocks of Christmas ornaments and treats for the outdoor markets.[29] The infusion of bright color and wintergreen fragrance into the normally drab streets of the city affected all but the most reclusive of Jewish immigrants. As a daughter of Serbian Jews remembered of her youth in New York City, "for us a need was filled at Christmas time by the gaily decorated wares that were spread out by the street merchants."[30]

Accentuated by the yearnings of children exposed to the ubiquitous ritual of gift giving, the impulse to buy Christmas presents welled up among the multitude of Jewish newcomers. On Christmas Day, 1904, feature stories in the *New York Tribune* and the New York *Forward* documented the extent to which the alien custom had been adopted by Jews. "Santa Claus visited the East Side last night, and hardly missed a tenement house," the *Tribune* declared, adding the patronizing remark that "in the greatness of his heart . . . he forgot that there was a religious significance to the day for which he has come to be the patron saint, and dispensed his favors regardless of creed or caste." In the same fatuous tone, the newspaper stated that "in the homes of the poor Hebrews, as well as of the well to do, Christmas is being celebrated with never a thought that it is the birthday of Him whom their forbears crucified more than nineteen centuries ago."[31]

Despite the attitude of pretentious bigotry behind this report, its findings were substantiated by the Jewish press. Under the title "They Are Pious, But They Observe Christmas Too," the Yiddish daily *Forward* claimed that many Jewish families, including "freethinkers" as well as observers of the faith, bought Christmas presents to satisfy the demands of their children. Yet children were not the only recipients of Christmas presents. Spouses and neighbors in the tenement houses were also seen exchanging gifts, some of which, expensive beyond the purchaser's means, were bought on the installment plan.[32]

The sudden popularity of gift giving among Jewish newcomers reflected not an inclination toward Christianity but an effort to embrace the

American spirit. "Who says that we are not Americanizing?" the *Forward* asked rhetorically, in the knowledge that the buying of presents in the Christmas season, for which Jewish newcomers showed such passion, constituted "the first thing that demonstrates that one is not a green-horn."[33] Through the ritual of gift giving, newcomers demonstrated their devotion to the belief in monetary generosity that reflected the American perspective of material abundance. Acknowledging the importance of liberal spending to the urban American, an official of a large East Side synagogue reported that many local leaders encouraged the practice of holiday gift giving on the premise that "it will do one no harm to open up his purse once a year and give generously where friendship dictates."[34]

Sometimes oblivious to the motive that led newcomers to accept the idea of the Christmas present, local critics made a ritual of hurling condemnations at the multitude each December. Parents were rebuked for giving gifts to settlement workers, for contributing toys for the decoration of public Christmas trees, and, of course, for exchanging gifts within their own circles.[35] Appalled that devout Jews would indulge their children's desires for Christmas presents, one social commentator imagined "how the soul-commanding voice of Isaiah . . . would chide the people for this error—could he but speak to-day."[36] The scriptural theme of religious backsliding was evinced poignantly in a 1907 editorial called "Our Greatest Enemy." Arguing that the subtle influence of American habits of consumption posed as great a problem as the tyrannical force of religious persecution, the commentary admonished that "we do not want death from pleasure, just as we have not wanted death from trouble."[37]

These spirited prophecies reflected the confusion that had arisen from the proximity of the secular Christmas to Chanukah, but they would not be borne out by the course of events. The adoption of gift giving implied the alteration of a Jewish festival, not the acceptance of a Christian belief. It was this practice that identified the American Chanukah. Despite the fiery criticism that poured from its pages, the tradition-minded *Yiddishes Tageblatt* itself sanctioned the shift in popular custom. Striking an analogy between the ancient conflict of Greek and Jewish culture and the struggle taking place in urban America, the newspaper called not for the abolition of gift giving among Jews, but, instead, for the use of presents as a means of bolstering the enthusiasm surrounding Chanukah.[38]

Ridley's department store on Grand Street, a major retailer of the Lower East Side and a faithful advertiser in the *Tageblatt*, articulated the alteration of Chanukah in an advertisement of December 1897. "The spirit with which all Americans wait for the joyous Christmas grows ever stronger and stronger with the passage of time," Ridley's exclaimed, "and

Chanukah gifts with Christmas presents go hand in hand. There is only a difference in name."[39] The spirit of Christmas to which the advertiser referred was clearly not that of a single religion. It seemed to be an ecumenical spirit of buying and giving, of festive consumption tempered by the flame of generosity.

In the ethic of consumption, Chanukah and Christmas had discovered a common denominator. Advertising in the Yiddish press mirrored that of the metropolitan newspapers, promoting the notion that new products were as pertinent to Chanukah as they were to Christmas. The fundamentally secular content of the festival was illustrated in an advertisement of the Schubert Piano Company, a firm with stores on West 33d Street in Manhattan and on Fulton Street in Brooklyn. Appearing in 1911, the advertisement urged "A Piano or Player Piano for Chanukah" and showed a picture of Santa Claus moving a piano into the living room of a young couple.[40] In the European setting, it would have been inconceivable that a Christian saint enter the psychic world of Jews. In urban America, where Saint Nicholas had been stripped of religious significance and converted into a herald of consumers, he could be accepted gracefully by the multitude of Jewish newcomers.

Through the winter rite of consumption, the majority of newcomers found the easiest way to incorporate an American attitude into Chanukah. The Jewish and American traditions could also be combined in the sphere of art, but this required an effort that many people were not prepared to make. In December 1900, the Educational Alliance of the Lower East Side staged a dramatic production that exemplified the artistic method of seeking such a harmony. Founded in 1889 as the Hebrew Institute, moved in 1891 to a stately five-story building on the corner of East Broadway and Jefferson Street, and renamed in 1893, the Educational Alliance was a civic center designed by affluent and well-established German Jews to expose the eastern Europeans to American beliefs and values, and to the fine arts. The primary cultural event of the holiday season in 1900 was the pantomime performance of Henry Wadsworth Longfellow's poetic five-act play *Judas Maccabeus*.

Composed in December 1871, with the spirit of Chanukah inspiring the poet's imagination, Longfellow's work contained a number of poignant scenes evoking the desperation of Jews besieged by Greek culture. Highlighting the dilemma of the Jew who submitted to the ways of the politically dominant Syrians, the high priest Jason mourns his own downfall, near the end of the play, by crying, "I am neither Jew nor Greek, but stand between them both, a renegade to each in turn."[41] Amplifying the play's message about the dangers of assimilation, the passion of the performers elicited a strong response from several audiences, which were composed mainly of young Russian Jews.[42]

In the production of *Judas Maccabeus*, the spirit of Chanukah was expressed through American art. Satisfying to the few who enjoyed serious theater, the Alliance's presentation was missed by the multitude of Jewish immigrants who honored the holiday in the arena of the department store and the street market. In their activities, the spirit of the American consumer was expressed through the holiday of Chanukah.

Whereas art served to heighten the spiritual meaning of Chanukah, the popular approach to fusing Jewish and American culture required that the essence of the holiday be discounted. Although Chanukah could appropriately be called the Festival of Lights as long as the menorah endured, the holiday's other traditional name, Festival of Dedication, sounded hollow in America. As a commemoration of the heroic rededication of the Second Temple, the festival had lapsed. Even in the Jewish calendar of eastern Europe, the message of Chanukah may have been subordinated to the festivities of dreidel-spinning and cardplaying that had been grafted onto the holiday during the Middle Ages. Yet, in America, the omnipresence of Jewish values had been shattered, and the spiritual basis of Chanukah had been obscured all the more by the focus on gift giving.[43] The festival fell prey to the same charge of superficiality that plagued the secular Christmas. For many newcomers, it had apparently become a time of celebrations that were not specifically Jewish and that had no relevance to the character of the holiday.[44]

The evolution of Chuankah during the first generation of immigration from eastern Europe reflected the effort of Jews to balance the flexibility of American urban culture against the rigidity of ideological commitment. By infusing an essentially American practice and attitude into the traditional form of Chanukah, newcomers tried to bridge the yawning chasm between their old world and their new one. Preferring involvement in American society to seclusion from it, they inevitably blunted the Jewish point of view. Their approach stifled the meaning of Judah the Maccabee, but it generated an Irving Berlin, the immigrant from Siberia who composed the popular song of 1909 *Christmas Time Seems Years and Years Away* and whose 1942 classic *White Christmas* would show the potential of American city culture for fusing the traditions of residents and newcomers.

Whereas Chanukah was altered in order to facilitate the Jews' participation in the central American rite of consumption, and Sukkot was modified in order to express the Jews' appreciation of American abundance, Passover infused the Jewish belief in the dignifying power of luxury into the American concept of the standard of living. On account of Passover's prestige among the Jewish holidays, this festival played a singular role in the revision of Jewish identity in America.

No Jewish holiday contained more regulations, required more preparation, and enjoyed more popularity than Passover. Commemorating the miraculous deliverance of the Jews from bondage in Egypt, this seven-day occasion was the foremost acknowledgement of God's covenant with the Jews. After the destruction of the Second Temple in 70 C.E., the unleavened bread, or matzoh, came to take the place of the sacrificial lamb as the symbol of the redemption assured by belief in the God of Abraham and Moses.[45] Neglect of the laws of Passover, which focused on the removal of all *khomets*, or leavened foods, from the home, was considered tantamount to rejection of the divine covenant.[46] Unlike other holidays, Passover had its own code of purity, which excluded a variety of foods that could conceivably rise from exposure to moisture, prohibited all contact with such foods, and required the purification of all vessels and utensils that had come into contact with them.[47] The uniqueness of the festival was exemplified by the practice of a Hasidic rabbi of late nineteenth-century Poland, who reserved special apartments of his two-story home for use only on Passover.[48]

The holiday stirred a profound sense of religious devotion and historical identity among eastern European Jews. The elaborate housecleaning and preparation of the feast for the Seder, the ceremonial meal that initiated the holiday, made the weeks before Passover a time of heady anticipation. An immigrant from Lithuania recalled that the people of his former shtetl "lived the whole winter for Pesach."[49] After the furniture of the household had been taken to the river for a cleaning, the dirt floor covered with fresh yellow sand from nearby hills and caves, the utensils of ordinary days replaced by special wine goblets, dishes, and tableware taken out of storage, and regular clothes replaced by the best available garments and shoes, the humble dwellings of Jews radiated a spirit of purity and holiness. On Passover, the joyous serenity of the Sabbath was intensified.[50]

Newcomers to America had special reasons for perpetuating this gem of the Jewish holidays. In Russia, the beauty of Passover had been accompanied by a peculiar anxiety, for, at this time of year, the underlying anti-Semitism of the populace was most likely to be aroused into an outburst of violence. Fear of the blood libel, the hideous accusation that Jews would kill a Christian child in order to get blood for the preparation of the Passover matzoh, filled the air of early spring with horrible visions of mass slaughter at the hands of a superstitious peasantry. As late as

1913, a Russian Jew, Mendel Beilis, was subjected to the absurd charge of committing the ritual murder of a young boy. In the United States, the specter of Christian fanaticism was weaker.

Coincidentally, in the same year of 1913, American Jews witnessed the trial of Leo Frank, the Jewish superintendent of an Atlanta pencil factory who was spuriously accused of murdering a young female employee and who, two years later, was dragged from the state penitentiary by twenty-five armed men and lynched. Yet, this famous instance of rabid anti-Semitism was, as Abraham Cahan noted several years afterward, an interruption of the general climate of religious tolerance prevailing in the decades before World War I, when "the Jewish immigrant almost did not know that there actually was such a thing as anti-Semitism here."[51]

The American Passover became an important time of reflection on the new conditions of Jewish life. Emphasizing the continued plight of his people in Russia, a journalist stated in 1898 that the Jews of the United States "as in no other country in the world," ought to celebrate "this feast of the deliverance of our forefathers, as a free people, with deep felt gratitude."[52] The comparative comfort of immigrants in urban America yielded a sense of thanksgiving, but it dulled the edge of a distinct Jewish identity that in eastern Europe was continually sharpened by oppression.

In the atmosphere of the American city, Passover came to serve as a bulkhead of Jewish identity, checking the powerful tendency to identify with American ways. It reminded Jews that they possessed a culture different from that of their "host" society.[53] The ongoing struggle of relatives left behind in Russia, Austria-Hungary, and Rumania became a focus for the collective memory of American Jews, whose relatively benign situation harbored the risk of forgetting about the social marginality that had long defined the Jewish people.[54]

Designated by the Torah (Deuteronomy 6:20–25) to be a time in which parents were obliged to inspire children with the history and principle of Judaism, Passover emerged also as the annual occasion for bridging the gap that separated American-reared children from their elders. Although restlessness impelled some young people to leave the table before the conclusion of the lengthy Seder, virtually all Jews attended a ceremony at the home of a relative or friend, if not a parent. Moreover, the fact that youngsters were observed singing traditional melodies "with greater earnestness" than they devoted to "Donkey-Monkey Business" showed that at least the rudimentary feelings of Jewish identity crossed the barrier of the generations.[55]

Finally, the symbolic matzoh was maintained in the uncongenial setting of urban America. "Even Jews who do not uphold Passover strictly," the *Forward* claimed in 1902, "concern themselves with the matzohs, because of the fear of embarrassing themselves before the neighbors."[56] By exerting pressure on each other at Passover, newcomers kept the anchors of cultural identity.

Although Passover continued to be a key to Jewish existence in the United States, its aura of sanctity disappeared. In a newspaper article that appeared before Passover of 1907, one newcomer pinpointed the corrosive effect of American material conditions upon the holiday. In Europe, he recalled, he used to look forward to Passover as soon as Sukkot ended in the autumn. His wife would then buy hens and chickens in preparation for the great holiday, and new dishes, spoons, glasses, pots, and pans would also be purchased well in advance. In America, however, the festival was prepared at the last minute. With two trips to the stores, his wife could prepare a complete Seder. There was no scouring and liming to do, because the walls were covered with wallpaper, as was the floor with oil cloth and carpets. "The whole year is by me Passover," he exclaimed, "clean and kosher!"[57] By narrowing the gap between the holy and the mundane, the ease of shopping and the commonness of luxury in the American city had eroded the distinction of Passover, dethroning the queen of Jewish festivals.

The decline of purification as the dominant theme of Passover was also rooted in the neglect of the special Sabbaths preceding the holiday. With special readings from the Torah and the Prophets, Sabbath Parah and Sabbath Hahodesh anticipate this theme. In particular, Sabbath Parah, which was named after the account of the red heifer (*parah adumah*), dwelled on passages from Numbers (1:22) that detailed a mysterious rite for purifying the defiled, and on passages from Ezekiel (16:38) that prophesied the time when God will purify the Jews and infuse in them a new spirit. The prefatory emphasis on purification appears to have been lost on many Jews in America, where Sabbath Parah, along with other special Sabbaths in proximity to it, were not well observed.[58]

As the theme of purification waned in the American Passover, the luxuries of the festival acquired a different meaning. Facilitated by the atmosphere of urban abundance, the acquisition of new things developed into an annual ritual that cohered with the American emphasis on the rising standard of living. Progress, rather than purity, came to be an important theme of the American Passover.

Although Chanukah had begun to gain importance as a time for shopping, Passover was the holiday that affirmed the dignifying power of luxuries, and, in America, this festival outpaced the others as an occasion for buying new things. The parade of people on the Lower East Side's main thoroughfare, Grand Street, around Passover in 1907, was likened to a "sea of new hats and new dresses . . . of beautiful color from the drugstore on the cheeks and beautiful color from nature on the faces." The bright appearance of Jews, enhanced "with jewelry both genuine and false," seemed to reflect "the holiday soul" that had come over them.[59] By donning fashionable new hats, a prominent part of dress at the turn of the century and one in which style changed quickly, "greenhorns" fresh from Europe could fit into the Passover crowd of Jews already familiar with American ways. The American Passover gave newcomers an opportunity to measure their acquisition of the basic luxuries of city life.[60]

In addition to the traditional idea of sanctifying oneself and one's household through the acquisition of luxuries, the practice of gift giving seems to have entered into Passover and escalated the importance of shopping for the occasion. Although Passover in Europe had not included the exchange of presents, the *Tageblatt* encouraged Jews, particularly young Jews, to augment the spirit of the holiday by giving gifts to their parents. For older immigrants who had difficulty adjusting to American life, Passover provided a welcome period of joy. The younger generation, it was argued, could increase the happiness of the holiday by honoring elders with a thing of beauty and value.[61]

The pulse of retail commerce in Jewish neighborhoods rose in the early autumn, for the High Holidays and Sukkot, and in December for Chanukah, but the intensity of shopping for Passover was distinctive. By late March, the advertising sections of Yiddish newspapers swelled to twice their normal size, and the street markets bristled with activity. Peddlers who usually sold fish or produce often discontinued these lines during the weeks before Passover, in order to sell new chinaware, tinware, and crockery, the products for which the holiday created a special demand.[62] The curbside inventory of all types of merchandise grew, as clothing, laces, ribbons, pictures, lamps, baskets, oilcloth, and fine foods all found a place in the "reconstruction" of the Jewish home and the material rehabilitation of its members. "The ambition of every Jewish housewife to have as many new furnishings in her home on this occasion as her purse can buy," a reporter observed in 1906, had turned the shopping weeks before Passover into a "harvest" for the street merchants.[63]

A novel ritual, the dumping of household furnishings into the city streets, showed that Passover in America had become a time in which many Jews upgraded their standard of living. With the holiday, the people of the East Side became "new and clean," the New York *Tribune* stated in a report on the Passover of 1902. They displayed new clothes and furniture, and the area took on "an unusual air of brightness," after the New York City street cleaning department "cleaned the streets into which all the abandoned furniture and bedding" had been thrown.[64] Gone were the days of hauling furniture to the river bank of the shtetl for a thorough cleaning. The rhythm of shopping in urban America demanded the replacement rather than the refurbishing of possessions.

Although not every item of every home was discarded at Passover, the dumping of merchandise on the streets assumed a remarkable scale, touching the poor as well as the affluent. In 1898, the "thorough renovating of Jewish homes once (at least) every year," was applauded as being of great psychological benefit, especially to poorer Jews whose existence in small and ill-ventilated tenement rooms was eased by the renewal of furnishings.[65] Well-to-do families tended to keep a special set of Passover dishes and utensils, but the majority of people reportedly took advantage of mass-marketed luxuries by discarding their wares, buying new ones, and then, after the holiday, using the newly acquired items on a daily basis for the rest of the year.[66]

The annual transformation of the household had become a well-established custom by the 1890s. In April 1896, while the great depression of the decade continued to burden urban workers, the dumping of possessions on the streets of New York was described as "A Jewish Custom that Gives Colonel Waring's Men Trouble," in reference to the industrious new head of the street cleaning department, Colonel George Waring.[67] It apparently took municipal workers several weeks to clear the Lower East Side of the tremendous amount of bedding, furniture, and kitchenware left on the pavement before and during Passover, an amount that was already considered typical despite the economically depressed conditions of the preceding years.

By providing an annual occasion for the acquisition of new products, Passover underscored the American belief in the value of a rising standard of living. Given the decline of traditional Judaism in America, luxuries served no longer to substantiate the Jewish sense of holiness. Instead, they symbolized the faith in social progress that moved many Jews seeking to fit into American society. The ritualized demand for new products gave newcomers reason to believe that they were "greening themselves out," upgrading their level of material life in the manner of urban Americans. Passover thus enabled immigrants to retain an important element of communal identity while it sanctioned a basic American attitude.

As Jews secularized their view of festive consumption, they inspired a democratic appreciation of luxuries that suited the new society. The

Acknowledging abundance—under the *sukkah* of a New York City household, 1891. [From *Century Magazine* (January 1892)]

A street market in Vilna, Lithuania. 1920s (?). [Courtesy of the YIVO Institute for Jewish Research]

Opposite page:
A street market in New York City. Hester Street, c. 1905. A Uneeda Biscuit wall sign presides over the background. [Courtesy of the New York Public Library, Division of Local History]

Fashion was woven into Jewish holidays in America. Late 1890s (?). [Courtesy of the YIVO Institute for Jewish Research]

Consumption and courtship. Dated January 13, 1891, the back of this photograph of a carefully dressed young woman, Rosy Swowsky, bears the message "presented to Alexander Lerman." [Courtesy of the YIVO Institute for Jewish Research]

The china display of a New York tenement parlor, circa 1905. [Courtesy of the New York Public Library, Division of Local History]

Opposite page:
A shopper's-eye view of Orchard Street, circa 1905. [Courtesy of the New York Public Library, Division of Local History]

Jewish women were identified as smart shoppers; buying fabric on Hester Street, circa 1898. [Courtesy of the New-York Historical Society, New York City]

Sabbath had long been viewed as a respite from the monotonous and degrading aspects of daily life, a time in which individual Jews were dignified by the "additional soul" that entered them on Friday evenings. Yet it was on Passover that the notion of dignifying the ordinary person through celebration attained highest expression. The Passover Seder was thought to confer an aspect of royalty upon its participants. Jewish fathers, mothers, daughters, and sons were commonly referred to at this time as kings, queens, princesses, and princes.[68] In the old world, the elevated dignity of the individual derived from the veneration of the Lord to which the Jewish holidays were devoted. As a subscriber to the divine covenant, the humblest Jew was entitled to a status of grandeur.

In urban America, as the cloak of religious sensibility fell away, and as the dignity of the individual became purely a secular matter, the consumption of products in honor of Passover inevitably took on a different light. Simply by virtue of being an American consumer, the individual was endowed with luxuries that had once been intended for the keeper of the Jewish faith.

The subtle shift of attitudes was illustrated in the advertising of clothier Moe Levy, an immigrant from Russia who was one of the few clothing retailers to achieve a broad regional following prior to 1920. In the Passover season of 1906, by which time Moe Levy and Company owned three stores, two on the Lower East Side and one in Brooklyn, one of the retailer's full-page Yiddish advertisements declared: "On Passover the man is a king, the woman is a queen, and the children are princes and princesses. When the king sits on his Passover cushion and his royal children ask him the four questions, and the queen smiles and becomes full of delight, one feels then a rare pleasure and one wants to pour a sixth glass and toast 'To Life' to Moe Levy and Co. who clothes all well-dressed Jews and their children with the best and finest clothes . . . in honor of Passover."[69] In the secular setting of the United States, the acquisition of fine products ceased to uphold the dignity of the Jew as a Jew. Instead, it dignified the Jew as a consumer.

In altering the symbolism of luxury that sustained the holidays of Sukkot, Chanukah, and Passover, Jews demonstrated an eagerness to create a new cultural identity that wuld combine aspects of Judaism with an American sensibility. As clothiers like Moe Levy were well aware, the act of dressing stylishly was fundamental to the quest for identity in the American city. For most newcomers, it would be the foremost symbol of Jewish commitment to the principle of becoming an American.

PART III

The Democracy of Luxury

ᥱ᠗᠕| 5 |ᥱ᠗᠕

The Clothing of an American

In the spring of 1902, a photography studio on the Lower East Side
of New York City was presented to the Yiddish readers of the *Forward*.
Soon to become the nation's leading foreign language newspaper because
of its sensitivity to immigrant life in the American city, the *Forward*
found this studio to be the last stop for newcomers completing a rite of
passage into American society. The ritual was a simple one. It consisted
of having one's picture taken in a newly acquired suit of clothes.

The photographer who was interviewed by the newspaper explained
that many Jews who had just arrived from eastern Europe passed through
his studio. Dressing themselves up in a suit of ready-made American
clothes, usually with the help of already settled relatives and friends, the
"greenhorns" came to be photographed. The pictures were intended to
show relatives back in Europe that the newcomers had attained, with
almost magical swiftness, the outward signs of social dignity. To enhance
the image of a sudden transformation from impoverishment to prosperity,
the photographer kept a watch and chain, a tiepin, and other pieces of
jewelry on hand for the picture, in case the "greenhorn" had not yet
obtained them.

The meaning of the ritualized change of appearance to the newcomer was exemplified by one young woman whom the photographer recalled. Pleased at how well her initial photograph had come out, the woman said that she would be willing to pay fifty cents for another sitting. When she returned for the second session, she had replaced her previous, somewhat gloomy outfit with a bright new shirtwaist that was intended to impress her relatives in the old country. This incident prompted the *Forward* to subtitle its article, "Whom to Photograph—the Girl or Her Silk Waist?"[1]

Many newcomers perceived American dress as a means of upgrading their traditional status. The concern of Jewish immigrants with American fashion, however, was extraordinary. Their comparatively rapid acceptance of the urban vogue reflected a powerful desire to fit into American society. Intense individualism and social competition reinforced the interest in American appearance, as did the heavy involvement of Jews in the garment business and retail trade of the nation's fashion center. Yet, above all, it was a passionate commitment to American society that led most Jews to view clothing as an important symbol of cultural transformation.

Dress has been recognized as a key aspect of the individual's integration into society. By conforming to prevailing standards of appearance, people express not only their desire to participate in important social activities but also their hope that others will accept them as participants. A flexible form of silent communication, dress can convey one's mood at a specific time, and it can also reflect one's general temperament and values. As a highly sensitive gauge of momentary feelings or a rough indicator of social attitude, in addition to its other functions, clothing helps people establish their identity as individuals and as members of a group. Like language, appearance must be understood in order to be meaningful. When a person's dress registers in other people the same associations that are intended by the wearer, then it has functioned as a mode of communication.[2]

On the most general level, clothing became a means by which Jewish immigrants announced their desire to fit into American society and to identify themselves as American Jews. Within the small circle of friends and family, the latest styles of dress may have communicated any number of messages about the personal identity of an individual, but, in the immigrant world at large, they were clearly understood as a sign of "Americanization." A newcomer hoping to outgrow the label of a greenhorn could count on the fact that other immigrants would interpret a new suit of clothes as a touchstone of American identity.

Jewish newcomers recognized how new garments could blunt the bitter memories of persecution that seemed to be embedded in old clothes from across the sea. In *The Promised Land*, a memoir of immigration from Russia to the United States during the 1880s, Mary Antin remembered how her family, almost immediately after arrival in Boston, purchased American clothes in a department store to rid themselves of their "hateful homemade European costumes," as if the suffering and impoverishment of the Russian Pale would be symbolically obliterated and the desire to be involved in the new society visually affirmed.[3]

The significance of appearance as a form of identification with American society was a recurrent theme in the fiction of Abraham Cahan, which offered unique insight into the psychological adjustment of Jews in the American city. In *Yekl: A Tale of the New York Ghetto*, a short novel published in 1896 to the praise of American writers, Cahan made clothing the initial focus of tension between Jake Podkovnik, a Jew who had been in America for three years and Gitl, his wife, who had recently arrived at Ellis Island. To Jake's American point of view, Gitl's bulky garments and traditional wig appeared "uncouth and un-American" and he immediately bought her a new hat and a corset to serve as an incentive for discarding the traditional outfit.[4] In his full-scale 1917 novel, *The Rise of David Levinsky*, Cahan wove personal recollections about his early days in America in 1882 into the story of a Talmudic scholar turned American businessman. The day of his arrival in New York City, David Levinsky was treated to a new suit of clothes, a hat, underwear, white handkerchiefs—the first he had ever owned—collars, shoes, and a necktie, and to a trip to the barber shop, where his hair was trimmed and his side locks shorn. Afterward, when he eyed himself in the mirror, Levinsky was amazed at the change in his appearance, which seemed to have wrought a change in his entire identity.[5]

Cahan's fiction explored the Jews' intense identification with the urban American lifestyle that was epitomized by fashionability. After the Civil War, which stimulated the mass production of clothing through the uniforming of soldiers, dramatic changes in the production and marketing of clothes allowed the multitude of city people to enter the fashion cycle. The mobility of urbanites, the entrance of women into the public domain as shoppers, employees, and students, the increase of white-collar work for both men and women, and the refinement of urban entertainment, as indicated by the rise of vaudeville, called for lighter, finer clothes than the heavy woolens and flannels of an earlier day. By the 1880s, stylish ready-made suits of clothes had become the norm for American men and boys, and, in the following decade, the rise of the shirtwaist expedited the mass marketing of women's garments as well. During the first decades of the new century, the continued simplification of women's dress made a tremendous industry out of a craft that had been monopolized by custom tailors only a generation before. The sudden rise of popular fashion was mirrored by the increasingly sophisticated clothing advertisements of metropolitan newspapers and mass magazines.[6]

As a result of urban demand, and of the new machinery, labor techniques, and department stores that combined to meet that demand, American dress was revolutionized. For the first time, a large variety of inexpensive yet expensive-looking clothes came into the possession of ordinary people. The effect of the change was highlighted by the observations of Guiseppe Giacosa, an Italian dramatist who toured the United States in 1898. Noticing the apparent affluence displayed in the dress of passengers on a New York City elevated train, Giacosa commented that "no European would be able to pick out by eye" the great variety of occupations, incomes, educational attainments and cultural backgrounds that separated the people on the train because "the shape and texture" of their clothing showed "the same care, the same cut, and almost the same easy circumstances."[7]

Urban immigrants recognized the prestige of American dress to varying degrees. How they responded to the new way of clothing was determined largely by their prior familiarity with Western fashions and by their commitment to American society. Chinese sojourners were accustomed to Asian standards of dress and appearance. In addition, for a considerable time after arrival in America, they kept their sights set on returning home. Reflecting these realities, as well as their social ostracism in the United States, they showed comparatively little interest in dressing like urban Americans. In a letter to a friend in Hong Kong, one immigrant who had lived in Los Angeles and San Francisco recorded his feeling that the great variety of shoe, hat, and garment styles enjoyed by the American consumer symbolized a social chaos that contrasted with the comforting uniformity of Chinese life. "There is no uniform mode of dress or manner of living," he wrote, "no system, regularity or order about anything, but all is a jumble of confusion."[8]

Mexicans, too, displayed ambivalence about American dress, even though they were more familiar with Western fashion and were themselves the originators of the Western cowboy look. Because of the proximity of their native land, Mexican-Americans stayed in close touch with traditional standards of behavior. Thus, while settlers in a city like El Paso wore American clothes, the latest newcomers criticized them for adopting this and other external features of a society that spurned them. The nearness of Mexico promoted this sort of reciprocal condescension.[9]

European immigrants found American fashion more completely acceptable, though there appear to have been differences in the pace of assimilation. The Irish seemed to pick up American habits more quickly than other non-Jewish newcomers. Like the Jews, the Irish were "true immigrants," intending to settle rather than return home. In addition, they had already been exposed, more than they would have liked, to British standards of appearance. Because young Irish women were more able than their men to advance socially in America, they, in particular, strove to be stylish.[10]

The multitude of eastern and southern European immigrants to urban America showed the same tendency, if not the speed of the Irish. In an extensive survey of wage earners in Homestead, Pennsylvania, around 1910, Margaret Byington observed that the steel city's Slavic immigrants liked to buy clothes at the local department store, because these "evidently gave the wearer a proud sense of being dressed like other Americans."[11] It is impossible to chart precisely the pace and degree to which newcomers from various ethnic groups adopted American dress. Nonetheless, it was generally true that Italians, Slavs, Poles, Russians, and others alike interpreted their new command of material goods in terms of the social categories of their native lands, where aristocrats had monopolized fineries.[12] The ready-made suits and derby hats of urban Americans became, by the old standards, aristocratic in caliber.

As common laborers, newcomers often gained little prestige in America, but as consumers they could lay claim to a type of nobility. Reflecting on the adaptation of an Italian shoe shiner in New York City during the first decade of the twentieth century, journalist Walter Weyl was able to emphasize the "revolutionary" change in self-image that was assured by the American style of consumption. When he began his career in New York, the Italian was amazed that a fellow shoe shiner possessed a derby hat, a stiff white shirt, a white silk tie, a scarf pin, and brilliantly polished shoes. Realizing that "in America, even a 'shiner' could be a Sunday afternoon *Signore*," the newcomer soon acquired the same outfit.[13]

Although most immigrants felt the pressure and the delight of dressing like an American, Jews, as a whole, appeared to be unusually attuned to urban fashion. In the summer of 1900, the *New York Tribune* devoted an article to the stunning appearance of the Jewish district. "Grand Street is Broadway plus Fifth Avenue," the newspaper observed of the area's major thoroughfare—"its wide sidewalks show more fashion to the square foot on a Sunday than any other part of the city."[14] The rise of stylishness was not restricted to New York City, even though this was the hub of both Jewish immigration and American fashion. In Chicago, which had the second largest population of American Jews, a reporter who studied the adaptation of 1,946 young Jewish immigrant women around 1913 observed that "great stress" was laid "upon clothes and the desirability of 'looking well.' " She concluded that "perhaps no other immigrant" was "so eager to become Americanized as the Jewish girl," whose relatives "almost immediately upon the girl's arrival" bought for her "American clothes, usually a suit, a large hat, and not infrequently the wherewithal to fix her hair in an American fashion."[15]

A distinctive vocabulary of style emerged in Jewish neighborhoods. By the 1890s, the terms "ladies" and "gents," rendered with a heavy Yiddish accent, had entered common usage, as was indicated by the abundant clothing advertisements of the Yiddish press. Unlike the traditional designations of men and women, these words injected the notion of stylishness into the definition of human beings. They summed up the phenomenon of attaining instant gentility through stylish attire, because anyone who obeyed the laws of fashion was a "lady" or a "gent."

The prevalence of style was evoked by other passwords as well. Not only did the Lower East Side have its share of "sports," but there were several levels of sophisitication that seemed to warrant distinctive terms. The "hot sport" was the "sport" to a superlative degree; the "stiff" was always à la mode in regard to collars, and would never be seen wearing a stand-up collar when a turned-down was in vogue.[16] The male "coquettes" of the Jewish quarter were a subject of commentary for the *Forward*, which ran feature stories such as the one detailing the fate of a yeshiva student from eastern Europe who had turned into a womanizing "dude" in New York City.[17] Although the spirit of acquistiveness was a target for the socialist editorials of the *Forward*, this popular newspaper was also captivated by American fashionability. In a 1911 article on the importance of stylish dress among Jews, it stated simply that "style is the essential thing—something either suits or it doesn't."[18]

The youthfulness of Jewish immigrants underwrote the enthusiasm over modern fashion. Although the statistics of immigration do not include precise divisions of age, it was evident that the group contained many young people. Between 1886 and 1898, 128,655 Jewish newcomers, amounting to 34 percent of the total, were under the age of sixteen. Subsequently, in the period 1899–1909, 245,787 incoming Jews were under fourteen, equaling about 25 percent of the total. This compared to 17 percent for the Germans, 12 percent for southern Italians, between 9 and 9.5 percent for Poles, Slovaks, and Hungarians, and 5 percent for the Irish. Despite their generality, these figures leave little doubt that many Jews arrived in the United States at an age that was, or would soon be, ripe for the appeal of American fashion.[19]

The Clothing of an American

Social tension within the group also motivated individuals to perceive new clothing as an important means of self-expression. The display of luxury enabled newcomers to jockey for position in a social milieu that upset the traditional social hierarchy. Clothes and jewelry thus became a provocative but civil way to vent old jealousies and to express social aspirations that had smoldered in eastern Europe.

Musician Samuel Chotzinoff vividly recalled how neighbors on the Lower East Side would assert themselves socially through material display. Having immigrated from Russia in 1897, Chotzinoff's family struggled to make a living in New York City. Yet, despite its relative poverty, the family possessed a measure of the scholarly attainment that generated social respect in the shtetl. Chotzinoff's maternal grandfather had been a prominent rabbi, and his father was a Hebrew teacher, an occupation that occupied the lowest position on the Jewish scholastic ladder but still required enough education to be considered socially superior to manual work. At a dinner given in honor of Chotzinoff's sister, Leah, and her prospective husband, the boy saw how the conspicuous consumption of the groom's family vied with the old-fashioned dignity of his own household. The fiancé was a housepainter, and the son of a housepainter. He and his family paid tribute to the Chotzinoffs by giving the head of the table to Mr. Chotzinoff. This traditional act of deference, however, was minimized by the fact that the groom's mother dressed more flamboyantly than Mrs. Chotzinoff, whose imitation mother-of-pearl "appeared insignificant alongside Mrs. Kalb's gold watch and chain."[20]

Unlike many other immigrants, the eastern European Jews constituted a coherent society with internal tensions that stimulated people to compete for prestige. Most Christian immigrants to America were peasants who had detached themselves from the old social order to seek their fortunes abroad. But Jews, whose suffering touched people on every step of the social hierarchy, virtually transplanted an entire society to the cities of the United States. Tailors and shoemakers, bakers and glaziers and furriers and merchants, Talmudic students and intellectuals, all came to America.[21]

The spirit of competition within this uprooted society was exacerbated by Jewish egalitarianism and individualism. Although differences of education, wealth, occupation, and lineage divided the people of the shtetl, the Jews of eastern Europe did not believe the social standing of a man to be predetermined. Success in religious scholarship or in business was available to almost anyone with the talent and the initiative to pursue it. Furthermore, laymen were credited with the ability and the right to assert their own viewpoint despite the statements of those in power. As authority within the community usually sprang from knowledge of the Torah and the Talmud, anyone who was versed in these sources could challenge the opinions of rabbis and officials. By trying to give all males the opportunity to educate themselves in the Law through a well-established hierarchy of schools, Jews affirmed their belief in individual aspiration and striving.[22]

In the secular American environment, Jewish ambition displayed itself vividly in the garment industry, where Jews were extensively employed. The innovative task system that the newcomers from eastern Europe had introduced into the business stemmed from the Jewish ideal of self-employment. According to an analysis made by the United States Industrial Commission in 1901, the retarded growth of large-scale factories in the clothing industry could be attributed to the desire of Jewish workers for the freer setting of the sweatshop and for the opportunity to increase their level of pay through piecework. "The contractor's shop is a sort of ideal worked out by this individualistic people," the Commission reported, "which holds out a fair hope to everybody of some day becoming his own boss, and, to a certain extent, of being his own boss while still at work in the shop."[23]

As a force behind consumer behavior, Jewish individualism contrasted with the comparative collectivism of other immigrants. Despite the significant ethnic difference among them, peasants from eastern and southern Europe tended to share a communal ethic that overrode the desires of the individual. Italians made many decisions, including decisions about what products to buy, in light of the needs of the extended household. The home, for example, was beautified not simply to meet American standards of decoration, but because it was considered the shrine of a household-centered world.[24] In the traditional culture of Polish immigrants, possessions such as clothing and furniture, like land, belonged not to the individual but to the family. These things were allocated for personal use, but their ownership was understood to be familial.[25] Although Italians and Poles enjoyed a new personal freedom in America, the persistent presence of such group-centeredness probably inhibited individuals from exhibiting too much personal ambition in their dress and public manner.

The explosion of social aspirations among Jewish immigrants was ignited by the atmosphere of competition in urban America, which allowed poor people to vent simmering resentments against those who had been their social superiors in eastern Europe. A Yiddish cartoon of 1909 characterized the social competition of these newcomers. Depicting a scene that was allegedly witnessed by a shopkeeper, the illustration showed two Jewish women, one obviously poor and the other elaborately dressed, passing each other in the street. Before she had immigrated, the well-dressed woman had beeen a servant to the one who had ended up poor in America. Now, she flaunts a sophisticated appearance in the face of her former employer.[26]

One of the most striking aspects of life in America, the inversion of old social relationships led many newcomers to the conclusion that America was a "farkerte velt," an upside-down or perverse world. Whereas the zenith of Jewish society in eastern Europe belonged to Talmudic scholars, these men were held in less regard in the American city, where hustling businessmen and politicians set the tone of existence. As the sages of the East Side dwelled ignominiously in rundown apartments, newcomers of a more practical bent made a substantial living by plying the needle and the pushcart.

In the flush of new economic opportunities, men with little but energy and nerve rose while others who once had social position met with bad luck or simply failed to adjust to the American way of doing business. In 1903, the daughter of an East Side carpenter told a journalist that her father worked for a real estate speculator who had formerly worked under her father in Russia, and she explained that this turn of circumstances bore out the popular saying that in America "a mister becomes a shister (shoemaker) and a shister a mister."[27]

In the kaleidoscopic milieu of the American city, the display of American possessions became a criterion of prestige, one that contrasted sharply with the traditional notion of *yikhes*, on which prestige used to depend. Along with scholarly distinction and wealth, yikhes was a critical ingredient of social status in the old world of the Jews. Loosely equivalent to the English concept "civilized," yikhes denoted a nobility of spirit, a compassionate involvement with other people that the Jews associated with great scholars and benefactors. Yikhes was often linked to a person's lineage, although poor comportment could negate the accumulated dignity of ancestors, and distinguished conduct could lift an individual from obscure origins to a position of respectability. The value of yikhes barely survived in America, where lineage and breeding were usually subordinated to the economic accomplishments of the moment. In a letter to his relatives in Europe written in 1783, Haym Salomon, the Polish-born financier who furthered the cause of the American Revolution, remarked that "your *yikhes* is worth very little here."[28]

The acceptance of stylishness as an element of prestige among Jewish newcomers was reflected most clearly in the ritual of courtship. In traditional Jewish culture, three qualities determined the desirability of a prospective mate: scholarship, wealth, and yikhes. But, in urban America, where familiarity with American ways had become a priority, stylishness was viewed as a social asset. As a youngster in New York City, Elizabeth Stern had written letters in Yiddish for neighbors who wanted to tell relatives in Europe about the new life in the United States. These letters "would tell of the grown daughter's beau," Stern recalled, "dwelling particularly upon his earning capacity and the fact that he 'was stylish.' "[29] Just as yikhes, the quality of civility and honor that impressed the Jews of eastern Europe, had waned in the United States, so the American type of yikhes, the instant gentility that came with luxurious possessions, rose as a factor in the arena of courtship.

In contrast to the elements of yikhes, which were accumulated gradually by a minority of Jews, the attainment of prestige through the display of possessions was accessible in short order to the majority of immigrants. Among newcomers, the signs of becoming an American served as an important criterion of social standing. Thus, Jews spoke of the initial period of learning American ways as a time of "purification" and they looked approvingly on a person who had turned from "green" to "yellow," a vital transition in the making of an American. For the same reason, one of the most frequently asked questions in immigrant neighborhoods was, "how long have you been in America?" In a land where so many residents were newcomers or the descendants of newcomers, the degree of familiarity with American life carried considerable weight in the opinion of the public.[30]

Along with American speech, American ways of consumption constituted a powerful symbol of social status for most Jewish newcomers. Marie Ganz, a well known political activist of New York City in the 1910s whose family had immigrated from Galicia in 1896 when she was five years old, recalled in her autobiography the American-style yikhes of a young man who lived in her tenement house. Although the neighbor did not earn much money, he was "an Amerikaner." Ganz noted that he had been in America at least three years, and that he was known to have spoken in English over the telephone. Furthermore, he bought beer "by the bottle instead of in the customary tin pail," and he and his brothers possessed a sateen quilt that had once been "hung on the line for all to see."[31] In the calculation of prestige, these attributes and possessions mattered more than the relatively humble financial condition of the newcomer.

Clothing was the simplest and most obvious way for newcomers to announce that they were settling into American society and gaining an appreciation of the modern urban lifestyle. It represented both the attainment of a degree of social status and the intention of pursuing the American standard of living.

The destination of immigrants had much to do with the specific ways ✂ they adapted to American society, and, for the majority of Jews, settling in New York City meant intimate contact with the world of fashion. Whereas many Poles looked for unskilled jobs in the steel industry and thus settled in industrial towns like those of Pennsylvania, Jews from the same part of the old world concentrated in major cities, where they would work in skilled and semi-skilled trades and in retailing, the occupations for which they were prepared. In Chicago, Philadelphia, and Boston, they became garment workers, merchant tailors, and retailers, but in New York City, they did so in massive numbers. Italians also worked in the clothing industry, but this line of work did not define their economic identity as it did that of Jews. Like Polish immigrants, Italians included large numbers of unskilled laborers. Digging coal, forging steel, laying railroad track, and building bridges did not bring newcomers into contact with the trends and nuances of American fashion. The manufacture and sale of ladies' underwear, children's dresses, and men's suits did. Working regularly with the fabric and millinery of America's most fashionable city, the great majority of Jews cultivated a sharp awareness of American dress. Questions of design, color, and fit became second nature to them.[32]

As employment in the clothing industry gave many Jews a surer awareness of how to dress stylishly, the emergence of a "new" middle class of white-collar employees intensified the general Jewish response to American appearance. The rapid expansion of white-collar positions during the last decades of the nineteenth century increased the importance of personal appearance to the modern urban identity. In 1870, there were roughly 342,000 professionals in the United States. By 1900, the number had grown to approximately 1,711,000. Workers in clerical and related types of labor multiplied twentyfold, growing from about 82,000 in 1870 to around 1,718,000 thirty years later. From a position of numerical insignificance, white-collar employees had risen to the status of a fully constituted group, containing nearly 5 percent of the American labor force.[33]

In New York City, the proportion of white-collar workers was much higher. By 1910, the clerks, salespeople, and managers of New York's industrial firms comprised 100,000 people and amounted to 18 percent of the industrial work force. In addition, many thousands of people were employed in the city's extensive network of retail stores, wholesale and importing firms, insurance and financial companies, and municipal departments.[34]

In contrast to many of their parents, who had labored in dirty factories, sweatshops, and fields, the young clerks, agents, and salespeople who turned the gears of the business world had to dress well. The female clerk, in particular, had to look "like a woman of fashion," despite wages that were not up to the task.[35] As the New York State Factory Investigating Commission noted in a report of 1915 that examined the nature of work in retail stores, the pressure to be fashionable came not so much from employers as from "the public's often unconscious demand that sales clerks be well appearing."[36]

Many retail clerks found the vogue to be a challenge, and their role as arbiters of fashion helped to spread the creed of stylishness throughout the social spectrum of the city. In 1899, Greater New York had about twenty-five large department stores employing an estimated 30,000 people, the majority of whom were sales clerks.[37] Predominantly young women from financially modest homes, these retail clerks showed a flare for the vogue that made the shopgirl into a famous city "type." William Sidney Porter, whose short stories reached millions of people in the years around 1910 under the pseudonym O. Henry, paid homage to this product of American urban life in the story "The Trimmed Lamp." Porter focused on a young department store clerk from a poor family who "absorbed the educating influence of art wares, of costly and dainty fabrics, of adornments that are almost culture to women" in the hope of attracting a rich mate.[38] The expansion of white-collar work gave a new importance to stylish appearance, and the social aspirations of retail clerks infused the ethic of fashionable dress throughout the social hierarchy.

The involvement of young Jews in white-collar occupations sensitized Jewish newcomers in general to American standards of appearance. A broad sample of New York's eastern European Jewish population in 1905 showed that nearly one-half of these people were employed in white-collar work, which included shopkeepers, manufacturers, professionals, clerks, and peddlers. Since 1880, when a substantial proportion of shopkeepers and merchants had already indicated the drift of Jewish labor, not only had the percentage of professionals and upper-echelon businessmen increased, but the ranks of lower-echelon, white-collar workers were composed increasingly of retail clerks and salesmen, insurance and real estate agents, and less of peddlers, whose relative numbers declined markedly.[39]

The growing popularity of this sort of white-collar work among Jews was evident in Europe as well. In Vienna, which attracted Jewish newcomers from central and eastern Europe after the constitution of 1867 abolished restrictions on domicile, officeholding, and occupation in

Austria-Hungary, a greatly disproportionate number of Jews had established themselves as clerks, salesmen, and managers by the early twentieth century. As non-Jewish Viennese were not similarly attracted to lower-echelon white-collar work, these occupations acquired a distinctly Jewish character.[40]

In contrast to the relative isolation of Jewish clerks in Austria, Jews in America flowed into what was becoming a mainstream of white-collar employment. Consequently, their behavior reflected not the dictates of an ethnically defined occupation but the social mores of urban Americans. The "East Side Observer" of the *Yiddishes Tageblatt* remarked, in the winter of 1900, upon the tendency of young bookkeepers, clerks, and salesmen from the Lower East Side to promenade on Sundays in the affluent area of uptown Madison Avenue. "The young fellow dressed in the extreme height of fashion, from silk tile [a high, stiff hat] to patent leathers, who you might imagine is a banker or the son of one," exclaimed this social critic of the ghetto, "is neither one or the other, but he is just a simple salesman at so much per."[41]

Epitomizing the comparatively urban background of Jewish immigrants, the presence of sophisticated retail clerks from eastern Europe accentuated the concern with style among white-collar Jews. By 1903, these young men from Russia, Rumania, and Galicia composed a large enough group to organize a labor union of clerks in the retail dress goods business, starting out with about one hundred and fifty members who worked in approximately forty stores on the Lower East Side. Three years later, there were reportedly over two hundred clerks employed in approximately fifty large dress goods stores in the same area. In the old world, these men represented a special type—young, single, and sophisticated, they were the envy of Jewish youth in the cities. In the United States, they continued to be socially active, spending most of their free time at events such as weddings and balls in order to make contact with a wide range of prospective customers. Reputed to be skilled at making conversation with a largely female clientele and simultaneously making large sales, these clerks often saved up enough money to form partnerships and open their own stores. In eastern Europe, the dress goods clerk served as a social model for the minority of young and secular Jews who lived in the big cities, but in America he became a model of success and stylishness for the majority of young people in the urban world of immigrants.[42]

Even by comparison with the flamboyant young men of the Lower East Side, the Jewish shopgirl was identified as the taste-setter for the Jewish community at large. Keeping a good appearance and a savings account in order to attract a husband, the Jewish shopgirl dressed "almost as expensively as any other class of working women, probably more so," the local press observed. The nature of her work had given her "a taste and a desire for the 'best' and the most attractive that can be found."[43]

The influence of the retail clerk on the attitude of many newcomers toward American fashion was pointed out clearly in "The Autobiography of a Shop Girl," an article that appeared in *Frank Leslie's Popular Monthly* in 1903. Stating that a relatively large percentage of department store sales clerks were Jews, either the children of immigrants or immigrants themselves, the anonymous author, a woman from a comfortable household who worked for several years in a New York department store, described a visit to the home of a Jewish coworker called "Bessie." Bessie's father was a carpenter, her oldest brother a finisher in a sweatshop, her aunt and nephew who boarded with the family were a newsstand proprietor and an insurance agent, respectively. "Of this heterogenous family," the writer commented, "Bessie, the department store girl, was the queen—for she was a saleslady! She gave tone to everything. She dictated fashion to the whole tenement house, and everybody in it imitated her and envied her."[44]

Even though slightly more than half of Jewish breadwinners were blue-collar, they had social aspirations which made the white-collar men and woman particularly influential. Jewish workers did not conceive of themselves as a proletariat. They were influenced by the socialist bias of the Yiddish press and some local leaders, and they did generally believe that the manual laborer was an important factor in society, a conviction that was expressed through their leadership in the unionization of the garment trades. Yet, like many American workers, Jews did not allow pride in labor to interfere with the desire to identify themselves socially as members of the broad middle class. As a result, they were determined to push their children out of the manual trades and into white-collar jobs. The older generation envisioned for Jewish youth some kind of work that would be "higher than the dirty work in a factory," as the *Forward* reported in a feature story on the occupational goals of Jewish newcomers.[45]

In 1902, Edward Alfred Steiner, an Austrian immigrant who studied the immigration from eastern Europe, gave a description of a meeting held by a Lower East Side mutual aid society that illustrated the connection between the aspirations and the appearance of the Jewish worker. The association had about eighty members from the same region of Russia. Nearly all were manual workers, albeit with varied incomes. Fifteen were Republicans, twenty were Democrats, two were Socialists, and the remainder had not yet become citizens. Most of them knew English fairly well, and in their meetings they observed all the ceremony of a typical American lodge. "To one who has seen these people in their old environment the change seems miraculous," Steiner commented— "the men wore the very best and cleanest clothing, and the women were inoffensively stylish."[46] Rather than use clothing to reflect a distinct identity as blue-collar workers, these newcomers conformed to the standard of fashionability that ruled the majority of urban Americans.

In this respect, Jews replicated the distinctive attitude toward clothing that had distinguished American workers. By dressing well, American laborers strove for equal respectability with more affluent people. Visitors to the United States often commented on the popularity of fancy dress among laboring people, and the fictional representations of the nineteenth-century wage earners, Mose the Bowery Boy and his girl-friend Lizzie, were adept at spending money on flamboyant clothing.[47] Household budget studies conducted in the early twentieth century indicated that "the importance placed on clothing" by American workers contradicted the theories of pioneering German statistician Christian Lorens Engel (1821–1896), who hypothesized on the basis of European budget studies that the proportion of income devoted to clothing would remain relatively constant as income increased.[48]

Jane Addams, a founder of the Hull House social settlement in Chicago (1889) and a keen observer of city life around the turn of the century, explained that poorer urban people dressed in style because they sought "to conform to a common standard which their democratic training presupposes belongs to us all." Speculating that American democracy may have been developed much more fully in regard to dress than in regard to other aspects of life, Addams pointed out the logic behind the fact that young working women spent money on clothes "out of all proportion" to that which was spent on other items—the person with "little social standing" knew that in the anonymous public domain of the American city "her clothes are her background, and from them she is largely judged."[49]

For Jewish newcomers, American dress represented something more than a means of asserting social respectability. The new suit of clothes gave physical form to the essentially spiritual undertaking of aliens striving for membership in a new society. It became a means of cultural transformation. Only the concept of *transformation* adequately conveys the impact of new material standards on these eastern Europeans. This was the theme taken up by the Yiddish press, which dwelled on the tantalizing idea of transforming one's self-image through the purchase of things. "Beauty on installment, beauty to rent, beauty a little, beauty a whole lot," the *Forward* proclaimed in a 1904 feature of a New York City beauty salon, "beauty for a year, for a whole lifetime, beauty only until marriage comes—these are various things that one can get nowadays, if someone wants to be beautiful."[50] Echoing the fascination of newcomers with the modern practice of altering the outward appearance, the newspaper reported faithfully on the latest techniques of cosmetic surgery that enabled the city's elite to extract "beauty from ugliness."[51]

As an "Americanizing agency," the Yiddish press served its audience not only by detailing the English language and American customs, such as fashion, but, moreover, by evoking the deep sense of self-transformation that pervaded the Jewish quarter of the American city.[52] Stories on the ins and outs of fashion blended with advertisements in which dentists drew large pictures of perfectly toothed mouths, patent medicine vendors depicted the metamorphosis of impotent and ugly people into virile and beautiful ones, and clothiers demonstrated that clothes "made" the American man and woman. Permeating Abraham Cahan's newspaper, the *Forward*, as it did his novels about David Levinsky and Jake Podkovnik, the theme of remarkable personal change sharply reflected the psychology of Jewish adaptation to America. Although it was only one of several key components of the urban standard of living with which Jews would establish an American identity, stylish dress emerged as the foremost symbol of Jewish transformation in the American city.

Behind the dramatic change in the self-concept of Jews was a key figure in the immigrant world, the Jewish homemaker. As managers of domestic consumption, women would help determine the Jewish response to American society.

ᘒᘓᕦ 6 ᕤᘔᘓᗅ

Jewish Women and the
Making of an American Home

Jewish women served as a catalyst for the adaptation of newcomers to the American standard of living. The increased prospects for consumption in urban America enabled Jewish homemakers to magnify their already powerful influence over family life. Through an expanded role as consumers and as managers of household consumption, these women smoothed the transition to a new way of life and emphasized the importance of new products to the cultural adjustment of Jews.

"There is no greater change from Eastern Europe to America," observed David Blaustein, in an address to the New York State Conference of Charities delivered in 1903, "than the change in the life of the women."[1] The foremost change experienced by women who had come to the United States involved personal freedom, particularly in marriage and career. The possibilities of freedom in these areas were conveyed brilliantly in the life of Emma Goldman, the prominent Russian Jewish anarchist who advocated the complete equality of the sexes during the thirty-three years that she spent in America before her deportation in 1919. Yet, most women, who ultimately married and raised children, expressed their new freedom within the confines of domestic life. The most conspicuous between the domestic power of women in America and in Europe was the magnitude of decision and control over family consumption.

Jewish immigrant women have often been characterized as old-fashioned and anxious about protecting their families from the pace of change in urban America. One of the more memorable images of the Jewish mother was composed by Henry Roth, whose rich novel of a Jewish immigrant family in New York City in the first decade of the twentieth century, *Call It Sleep*, was published in 1934. In Roth's story, the young mother lived in awe of the American city, rarely venturing beyond a small radius from her apartment. Periodically, with intense nostalgia, she dwelled on the picture of a farm that hung on the living-room wall as a reminder of the world left behind. The woman's conservative role in the family was emphasized by her being the sole emotional sanctuary for her son, a sensitive child abused by the outer world of callous men and rough boys.[2] The nostalgic image of the old-fashioned woman has also entered the historical literature. Jewish women have been portrayed as the primary force shielding the immigrant family from the supposedly pernicious temptations of urban consumption.[3]

In fact, the positive attitude of Jews toward new products and habits of consumption hinged on the activity of Jewish homemakers. Being the arbiter and director of domestic consumption was not a new experience for Jewish women—this had been one of their major responsibilities in the more traditional culture of eastern Europe. As consumers within the limited material environment of the shtetls and cities of the Pale, they laid a foundation for the larger role acquired in the United States.

The dynamic role of women in Jewish domestic life was summed up in the concept of the *baleboste*. A term without equivalent in English, baleboste was a Yiddish adaptation of the Hebrew phrase *baal-ha-bayit* which literally means "owner of the home" and implies the control of a household. It exemplified the capacity of Yiddish, which was essentially a variant of German strongly influenced by Hebrew, to use Hebrew words in order to expand the meaning of common concepts. Although Yiddish borrowed many words from German, the German word for housewife—"hausfrau"—was replaced by the Hebrew term "baal-ha-bayit," a phrase that magnified the Jewish conception of the woman's role in the home. As the masculine ideal in the traditional Jewish culture of eastern Europe was that of the scholar whose total attention focused on the study of Torah and Talmud, the complete direction of domestic affairs was considered the prerogative of women. As the term baleboste implied, the role was not underestimated.

Jewish women had inherited the task of overseeing an elaborate system of consumption that originated in the scriptural identification of pure and impure things. Despite the incipient decline of traditional Judaism in the late nineteenth century, particularly among urban people who viewed themselves as progressive thinkers, the majority of eastern Europeans appear to have maintained the observance of Jewish law, a central part of which was kashruth, the concept of purity in the preparation and consumption of food. The Jewish dietary code required of women scrupulous attention to the quality and preparation of food eaten by their families. In addition, the custom of honoring the Sabbath and holidays with special foods, clothes, and tableware added to the task of the baleboste the need to acquire and maintain luxury items with which to relieve the ongoing pressure of material scarcity. With white tablecloth, brass candlesticks, silver wine goblets, loaves of challah—the long, braided white bread rich in eggs—and a crowning dish of chicken or fish, the baleboste performed the wonder of creating a Sabbath atmosphere that consistently evoked affection in Jewish memoirs of eastern European life.[4]

Enhancing the role of the baleboste as an arbiter of consumption, Jewish women frequently involved themselves in the domain of petty commerce, where they sharpened their familiarity with the quality of merchandise and the activity of bargaining. The ideal of freeing one's husband for the study of the Law had made an unofficial commercial career a logical pursuit for Jewish wives. Under the economic duress of the late 1800s, the presence of women as shopkeepers became conspicuous. In an investigation of economic conditions among the Russian Jews shortly after 1900, Isaac Rubinow found that the income of many petty merchants, whose ranks had swollen since the 1880s, was so small "that the wives are forced to sell something so as to earn a few cents a day."[5] Although their inventory of goods was limited by the reign of scarcity in the Pale, women operated a substantial number of the small stores in the region. In some places, they established a rudimentary form of the catering business, selling expertise in cooking and baking to local families preparing a *simkhe*, or celebration.[6] Despite the lack of statistics about women in commercial occupations, the scope of their involvement was suggested by a journalist who in 1898 observed of Bialystock, the second largest city in Lithuania, "generally the women are very much engaged in trade."[7]

In the more sophisticated material setting of American cities, the continuing involvement of women in retail trade produced familiarity with a higher grade of merchandise. Venturing successfully into the marketing of foods, garments, artificial flowers, and specialty items for American consumers, Jewish women sometimes attained public recognition for the high quality of their products.[8] Though limited to a minority, these commercial ventures benefited the community of Jewish women, as the knowledge of the entrepreneurs circulated among the multitude of shoppers. The engagement of women in trade enhanced the skills of Jewish consumers, but it was secondary to the activities of shopping and home management with which the majority of women were concerned. Through these activities, Jewish homemakers in America realized their potential as accomplished consumers.

The culmination of the Jewish woman's skill as a consumer in the United States depended on the belief that Jewish wives should avoid wage labor when possible. Out of deference to the role of the baleboste, an extremely small proportion of wives sought official employment. In 1911, a government investigation of immigrants in cities reported that in only 4.4 percent of the 297 Russian Jewish families surveyed did the wives take on official employment. The average percentage for all groups was 30.7 percent. Furthermore, between 1910 and 1925, the percentage of Jewish wives working for wages declined, whereas it increased for other groups of immigrants. Yet the father's income was not the sole support of most Russian Jewish families. Nearly 60 percent of wives contributed to the family income, often by taking in boarders. Twice as common in Russian Jewish homes as in the homes of other groups, this practice was more suited than was industrial labor to the role of the baleboste.[9]

Unlike many other immigrants, not only did Jews arrive with the motivation and the family structure for resettlement, but they endowed women with great authority to run the household economy. The significance of this factor appeared in comparison to Irish immigration. Like the eastern European Jews, most Irish newcomers were drawn by persecution to view America as a final destination, and they also included a large number of women. Irish women similarly aimed to raise their households to "lace curtain" status, and they had some commercial experience. Though probably not as extensively as Jews in eastern Europe, they entered the marketplace in Ireland by peddling household wares at local fairs, and running small shops in the towns. Yet, the rigid segregation of the sexes among the Irish made it more difficult for these homemakers to control the income and the consumption habits of their husbands, who tended to spend their money on drink and frivolities.[10]

The circumstances of the Irish suggested that household consumption was affected by the nature of domestic relations, and not simply by the amount of time the woman spent at home. Like eastern European Jews, Germans and Italians also tried to keep women at home as much as possible. But the patriarchal nature of these families made it difficult for housewives to exert full power over the family's habits. Compared to other European newcomers, Italian women were sheltered from American ways—they generally saw their role as one of maintaining traditional ways in opposition to outside influences.[11] Many German women also stayed home, as was indicated by several government surveys of immigrant households, which showed that they had a relatively low rate of participation in the work force.[12] Yet, German men upheld the deeply rooted custom of spending money on drink and entertainment at beer gardens and saloons, a habit that impaired the homemaker's ability to direct domestic consumption.[13]

The position of the Jewish woman as the manager of domestic consumption was buttressed by the comparative advantage of Jewish men in the work force. Remarkably few Jews were unskilled workers, whereas the Italians, Poles, Irish, and to a lesser extent Germans included a considerable number of common laborers. The concentration of Jews in skilled and semi-skilled trades and in white-collar occupations constituted one of the group's outstanding features.[14] Thus, Jewish homemakers rested on a comparatively sound economic base. Unlike many Italian women, they were not generally forced by the low wages of husbands to spend a lot of their time at home making artificial flowers, sewing garments, and doing other low-paid task work for local contractors.[15] Along with their low rate of alcoholism and their respect for their wives' domestic authority, the higher occupational status of Jewish men may have added an element of refinement to the home. In organizing household expenses and furnishing her apartment, the baleboste faced fewer man-made obstacles than did other immigrant women.

Emphasizing the role of the baleboste in the American city, Jewish women were able to increase their control over domestic consumption. In this respect, they approximated the situation of many American housewives. H. L. Mencken's sardonic remark that America was "a land where women rule and men are slaves" reflected at least one aspect of the relation between the sexes.[16] Prominent social workers and home economists agreed that the American wife was the "general purchasing agent" and the "financier" of the family, in both blue-collar and white-collar homes.[17] In the age of mass consumption, this was no small task. As new technology increasingly relieved women from backbreaking housework, the sophistication of the urban marketplace introduced the mental strain of intelligent consumption. "Housekeeping," explained Ellen H. Richards, a leading author on American domestic economy at the turn of the century, "no longer means washing dishes, scrubbing floors, making soap and candles; it means spending a given amount of money for a great variety of ready-prepared articles and so using the commodities as to produce the greatest satisfaction and the best possible mental, moral, and physical results."[18]

The energy of many urban American women had come to be invested in the activity of shopping, which offered Jewish women from eastern Europe an entirely new arena in which to sharpen their powers of discrimination as they widened the horizon of their demands. "Any one who thinks that all the good food is consumed in the upper end of the city . . . can learn something these days by visiting the open-air markets in the East Side," exclaimed a reporter for the *New York Sun* in 1900, on describing the active demand "among the wives and daughters of the East Side tailors" for expensive fish and imported vegetables—including dried mushrooms at eighty cents per pound![19]

The distinctive street markets of New York City allowed the accumulated experience of Jewish shoppers to surface in public, where it drew the attention of observers. In the first major report of the federal government on street marketing in New York City, published in 1925, the skills of Jewish women as consumers were a source of comment. The report noted how, amid a crowd of ten or twelve others, they would judge the merchandise on a pushcart solely by eye and simply call out the desired quantity. "The women of the Jewish race," it was concluded, "are rarely deceived when trading with the vendor."[20]

Through bargain hunting, these homemakers could obtain good-quality products for their families without compromising their sense of fiscal responsibility. The practice of bargain hunting was widespread in the United States as a result of the nation's peculiar social structure. In Europe, consumption had been profoundly influenced by a customary class structure, in which the aristocracy enjoyed luxuries carelessly while the multitude of working people lived in stoic want. American society, however, seemed to develop within the extremes of wealth and poverty, revolving as it did around a large population of people with moderate incomes but great expectations of comfort. In the early 1830s, Alexis de Tocqueville astutely observed the prominent tendency of the society that encouraged all to imagine affluence and that enabled many to attain a position of sufficient comfort to keep such an imagination. Tocqueville saw a multitude of Americans "whose wants are above their means, and who are very willing to take up with imperfect satisfaction, rather than abandon the object of their desires altogether."[21]

As a result of this tendency in the American population, bargain hunting—the search for good products at low prices—emerged as the definitive feature of urban shoppers and urban shops. Reporting on the enthusiasm with which consumers of all social classes redeemed manufacturers' coupons for gifts available at bargain outlets, the *New York Times* asserted in 1899 that city shoppers were driven by "the bargain-counter spirit."[22] The development of American retailing was defined by the passion of the people for bargain hunting. The two most prominent merchants in the United States during the nineteenth century were Alexander Turney Stewart, the New York City retailer who introduced many methods of modern selling between the 1820s and 1860s, and John Wanamaker, the Philadelphia department store owner who succeeded Stewart as the model of retail technique from the 1870s to the early 1900s. Both of these men had a distinct ability to locate, remake, and market products of good quality that could be sold at unusually low prices, an ability well-suited to the temperament of shoppers with moderate incomes and elite aspirations.

By the 1880s, bargain counters were becoming a normal part of American department stores. Established in 1879, the bargain basement of Marshall Field's store in Chicago enjoyed a booming business, expanding within a decade to include thirty departments of specially made, less expensive items in addition to discounted merchandise from the main store. By 1906, it had become a complete store in itself, with a volume of sales that kept pace with that of the original department store above and thus sustained the reduced level of prices. The trend at Marshall Field's was duplicated elsewhere, as merchants recognized the desire of urban people for potentially expensive products that did not carry a high price.[23]

By virtue of the important position of Jewish women as consumers, Jews were able to excel at the American custom of bargain hunting. In contrast to haggling, which revolved around the ability of a consumer to negotiate a lower price through clever talking, bargain hunting depended upon the activity of shopping. Emphasizing the value of spending time to investigate the comparative prices of merchandise, the baleboste turned the Lower East Side into a haven for bargain hunters. The bustling activity of Jewish shoppers was well depicted in a report of a fire sale held at a large store on Avenue A between Fourth and Fifth Streets in March 1899. The bargains on salvaged household furnishings drew tremendous crowds, causing a "riot" that required the supervision of the police and fire departments.[24]

The demand of Jewish shoppers for fine merchandise at discounted prices guided the development of retailing on the Lower East Side. In the 1880s, there emerged outlets known as "cheap stores" that marketed good-quality groceries and foodstuffs at moderate prices.[25] The evolution of Grand Street into a retail center also reflected the character of the newcomers as consumers. According to the *Tageblatt*, several large department stores that occupied this thoroughfare in the 1880s gave way to Jewish businesses because of their failure to understand "the psychology of the Jewish consumer," who wanted "more 'money's worth' with less ta-ra-ras."[26]

By enabling newcomers to view the spending of money as a means of saving money, bargain hunting legitimized the purchase of luxuries. During Jewish holidays, "Now Is Your Time to Save Money" became a familiar slogan of merchants on the Lower East Side whose businesses thrived on the desire of consumers to economize through calculated consumption.[27] Endemic to the situation of urban Americans, the custom of bargain hunting appealed to Jews as a way to reconcile the persistent need to save money with the intense desire to participate in the American pursuit of luxuries.

Not only as an economic exchange, but also as a social focus for urban women, shopping attracted newcomers. Through the institution of the department store, American women established the social ritual of shopping, which included getting together over lunch, and making comparisons of purchases with an eye to the fashion cycle. Although shopping limited the scope of female behavior by keeping women safely within the orbit of domestic affairs, it also provided an exhilirating freedom from the monotonous confinement of the home.[28] Substituting the Lower East Side's emporium of street markets and small shops for the palatial surroundings of the department store, Jewish women found similar satisfaction in the ritual of shopping. Describing Jewish shoppers on Hester Street in the autumn of 1895, the *New York Tribune* noted that "the pleasure they take in the excitement of marketing" dispelled any signs of stress from the faces of these immigrants. Shopping casually amid the intense barter of the street, they were "out to see and be seen as much as to buy."[29]

As an outlet for the personal striving and social competition that men found in the occupational world, shopping permitted newcomers an individualism that barely existed in eastern Europe. In 1906, under the provocative title "They Make Visits to Display Their Hats and Dresses," the *Forward* gave an account of two immigrant women who had adopted the American form of competitive shopping. One, from Berdichev, a city in the Ukraine, was the wife of a superintendent of a fire insurance company, and the other, from a shtetl, was married to a wage earner. Before her husband became a superintendent, the Berdichev woman was poor. Unable to dress nicely, she withdrew as much as possible from her circle of *landslayt*—people from the same region in Europe. Once her husband attained his position and earned forty dollars a week, she made a habit of wearing expensive outfits and visiting her friends. The wife of the wage earner, tired of these obvious displays on the part of her acquaintance, invited the Berdichev woman for a visit in two weeks. By that time, she had bought an exceptionally fine outfit which outclassed that of the superintendent's wife.[30]

In the realm of consumption, the American woman was ideally to be as up-to-date and time-conscious as the American businessman. The ethic of progressive consumption gradually infiltrated the concept of the baleboste in America. Yiddish advertising gave the best reflection of the changing ideal. Playing on the rhyme of the Yiddish words for yarn and lose—*gorn/farlorn*—a 1902 advertisement for Fleisher's yarn, a major American brand that was steadily promoted in the Yiddish press, contended that "a smart baleboste has no time to lose. She knits only with Fleisher's yarn."[31] The domestic equivalent of the popular American axiom "Time Is Money" found its way into the world of the Jewish newcomer.

The value of being up-to-date, as well as time-conscious, was reinforced by Yiddish advertisements. Fels Naptha soap, the well-known brand of a Jewish soap manufacturer, was regularly advertised with the character of "Aunty Drudge," a matron who instructed readers in the progressive approach to cleaning. At times, a drawing of an attractive, fashionably dressed young woman helped to convey the message that Fels Naptha would help keep a woman up-to-date.[32] When the New York Telephone Company began advertising in the Yiddish press near the end of the prewar period, it too reflected the idea of the Jewish woman as a progressive consumer. The advertising addressed "The Woman Who Keeps Herself Up-To-Date" and emphasized "A Telephone Makes Every Home Up-to-Date."[33]

Incorporating traits of the American consumer, the role of the baleboste extended to include control over consumption by other members of the family. "That a wife should accompany her husband in the store when he wants to buy a suit or a hat is with the Gentiles an old custom," the *Forward* exclaimed in 1905, "but to we sons of Israel this is just now becoming the way."[34] The newspaper depicted a scene that typified the new division of labor in regard to domestic consumption. Having just bought a new suit, the husband returns home to the scrutiny of his wife. She does not like the color, the suit does not "lie" quite right, and other problems arise. Inevitably, they return to the store, where a dismayed clerk must then deal with the more discriminating consumer of the pair!

Through her command over the household's consumers, the baleboste initiated newcomers in the adoption of American ways. Unlike many other immigrant women, Jewish wives played an active part in receiving the newly arrived. American immigration officials took note of the efforts of the women to provide the "greenhorn" with a transition to American society. In one recorded case, a Russian Jewish family with seven children was met by the father's two sisters, who had been living in the United States for several years and who displayed the trappings of "a state of opulence that appeared to stagger the recently arrived brother."[35] The transition provided by these and many other women was based not only on the offer of temporary lodging and help in finding a job. It focused as well on instruction in the way an American looked and lived, lessons that primarily involved habits of consumption.

The baleboste also monitored and incorporated the demands of children for an American lifestyle. In the era of immigration from eastern Europe, the desire to give children greater educational opportunities was one reason for coming to the United States, and Jewish newcomers clearly emphasized the value of their children's success in America. The more sympathetic approach to childraising that had gained popularity in urban America during the late nineteenth century promoted the idea that the desires and the position of the young should be respected. Attracted by this notion, the Yiddish press excerpted advice about childrearing from leading American magazines. Jewish parents were told that American daughters had the right, not the privilege, to receive an allowance, and that American sons would turn into American gentlemen if they were treated as such at home.[36]

Given this type of respect, Jewish youngsters were able to persuade their elders to adopt American ways that they considered indispensable. Once children had entered the public schools, the pressure of conforming to American customs came powerfully to bear on the family. Schools taught the young that Americans were "the best, the brightest, the most educated and the strongest people in the world."[37]

Although parents often had to bridle at the insistent and sometimes insolent demands of their Americanizing children, Jewish mothers displayed an astute flexibility to the desire for a different lifestyle. In a memoir of the relationship between an immigrant mother and an American daughter, Elizabeth Stern, whose family had come from Russian Poland in 1891 when she was two years old, recalled the positive response of her mother to the new desire she felt on befriending non-Jews in high school. Once Stern began to yearn for a "sitting-room," her mother made provisions for one as soon as space allowed, even though the idea was completely foreign to her. Moreover, Stern commented, her mother strove to beautify the room by buying furniture, rugs, cabinets, a carpet, and by crocheting doilies and embroidering covers for the backs of chairs. "To the standards of the people I was coming to know," the daughter wrote of her mother, "she altered her standards, her speech, her dress. She even altered the whole plan of her home for me."[38]

The ability of Jewish women to respond to youth's desire for American ways reflected the enlarged role of the baleboste in America. Drawn by the sophistication of the urban marketplace, Jewish women sharpened the sense of discrimination about the material world that they had acquired in the traditional culture of eastern Europe. Through their skill as consumers, they extended the control of the baleboste over domestic consumption and thus facilitated Jewish adoption of American habits. Without the activity of women as arbiters of consumption, the pace and the form of Jewish adaptation to urban America would have been different.

Relying on a strong female presence as a base, Jewish immigrants gravitated toward American forms of leisure. Their foray into this area of American life would take them far from the city, as they turned the summer vacation into a custom for the ordinary family.

ᘉᘍ 7 ᖳᐰᘉᘍ

Urban Leisure and
the Vacation

The changing relation between the sexes in America promoted new forms of leisure among Jewish newcomers. Posing a stark contrast to the customary recreations of the old world, theater, vaudeville, movies, dances, and balls allowed men and women to socialize together in public. As a result, the American custom of treating came to occupy a place in Jewish life. While it acknowledged the rising influence of women and social competition over men, treating reflected the carefree attitude toward spending money that suited the perspective of abundance. The most striking response of eastern European Jews to American leisure, however, took the form of vacationing. By creating a distinctly Jewish version of the American vacation, these immigrants not only addressed the changed relationship of men and women, but, more importantly, they pioneered the concept of the summer resort for the masses. A distinctive feature of Jewish adaptation to the United States, the vacation came closer than any other custom to fulfilling the vision of the earthly paradise that Jews carried to America.

The changing relationship between women and men in Western society has long been recognized as a major force over habits of consumption, particularly leisure. Two of the earliest theoretical works on the rise of

116

modern consumption, Thorstein Veblen's *The Rise of the Leisure Class* (1899) and Werner Sombart's *Luxury and Capitalism* (1913), both observed that attitudes toward women shaped the consumption habits of society in general. Sombart argued that the "secularization of love" in European cities of the late Middle Ages escalated the concern of the affluent for the display of luxury, and Veblen recognized that endowing women with possessions enabled men to indulge their basic instinct for "conspicuous consumption."[1]

During the last decades of the nineteenth century, the demand of American women for a more active social life generated striking changes in urban leisure. In 1860, commercial entertainment played a minimal part in American life. After the Civil War, however, the rapid expansion of the urban population gave rise to a dynamic market for entertainment. The show business grew in many directions, as musicals, plays, extravaganzas, circuses, burlesque, drama, Wild West shows, and vaudeville all came into their own. Whereas an earlier generation had tended to seclude women from the leisure of the streets, which were identified as a place for crude masculine pleasures, the rise of vaudeville in the 1870s and 1880s heralded a new era in which impresarios produced a more "respectable" show for the enjoyment of mixed audiences of men and women. In the 1890s and early 1900s, respectable dance halls and amusement parks emerged as an important site for heterosocial activity, and the moving picture theater arose to compete with the vaudeville stage by attracting entire families. After 1911, the modern nightclub appeared, offering respectable men and women a new kind of informal social life.[2]

These new forms of commercial leisure were quickly incorporated into the urban American standard of living. The joint need of men and women for recreation and entertainment made vaudeville shows, theatrical productions, moving pictures, balls and dances, and trips to amusement parks a routine for city people. In 1915, a municipal report on living standards in New York City emphasized that these amusements were necessary for "a normally happy and self-respecting existence."[3]

The forms of commercial entertainment that city people in America took for granted were a novelty to the majority of immigrants from eastern Europe. Festivity in the old world revolved around ritual events such as marriages and births, and around the Sabbath and holidays. Although the emerging Yiddish theater provided entertainment in a few cities of the Pale until 1883, when it was outlawed, Jews had no contact with the variety of entertainment they encountered in the United States, where the emphasis on athletics and amusements seemed at first to be a strange characteristic. Contrasting the social life of Europe and America around the turn of the century, David Blaustein noted that there were not even pianos in the many shtetls with populations of several thousand Jews. Theaters were "something that the newcomer knows little about until he lands in America, and as for balls, which the young people have so many here—they are indeed rare in the villages and towns of Eastern Europe, though you sometimes hear that 'the Count of the village had a ball.' "[4]

Traditional Jewish culture discouraged entertainment not connected to religious events. Diversion from the study and the practice of the Law was viewed as anathema. The Talmud contained not only the admonition of Rabbi Akiba that "jesting and levity lead a man on to lewdness," but also the grim warning of Rabbi Jacob, another scholar of the second century: "He who is walking by the way and rehearses what he has learnt, and breaks off from his rehearsing and says, How fine is that tree, how fine is that field, him the Scripture regards as if he were guilty against himself."[5] Although these injunctions were observed as much in the breach as in the practice, there was a seriousness to the traditional Jews of eastern Europe that distinguished them from the surrounding peasantry. In addition to the emphasis on study and devotion, the concept of *takhlis*—purpose—dominated the Jewish sense of admirable behavior and stalled the spread of secular entertainment, which seemed useless.[6]

The encounter of Jewish immigrants with American urban leisure turned the Lower East Side of New York City into a place that abounded with commercial entertainment. "If the gas-bills of our downtown residents are not greater than they are, this is not the fault of the gas-trust," the New York *Forward* exclaimed in 1905; "the main reason for this is that the people do not sit at home at night."[7] By the 1800s, German residents of downtown Manhattan, including thousands of German Jews, had already set up a network of restaurants, beer and music halls, and theaters, onto which eastern European Jews grafted another heavy layer of establishments.[8] Condensed into the southeastern part of the city, a whole range of commercial entertainments flourished from the patronage of immigrants. In 1911, a study of popular amusements in New York charted one hundred restaurants and lunchrooms, seventy-three soda-water shops and stands, ten pool halls, nine dancing academies and halls, eight moving picture shows, two evening recreation centers, and one Yiddish theater within the area bounded by Grand, Chrystie, East Houston, and Suffolk Streets, which comprised less than one-third of a square mile.[9]

The immense popularity of the Yiddish theater testified to the appetite for secular entertainment among the newcomers. Originating in eastern

Europe during the late 1870s, the Yiddish theater quickly became a major cultural institution of the Lower East Side. Into the standard fare of romantic musicals, popular adaptations of classical drama, and dramatic renditions of soul-stirring events, it mixed the motifs of immigrant life in America. At the turn of the century, patronage of the Yiddish stage supported over one thousand shows a year, accounting for the annual sale of an estimated two million tickets. In 1910, despite keen competition from vaudeville and moving pictures, as many as twenty-five thousand tickets were sold each week.[10]

Though the Yiddish stage remained a vital social institution, American forms of entertainment with few artistic pretensions attracted growing numbers of Jews. After the turn of the century, the fast-paced vaudeville show of popular comedians and singers, magicians and acrobats, appears to have gained popularity with the "lighter element among the Jewish theatre-going population" that rebelled against the "seriousness" of the Yiddish theater.[11] Like the Yiddish theater, though, the vaudeville house combined entertainment with lessons about American life. Comics and singers helped immigrants to feel more at home in a multiethnic society, as they poked fun at the stereotyped traits of their own and other groups.[12] African-Americans suffered from disparaging vaudeville routines, but Europeans were well enough integrated into American society to ameliorate this kind of humor. The rise of prominent Jewish vaudevillians like the team of Weber and Fields and singer Sophie Tucker solidified the connection of Jews to vaudeville entertainment, by proving that the medium could be adjusted to suit Jewish interests and tastes.

The movies provided an ideal setting in which immigrants could find the right combination of fun and social education. First appearing in 1896, the moving pictures gained a large audience after the introduction of the nickleodeon in 1905. A number of characteristics of the early cinema particularly appealed to immigrants. Silent film required no understanding of English, and the informality of theaters, which were often located in immigrant neighborhoods, invited whole families of movie-goers to congregate, eat, and chat with friends during the show. Although filmmaking demanded a considerable amount of imagination and artistry, early films were short, usually lasting fifteen or thirty minutes, and they did not burden audiences with complex themes. Instead, they depicted many subjects and scenes of American life, from the street peddlers of the familiar city to the cowboys of the mysterious West, from the contrast between rich and poor in New York to that between settlers and Indians on the Great Plains. An excellent medium for communicating American habits and values, the movies attracted newcomers of all backgrounds.

Even Italian women, whose social life was usually restricted, regularly attended the picture shows, which immigrants considered suitable for both women and men.[13]

Given the youthfulness of eastern European Jewish immigrants, and the comparatively high proportion of women among them, dances and balls naturally emerged as a hub of social life. The proliferation of dancing academies and halls on the Lower East Side of New York offered the most concise testimony of this. In *Yekl: A Tale of the New York Ghetto*, Abraham Cahan focused his descriptive chapter of the Lower East Side on a dance hall that occupied the first floor of a five-story house built for sweatshops. In the hall, from which music filtered outside into the crowds of Suffolk Street, there was a throng of immigrants, "an uproarious human vortex, whirling to the squeaky notes of a violin and the thumping of a piano" and struggling to keep the rhythm of the dancing "professor" whose periodic chants of " 'von, two, tree! Leeft you' feet! Don' so kvick —sloy, sloy!" trailed off toward the marble soda fountain at the end of the room.[14]

The fascination of Jews with dancing was witnessed as well by journalists and social workers. Jacob Riis's extensive survey of immigrant life in New York City in the late 1880s alluded to the proliferation of dancing schools on the Lower East Side and yielded the conclusion that young Jews were "inordinately fond of dancing," no matter how tired the day's work had left them.[15] In a comparative study of 1,476 American, German, Irish, Jewish, and Italian working women, published in 1910, the investigator found that Jews showed the most decided preference not only for theater but also for dancing and music.[16] Several years earlier, a sociologist studying the social life of a New York City block observed that Jewish residents were unusually "convivial," spending their leisure time "in calling upon one another, in parties, and in dances."[17]

In the arranging of balls, newcomers imbued an urban American recreation with a Jewish character and created the only Jewish festivity of metropolitan scope. From the early days of Jewish immigration, political parties and social clubs rented public halls for concerts and balls in the hope of raising money and increasing membership. Along with excursions, these events became the primary method of combining the urge for entertainment with the need for fundraising. During the first decade of the twentieth century, major institutions such as the Beth Israel Hospital and the *Forward* held annual affairs that attracted thousands of dancing donors. The popularity of balls was illustrated by the *Forward*'s masked ball of February 1, 1902, in the Grand Central Palace. Although the building was designed to hold ten thousand people, thirteen thousand tickets were sold, and three thousand costumed party-goers caused a riot as they tried to get into the Palace.[18]

The following January, the Beth Israel Ball at Madison Square Garden, to which all classes of the eastern European community were invited, evoked the vivid description of a local reporter. "For those who are accustomed to connect the East Side with poverty, the magnificence of the Beth Israel function must have been amazing," the journalist exclaimed, "the brightness, the sparkle, the gayety and tasteful, though elaborate dress, bore ample testimony to the truth of our contention that the East Side is an up-to-date, progressive community, which has absorbed all that is best and most attractive in 'Americanism.' "[19] By giving the ball a charitable function, or takhlis, Jews were able to legitimate secular gaiety.

Accustoming themselves to new forms of urban leisure that involved men and women together, Jews came to embrace the distinctly American custom of treating. Treating conveyed the perspective of abundance, which instructed consumers to present an image of financial ease regardless of their economic condition. Defined by the restless coexistence of high aspirations and moderate means, the majority of American consumers struggled to attain the trappings of affluence but tried not to reveal the necessity of struggling. As bargain hunting facilitated the attainment of luxuries, treating disguised the financial limitations that made bargain hunting a necessity.

The American pretense of financial ease produced a distinct attitude toward prices. During his first days in the United States, Marcus Ravage, a Rumanian Jew, encountered the American view of prices when he began peddling chocolates on the streets of New York. Perplexed that his treats failed to sell at the low price of one cent apiece, the newcomer was advised by a veteran peddler to charge a nickle instead of a penny for each chocolate, which had a wholesale price of two-thirds of a cent. To explain this bit of advice, the oldtimer stated authoritatively: "Your American likes to be charged a stiff price; otherwise he thinks you are selling him trash." Once Ravage began charging five cents for a chocolate, his business immediately increased.[20]

The pretense of not having to count each penny had become a vital element of the perspective of abundance, one that was reflected clearly in the system of rounded-off prices employed by various restaurants and retail stores. The distinctive method of pricing found at some quick-lunch restaurants of New York City attracted the comment of a journalist who accompanied immigrants from Russia to the United States shortly before World War I. In one such place, where the writer and his newly arrived friends had their first meal after leaving Ellis Island, the cashier gave out slips of paper with denominations of five cents printed on them. Once the customer received his or her food, cafeteria style, the cook punched out the appropriate price. Using the nickel instead of the penny as the smallest unit, this system relied on an expansive psychology of price that the author considered "part of the foundation of American prosperity."[21] The tendency toward rounding off prices, which was also basic to the rapidly expanding chain of "Five and Ten Cent Stores" created by Frank W. Woolworth in the 1880s and 1890s, reflected the desire of American consumers to create an appearance of financial ease, a facade of nonchalance about their budgetary situation that would distinguish them from those who plotted the destiny of every cent.

Such a facade was sustained as well by the practice of generous tipping. Whereas the European system of tipping revolved around the predictable allowance of a moderate sum of money, the American way was devoid of order, depending solely on the size of the customer's desire to make a show of affluence. In a 1900 feature on the custom, the *New York Tribune* linked excessive tipping to the relaxed social structure of the United States, which lacked well-defined social classes and well-established forms of conduct based on social class. Situated among people of varying fortunes and tastes, and reluctant to appear socially inferior, Americans tended to rely on tipping to create an image of affluence.[22]

Treating was a basic feature of urban leisure that allowed Americans to establish the appearance of financial ease, and its acceptance by newcomers was a prominent sign of the subtle change in outlook that came with the adaptation to material abundance. Appearing commonly in the sphere of public drinking, where men were expected to buy each other drinks as a display of generosity, treating was introduced through the saloon to the comparatively small number of Jews who were regular drinkers. In 1888, the Yiddish press criticized this American custom, lamenting the inevitable cycle of spending and drinking that faced the greenhorn—"he must drink with them, so as not to insult the treater, and he must treat, so as not to be considered 'stingy.' "[23] Whether in saloons or in the cafés, tearooms, and sodawater shops that seemed to be favored by Jewish immigrants, the practice of treating defined conventional drinking in the American city.

Yet it was not relegated to the public interaction of men. Treating permeated the entire domain of commercial leisure, in which many Jewish newcomers, particularly the young and unmarried, discovered and practiced the subtleties of this new kind of social communication. The practice served as a type of ground rule for social relations between men and women. Through it, women expressed their desire for a financially secure mate, and men strove to assert their eligibility by showing an American nonchalance about spending money.[24]

Dating provided the perfect arena for the ritual of treating. As the traditional authority of elders over youth waned in the urban environment, young people gained new opportunities to regulate their social life. Within the context of dating, they developed a standard of treating with which to estimate the acceptability of a suitor. As a focus of tacit communication between couples, the importance of treating was suggested by a conversation between two young women that was recorded by a journalist departing Coney Island in the summer of 1904. Comparing the amount of money spent by their dates on amusements, one reportedly said to the other, "You beat me again. My chump only spent $2.55."[25]

The desire for a successful marriage, which was defined by material as well as romantic aspirations, was a primary concern of many young Jewish immigrants, who embraced the American custom of dating with a fury. In an interview for the *New York Tribune* conducted in September 1900, a *shatkhn*, or matchmaker, of the Lower East Side commented ruefully on the passion of the young for deciding their own romantic destinies. To the detriment of his occupation, young Jews had come to believe "in love and all that rot," as they "learned how to start their own love affairs from the Americans."[26] As the traditional craft of the matchmaker dissolved, the daily newspapers emerged as a forum for personal interchanges. Echoing the intensity of dating in the Jewish community, the English page of the *Yiddishes Tageblatt* hosted a series of letters during 1899 and 1900 on what East Siders called "The Burning Question"—the question of finding a suitable mate. In the course of the dialogue, young people coined special phrases to express the magnitude and the precision of their expectations. The "$12-a-week man" described the man who did not earn enough money to provide a spouse with desirable luxuries, and the "five-room-and-a-bath girl" stood for the woman who sought a comfortable situation in marriage.[27]

Jewish courtship tended to focus on the woman's ability to amass an attractive dowry and on the man's capacity not only to prosper but also to entertain through treating. The preoccupation of many young women was pinpointed in 1906 by the *Forward*, which headlined one of its pages "They Come to America After a Dowry."[28] Observing the importance of the dowry to Jewish women, Katherine Busbey commented in her study of American domestic life that "a girl in another part of the city sings and dreams of love" while "the East Side girl thinks hard over how to scrape together a dowry to tempt a business husband, whether the business is that of owning a garment factory or a little soda-water stand on a street corner."[29]

On the part of men, familiarity with the nuances of treating signified a refreshingly optimistic attitude about the prospects of the future, an attitude that attracted astute women hoping to live in the style of the American. In "A Sweatshop Romance," Abraham Cahan depicted the significance of treating among young Jewish newcomers embroiled in the intricacies of modern courtship in the 1890s. The heroine of the story is disappointed by her suitor's habit of giving her a piece of fruit on their dates. Although fruit had been a luxury in eastern Europe, in New York City it was a common item that could not compare with the glass of sparkling soda or the other treats that had become part of social life in the American city. Interpreting the dull offering of an apple or a pear as a sign of stingy indifference, the young woman finds herself more attracted by the indulgences of a different suitor who "would treat her to candy and invite her to a coffee saloon—a thing which Heyman had never done."[30] As a ritual demonstrating the American ethic of liberal spending, treating constituted a departure from the inhibition and pessimism induced by the prevailing scarcity of eastern Europe. It reflected a willingness to strive for the material standards considered appropriate by city people in America.

The influence of treating within the Jewish community was epitomized by the rise of a new social creature on the urban landscape, the consummate treater known as "the sport." In 1903, the Yiddish press featured the escapades of a stereotypical Jewish sport as a subject of interest. Jake, the sport under review, is described in the act of treating two young Jewish women to a night on the town. He takes them to the theater, paying the comparatively large sum of seventy-five cents for each seat, buys them chewing gum for the show, and finally takes the ladies to a fancy restaurant, where they order sirloin steaks. The story reaches a humorous conclusion as Jake, unable to pay the dinner bill of $2.75, finds that he has outsported himself![31] Although the frivolous behavior of the sport grated against the traditionally serious charter of Jewish culture, the emergence of this stereotype proved the coercive power of ritualized treating. Many societies developed some form of treating as a way of expressing basic values. In urban America, the practice signified belief in the perpetuity of abundance and in money spent as a sign of social aspiration.

Within the realm of leisure, Jews found the vacation to be the most impressive component of the American lifestyle. Assuming immense popularity, the vacation gave newcomers a unique way to pattern the social relationships of men and women and to experience a profound sense of fulfillment about their expectations of American society. Not only were Jews alone among immigrants in adopting the full-fledged American vacation, but they also envisioned the summer resort as an appropriate destination for people of average means at a time when most wage earners and clerks contented themselves with a day trip to Coney Island.

The distinctive qualities of the American vacation were highlighted by the publication of Sholom Aleichem's *Marienbad* in the Yiddish press of New York City. In August 1911, the *Tageblatt* issued the first installment of this satirical, epistolary novel about affluent Polish Jews at a spa in Bohemia, written by the man whose sense of humor led him to be called "the Jewish Mark Twain" and whose prolific contribution of short stories, plays, and novels warranted the title "the father of Yiddish literature."[32] Focusing on the resort as a place where people cavorted under the pretense of needing therapeutic rest, Marienbad exposed the nature of the vacation in eastern Europe as a privilege of the affluent that was justified by the rationale of rehabilitation.[33] The full force of Sholom Aleichem's satire may have been lost on Jewish readers in America, who had come to understand the vacation as neither a class privilege nor a medical recourse, but as a social necessity for city people.

By adapting the vacation as a regular form of leisure for the majority of people, Jews from eastern Europe broke with the precedent of vacationing set by wealthy Americans. During the nineteenth century, summer and winter vacations had become a custom of the upper classes throughout the United States. Islands off the coast of Maine, the seashore north of Boston, Newport, Rhode Island, Saratoga Springs in upstate New York, the North Shore of Long Island, the New Jersey shore from the Atlantic Highlands down to Cape May—these and other spots became summer favorites, and a variety of locations in Virginia, the Carolinas, Georgia, Florida, and California accommodated wealthy people seeking respite from the cold winters of the North. After the Civil War, the boom in railroad construction increased the accessibility and variety of resorts as well as the popularity of "vacationing," a verb that was coined in the 1870s.[34]

German Jews who had built substantial careers in commerce and finance during the middle decades of the nineteenth century deviated little from the precedent of vacationing set by the American elite. In fact, the directness of their emulation ultimately resulted in a backlash of prejudice and discrimination. During the 1880s, the influx of Jews, presumably German, into the popular Atlantic Highlands of New Jersey stirred some real estate brokers to speculate about the potential decline of property values that these vacationers might precipitate in spite of their affluence.[35]

The most prominent incident of anti-Semitism of the late nineteenth century occurred in 1877, when Joseph Seligman, a German immigrant who had risen from peddling to the height of New York City banking, was refused admission to the Grand Union Hotel in Saratoga Springs, New York, an establishment that he had patronized for years. In response to this insult, one hundred leading Jewish merchants conducted a successful boycott of A. T. Stewart's great department store at Broadway and Fourth Avenue between 9th and 10th Streets in New York City, which was administered after the death of Stewart by Henry Hilton, the proprietor of the Grand Union Hotel who had rejected Seligman.[36] As this and other, less famous incidents of social ostracism suggested, vacationing among the German Jews appeared to follow in the tracks made by wealthy Gentiles.

Immigrants from eastern Europe inaugurated a style of vacationing that had little to do with therapy and that broke with tradition by including people from almost all areas and levels of society. Secular Jews and religious Jews, businessmen as well as wage earners patronized the farmhouses, boarding houses, cottages, and hotels that had converted the loose network of towns like Tannersville and Hunter in the Catskill Mountains of New York into a bustling resort area. In 1883, approximately 70,000 people, mostly affluent Americans, enjoyed a summer vacation in the Catskills. By 1906, the number of vacationers had jumped to 400,000, an increase that owed much to the rapid acceptance of this custom by Jewish immigrants from New York City.[37]

Unlike the Germans, these newcomers gave a distinctly Jewish complexion to the custom of vacationing. In one of the most vivid depictions of vacation life in the Catskills during the early twentieth century, Abraham Cahan narrated the sojourn of David Levinsky in an unnamed town that had several hotels and boarding houses, all but one of which were occupied by Jews. Levinsky's hotel contained a variety of immigrants from New York City—successful businessmen and professionals as well as less affluent salespeople, stenographers, bookkeepers, teachers, and librarians who often shared the rent of the posh resort's smaller rooms. The establishment featured kosher food, music adapted to the tastes of Jewish newcomers, and a special room used as a synagogue in the mornings and as a gambling parlor at night.[38]

The Jewish resort met the demand of immigrants who wanted the comforts of the countryside without the discomforts of a strange environment. Whereas German Jews tended to downplay their ethnic identity by seeking genteel accommodations, the comparatively traditional people who constituted the readership of the *Yiddishes Tageblatt* were commended by the newspaper in 1897 for not being ashamed "to sit on the piazza of a summer hotel and read a paper printed in Yiddish."[39] Some Jews from the eastern European community were content to accept the American model of vacationing, and these people patronized resorts that lacked kosher food in order to enjoy a refined atmosphere based on orderly and quiet service. Alongside these conventional places, however, not only in the Catskills but also in the older vacation spots on the Jersey coast, there grew up a type of establishment that conformed more or less to Jewish dietary laws and that operated in a way alien to the genteel tradition. These kosher hotels and boarding houses tended to be set up by entrepreneurs new to the industry of leisure. They were marked by unkempt yards, boisterous children, informal service, and good food. Attractive to elderly Jews as well as to youth, the development of a distinctly Jewish resort was essential to the rise of the vacation as a popular custom.[40]

The prosperity of the Jewish resort, and of the Catskills as a Jewish resort area, hinged on the enthusiasm of the majority of working people for vacationing. By the 1890s, a summer vacation had begun to be a normal expectation for Jewish wage earners. In the winter of 1891, a well-known Delancey Street restaurant owner bought the Arlington Hotel in the Coney Island section of Brooklyn, installed a kosher kitchen, set up a system of discount rates for large families, and began advertising regularly in the *Arbeter Tsaytung*, a weekly socialist newspaper with a respectable following of Yiddish-speaking workers. Advertisements for the Arlington pictured a well-dressed couple and a child strolling in front of the resort.[41]

The concept of vacationing in the mountains also came readily to the ordinary Jewish immigrant, as was indicated by the growth of the Jewish Working Girls' Vacation Society. The Society was founded in 1892 to accommodate girls who could not find suitable places through the New York Vacation Society or whose parents insisted on accommodations that upheld the Jewish dietary laws. Ten years after its establishment, the Society was sending more than one thousand Jewish girls on week-long vacations to the Catskills and to Long Island each summer.[42] In the summer of 1903, a reporter for the *American Israelite* interviewed people on the Lower East Side for an article that focused on the striking popularity of vacationing among Jews of modest means. "One would never think of an Italian laborer, or an Irishman working on a street railroad, sending his wife and children [on vacation] for the summer," the journalist stated. Jewish sweatshop workers, on the other hand, did so "year after year."[43]

The seasonality of the garment trades encouraged Jews to embrace the concept of the annual vacation, which meshed with slack periods of work. Accustomed by the fluctuations of the clothing business to save money from the busy season for use during slow months, well-employed garment workers were prepared to take leave of the city for two weeks or so between late June and mid-August. Illustrating how conventional the vacation had become by 1914, a number of workers in the knit goods industry, which was busy in the summer, scheduled their visit to the Catskills during the winter.[44]

The widespread aspiration of Jewish newcomers for a summer vacation arose partly from pressure for social conformity. Although the truly poor would not normally obtain the means for a stay in the country, most Jewish immigrants earned at least a modest living, and many would struggle to save enough money for a two-week summer holiday. Often, men sent their families to the resort while they continued to work. On the weekends they might take the train to upstate New York or the Hudson River ferry and the train to the New Jersey shore to be reunited with spouses and children. However the trip might be arranged, it was apparent in New York City that large numbers of Jews who were "not rich, and not even well-off" were willing to "strain themselves to afford it." Once average folk took up the idea, the summer vacation became contagious. "One Goes Because Everyone Goes," a Yiddish headline proclaimed in May 1906, leading into the story of a Jewish wage earner whose wife finally insisted on a stay in the mountains in order to avoid the embarrassment of not joining her vacationing landslayt each year. In the springtime, when Jewish neighborhoods buzzed with plans for upcoming summer vacations, those who could not spend the time between Passover and Shavuoth talking about a prospective secular holiday at the resorts suffered a sense of isolation from the currents of American Jewish life.[45]

As Jews familiarized themselves with the American vacation, they developed the same standards of sophistication that applied to other components of the American standard of living. In the 1880s, the Brownsville section of Brooklyn still had enough of its natural scenery to meet the desire of Manhattan residents for a bucolic setting. "When rent was six dollars a month and a sink could double as a bathtub," the New York Morgen Zhurnal stated two decades later, "Brownsville could pass for the country." The Jew of 1906, however, no longer raised an eyebrow about a month-long stay in the beautiful Catskill mountains, which had become common. By that time, "the latest thing among the wives" was "to inform friends that one is going to Europe for summer vacation."[46]

The cycle of rising expectations ultimately produced less of a penchant for Europe, though, than a demand for more luxurious accommodations in the well-established resort areas of New York and New Jersey.

The rise of the Jewish vacation was fueled by the importance of the baleboste in America. "All the little towns and farms in the mountains, and all the summer places by the sea are now packed with Jewish women who have come for a rest from their year's work," the *Morgen Zhurnal* reported in July 1906. Viewing this phenomenon as an achievement, the newspaper exhorted all Jewish men to "send your wife to the country" in appreciation of the dawn-to-dusk labor of Jewish homemakers. The summer vacation was perceived as "an absolute necessity" for hardworking men, too, but it remained above all a form of homage to the baleboste. Jewish newcomers in America developed the remarkably liberal conviction that a woman could not be a "good and healthy mother" if she did not have an opportunity to "change her routine and lead a life of peacefulness and joy."[47]

In addition to acknowledging the large influence of the baleboste, the vacation gave Jewish husbands their own brand of freedom from daily routine. Using the summer holiday to boast about how well they treated their wives, men hardly subordinated their own needs. At the summer hotels, they gained a reputation for spending virtually all their time playing poker. Often, husbands stayed in the city to work during the weekdays and then took the train to join their families in the Catskills mountains or at the Jersey shore on the weekend. During the weeknights at home in New York City, they were now able to socialize without the customary household rules. Typically playing cards, Jewish fathers appreciated that "when God permits one to have a 'full-house' and one takes to conversation, he isn't afraid that the wife will suddenly seize him and scream: 'Moshe, have you already forgotten where in the world you are? It's nearly dawn and you haven't stopped playing—I'm going down and tearing the cards in pieces!'"[48]

Partly because men might use the vacation time to escape from familial obligations, but also because of the hectic social schedule at the resorts, the "new freedom" of women generated its own type of labor. Vacationers who stayed at farm houses discovered a quiet that bordered on monotony, but those at the hotels entered a busy world. Though freed from the tedium of cooking and washing dishes, Jewish homemakers found themselves on display, having to change clothes several times a day to meet the demands of fashion, having to compete in conversation about their husband's economic prospects, and having to stay up late at night because, as one critic of the resorts remarked, "somebody feels like playing,

singing, or dancing." One young baleboste who was interviewed by a
Yiddish newspaper in 1907 related that she had vacationed in the mountains for eight consecutive years but ultimately found the social life at the
hotels too exhausting to keep up. Instead of the sustained period away
from home, she began taking her family on day trips to Coney Island,
Rockaway Beach, Long Branch, and other accessible beaches.[49]

Yet, despite the peculiar strains of the vacation, the custom apparently
served the needs of many Jewish spouses, and, in addition, it became an
important arena for matchmaking. In accounting for the expansion of
Jewish hotels in the Catskills mountains and along the Jersey shore, a
journalist observed that segregated Jewish vacationing derived more from
ethnic preferences, particularly about courtship, than from anti-Semitism. Preferring not to mix in marriage, both Jews and Gentiles maintained their own resorts, despite the fact that they might socialize in other
situations. Jewish mothers brought their daughters to vacation spots in
the hope that a suitable match might be found, and young single men and
women arrived with the same idea. Noting that Jews came to the hotels
"as much for matchmaking as for pleasure," the reporter explained that
"the strolling paths, the bathing places, the dining rooms, and the veran-
das of the hotels are the spots where the God of love does his biggest
summer business."[50]

As it attained a regular place in the life of Jewish immigrants, the
vacation heralded a new way of thinking. The prospect of relief from the
heat and congestion of the city attracted newcomers to the concept of
relaxation as a legitimate pursuit. In line with the old-fashioned view of
the vacation as a therapeutic activity, the disproportionate number
of Jews attending resorts was occasionally attributed to the Jewish preoccupation with health.[51] Yet it was clear that the summer jaunt in the
mountains or at the beach appealed to the deeply felt need of newcomers
to loosen the grip of traditional ideas about recreation as they escaped
temporarily from the congestion and dirt of the city. In April 1907,
shortly after Passover had ended, an editorial in the *Tageblatt* advised
readers to begin thinking about the coming summer vacation, which
would take the edge off the Jewish tendency toward incessant labor. "He
who can enjoy and does not enjoy," the paper exhorted in Talmudic
fashion, "commits a sin." Having bent the original Jewish concept of
enjoyment to suit contemporary wants, the editorial concluded, "the
summer holiday is here, let's all take from it what we can."[52]

The new mode of thinking wrought a new vocabulary to convey the
profound sense of release embodied in the vacation. Jewish vacationers in
the Catskills came to be known as "pleasureniks," people for whom

pleasure was central.[53] Other terms of description similarly emphasized the intensity of the vacationing experience. "We are all talking and thinking and dreaming of our vacation," a Jewish columnist stated in June 1899, as he discussed the fashionability of the yachting cap among young East Siders who were in the grip of the "vacation fever."[54] The use of the word "fever" manifested the extent to which the community had been overwhelmed by the urge to relax, and the coinage of terms such as "the summer man" and "the summer girl" suggested that people felt themselves transformed by the prospect of the vacation. The end product of the transformation was an individual whose habits of consumption were dictated by the buoyant spirit of the vacationer. The "summer girl of the Ghetto" displayed the light feeling of the season through the tasteful selection of shirtwaists to be worn on dates, vacations, and trips around town.[55] The "summer man" was known to leave the city for a weekend at Coney Island or Long Branch, New Jersey, where he spent money "with a rather astonishing agility."[56]

Jews explicitly described the vacation as a transformative experience. The stress of city life formed the background against which newcomers viewed the spiritual dimension of the secular summer holiday. "When you go to the country, your life is changed," one report contended. In the mountains, struggle ceased to be the defining quality of life—"no one is coming to grab you, and you are not trying to grab anyone else." Instead of the dourness and corruption that were apparent in the city, people in the country offered "a friendly greeting," and human relations took on a strange serenity. The world of the vacation was one in which people found their "feelings" restored and the soul regenerated.[57]

The spirit of vacationing was nourished in the faith that the future was full of good possibilities. It embodied the promise of American abundance in a particularly evocative way. To Jews in search of a Promised Land, the summer resort stood as the best approximation of earthly paradise that could be imagined. Abraham Cahan articulated this perception of the vacation in the words of David Levinsky, who says to himself as he gazes in wonder at the richly forested mountains and the deeply colored skies of the Catskills, "this is just the kind of place for God to live in."[58]

Although the Catskill resorts were a principal destination of eastern European Jews, the setting at the New Jersey shore illuminated the symbolic meaning of the vacation for newcomers. Once the exclusive domain of an American elite, the coastal towns of Long Branch and Asbury Park, and the smaller towns dotting the broad beaches to the south, represented a veritable crossing of the River Jordan into the ultimate land of leisure. During a visit to Asbury Park in August 1892, the year that his first novel, *Maggie: A Girl of the Streets,* was published, Stephen Crane observed the utter luxury of the resort. Leveling a critical eye at this place "of wealth and leisure, of women and considerable wine," Crane stated tersely that "Asbury Park creates nothing. It does not make; it merely amuses."[59]

By the late 1890s, Asbury Park and Long Branch were featured regularly in the advertising pages of the *Yiddishes Tageblatt,* and the tantalizing prospect of unmitigated luxury was not lost on Jewish readers. With an awareness of the impact that the New Jersey vacation would have upon his people, the promoter of Prospect House in Asbury Park referred to the resort as "a paradise in this world."[60] The Yiddish word for paradise —*gan-eden* or Garden of Eden—helped to stimulate a majestic perception of the deep sands, salty breezes, and spacious boardwalks that had made the Jersey shore a haven for the wealthy. As a possibility for the person of ordinary means, the vacation by the sea seemed to fulfill the promise of material abundance in the United States. It allowed Jewish newcomers literally to inhale the air of freedom and boundlessness that they had understood to be an elemental part of redemption in the new society.

As the summer holiday away from the city met the needs and aspirations of Jews, the possession of a piano in a parlor would enable these immigrants to deepen their response to American society within the confines of the home.

❧ 8 ❧

The Parlor and the Piano

Much as Jewish newcomers had appropriated the American habit of vacationing, they embraced the concept of the piano in the parlor, which had become an ideal of home furnishing during the late nineteenth century. More than any other product, the parlor piano represented the rise of the "common man" to a height of social respectability. For city people who were content to rent an apartment rather than buy a home, this possession carried the hint of affluence that the private homestead held for farmers and townsfolk. Though Jews were not the only newcomers to strive for the ideal of the piano in the parlor, they responded to it in a distinctive way that was shaped by Jewish culture. Mesmerized by the idea of a room devoted simply to "living," Jewish immigrants struggled to create a parlor in their small tenement homes. In adopting this component of the American standard of living, they were motivated by the old Sabbatical imperative to make the home into a sanctuary from the world of work. Meeting a number of needs, the piano emerged in many Jewish homes as a means of satisfying the group's extraordinary interest in American popular music, which turned into a medium of cultural adaptation, as an instrument for refining Jewish children and raising the social status of the household, and as a culmination of the effort to make the parlor a site for domestic tranquillity amid the turbulence of immigrant life.

When the consummate artist of the American city, Edward Hopper, executed a pen-and-ink drawing of an "East Side Interior" in 1922, he showed how the domestic atmosphere of small urban apartments was dominated by furniture. In the tenement room which was the subject of that picture, a sewing machine governed the surroundings.[1] Designed with the aesthetic touches of a piece of furniture, the typical sewing machine signified both the need to labor and the aspiration to luxury of the urban worker. For Jewish newcomers, however, the sewing machine was not the most impressive feature of the American home, particularly because the vigorous international marketing of the Singer Sewing Machine Company had made the product a common possession in Russia during the late nineteenth century.[2]

As a focal point of the busy tenement kitchen, the modern oven did have a tantalizing effect on immigrants. Louis Borgenicht, who immigrated with his wife from Hungary in 1889, remembered how the stove of the couple's apartment on the Lower East Side had become a psychological anchor for his wife during the first difficult year in America. "It was her pride and joy, and little enough she had then," Borgenicht wrote of his hardworking spouse, who viewed the stove, which she kept scrupulously clean, as "a sort of symbol" that helped her "to retain her self-respect."[3]

The gas stove, in particular, revolutionized the situation of the housewife and confirmed the high expectations of Jewish newcomers about the material conditions of American life. Memoirs of the Lower East Side agreed on the psychic importance of this new appliance, which obviated the necessity of chopping wood, making a fire, and cleaning out ashes. An immigrant from Serbia recalled how her mother watched with delight the spectacle of a flame appearing at the strike of a match, and how she "presided over that stove like a queen."[4] The apparent miracle of heat and light without wood or oil made the gas stove a popular luxury among Jews. By the late 1890s, when there were reportedly "hundreds of thousands" of gas stoves on the Lower East Side, the cheapness and convenience of the invention led Jews to speak of it as "a salvation for paupers" and as "a true delight and God's blessing for ever."[5]

Although the gas oven sanitized and expedited the chore of cooking, and boosted the image of the homemaker, the most symbolic part of the home was the parlor. No matter how technologically impressive, kitchen appliances were still beasts of burden. They were developed for people who had to do housework, rather than for those who could afford to hire servants. They created some leisure, but they could not alter the functional character of the average urban apartment, which accommodated the basic needs of eating and sleeping. In spite of cramped quarters, city people aspired to the leisurely character of affluent homes by instituting a parlor, or "living room." The prestige of the urban apartment hinged on this innovation.

The concept of the parlor was well-rooted in American society. By the late seventeenth century, many homes in New England included a parlor to display the family's prized possessions, one of which was usually the household's most expensive bed, well furnished with textiles. Cupboards stocked with silver, pewter, or ceramic objects may also have been a feature of the early colonial parlor, and fine linens and clothing were kept in parlor chests.[6]

By the late nineteenth century, the parlor existed apart from the bedroom, and, as a room devoted primarily to leisure, it had become a social ideal. The high aspirations for the average American home were illustrated by the "Workingman's Model Home" at the Chicago World's Fair of 1893. Part of the New York State Exhibit, the model home had two floors, the bottom one including a living room, kitchen, bathroom, storeroom, and hallway, and the top floor containing three bedrooms, each with a closet, in addition to one large closet in the hallway. This structure was considered ideal for a husband, wife, and three children.[7] Geared toward suburban or town life, the Workingman's Model Home contrasted clearly with the majority of city homes. Nonetheless, it indicated the popular striving for a home that was devoted partly to leisure, one that freed people from having to spend most of their time in the kitchen, a room defined by the requirements of domestic labor.

Confronted with limited space, urban workers improvised a parlor in an effort to refine the atmosphere of their homes. In the depth of the depression of the 1890s, the *Forum* magazine presented its readers with the "anatomy of a tenement street" in an unidentified city. The manner of dividing the home in this neighborhood was typified by a family of eight people that lived in a three-room apartment. The front room, one of two that measured twelve by fifteen feet, was made to serve two purposes. At night, it was a bedroom for the parents and the two youngest children. During the day, it was turned into a parlor, or sitting room. Furnished with a carpet, pictures, and other appropriate furnishings, this was "the show-room of the house."[8] The appearance of tenement parlors in New York City impressed an English traveler who toured America in 1896. The careful placement of vases, statuettes, and bric-a-brac on the mantel, and the general style of furnishing the sitting room imbued these homes with an "air of social self-respect" that was lacking in the dwellings of most English workers.[9]

✗ The American ideal of having a parlor, a room devoted to leisure, appealed to immigrants of various backgrounds, but Jewish newcomers appeared to be enthralled by it.[10] On his arrival in New York City from Rumania in 1900, Marcus Ravage was astonished at how the relatives with whom he first stayed had emulated American standards of home arrangement. At night their five-room apartment was strewn with sleeping bodies that included members of the family and a large number of boarders. Little floor space remained. Yet, during the day, Ravage realized that "the interesting fiction of an apartment with specialized divisions" was maintained.

> Here was the parlor with its sofa and mirror and American rocking chairs; then came the dining-room with another sofa called a lounge, a round table, and innumerable chairs, then the kitchen with its luxurious fittings in porcelain and metal; then the young ladies' room, in which there was a bureau covered with quantities of odoriferous bottles and powder-boxes and other mysteries; and, last of all, Mrs. Segal's and the children's room.[11]

Accustomed in eastern Europe to severely overcrowded housing, Jews were fascinated by the notion of the home as a place of refinement and leisure. In spite of the tumultuous state of affairs created by the arrival of relatives from abroad and by the need to raise money by taking in boarders, a concerted effort was made to realize the American ideal of home furnishing. The behavior of Marcus Ravage's relatives was not unusual, as was suggested by a report by Anatole Leroy-Beaulieu to the French Consistoire Israelite in 1904. Having visited the Lower East Side in the spring of that year, Leroy-Beaulieu was immediately struck by the good appearance of Jewish homes, many of which were arranged according to the prevailing American standards.[12]

The parlor appeared to have been incorporated into Jewish homes in the early years of the great immigration. Abraham Cahan, who arrived in New York City in 1882, recalled that the first household in which he boarded, that of a widowed peddler and her children, had a parlor with carpeting and good furniture. The home resembled one of a well-to-do family in Cahan's native city, Vilna.[13]

Echoing the impression that this household had upon him, Cahan posed the parlor as a major symbol of American social status in his short story "A Sweatshop Romance," which appeared in 1898. On meeting a couple from her native region in Russia, Mrs. Leizer Lipman, the wife of a small-scale clothing manufacturer, brought the newcomers to her apartment. In light of the fact that her social position in the old world had been inferior to that of her newly arrived guests, Mrs. Lipman was especially intent on demonstrating the progress she had made. As soon as they arrived at the apartment, which served also as a sweatshop, Mrs. Lipman announced, "Come, I want to show you my parlor." This marked the first step in the effort "to overwhelm them with her American achievements."[14]

Partly a sign of prestige in the new urban society, the creation of a parlor was, moreover, a consummation of the Jewish tendency to infuse luxuries with spiritual meaning. Commenting on the priority given to this special room, the New York *Yiddishes Tageblatt* stated in 1897 that "many a good housewife turns her parlor into a sort of Paradise, which only a select few are permitted to enter."[15] The careful attention given to the parlor appeared to reflect the same spirit of dedication with which eastern European Jews had traditionally joined material luxuries to the sublime world of the Sabbath and holy days.

Having understood fine things to be reflections of the divine state of peacefulness that filled these occasions, Jewish newcomers in America could hardly avoid associating the well-furnished parlor with a state of grandeur that was unimaginable to dwellers in the dismal lodgings of the Russian Pale. Elizabeth Stern, whose family had immigrated from Poland in 1891, remembered how her mother used to refer to the parlor she created in their apartment as the "Sabbath room."[16] The idea of a room devoted entirely to sitting, to leisure, was so foreign to Stern's traditional mother that it could be best assimilated through the familiar Jewish concept of honoring the Sabbath. Interpreted like this, the parlor took on a meaning that was spiritual in intensity, if not in content. In the secular setting of urban America, the Jewish sense of luxury in honor of God had fused into the American sense of luxury in honor of the individual. The parlor helped to complete that change.

The possession of a piano, which was the crowning feature of the parlor, offered the most eloquent testimony of the newly raised position of the ordinary Jew in the United States. In the cities of Germany and Austria, limited numbers of Jewish migrants who had advanced into the bourgeoisie found in the possession of a piano the sign of membership in an exclusive social class. In the cities of the United States, large numbers of Jewish newcomers were able to possess this luxury without becoming prosperous businessmen or professionals. For these Jews, the piano was a potent symbol of the American ideal of social equality.

No product better evinced the elevation of the ordinary person in America than the piano in the tenement house. "There was a time, in the memory of people now living, when the piano was considered an article of luxury," wrote advertising executive John Lee Mahin of Chicago in 1911—"it has now become a staple commercial product."[17] As early as 1866, when the New York City firm of Steinway and Sons developed an upright piano with the tone and durability of the square and the grand piano, the trend toward marketing a more affordable piano had begun.[18] In 1875, an official survey of the household budgets of 397 workers in Massachusetts uncovered the fact that a large majority of the families studied had a piano in their home.[19] In addition to its delicate construction, the artistic design of the conventional piano of the day made the instrument the prized possession of the average home. Epitomizing the striving of the multitude for an elite standard of luxury, mass consumption of the piano reached a high point in the period 1890–1910.[20]

The mass-marketing of the piano turned on the social aspirations of urban wage earners. In 1912, the trade journal *Advertising and Selling* discussed a successful promotional campaign for the piano that had been launched by the great Philadelphia department store owner John Wanamaker a decade or so earlier. Wanamaker had 275 pianos that he wanted to close out at 240 dollars each. His advertising manager decided that the only market for the pianos would be city people with relatively low incomes, who would have to be persuaded to buy not on the basis of the product's technical qualities but on the grounds that the piano would elevate the social standing of their children. Stressing the point that music was essential to a girl's education, and that parents would naturally want to give their children opportunities that they themselves had lacked, the campaign revolved around the slogan "Make Mary a Lady." With the help of an installment plan, the lot of pianos was reportedly sold within three days.[21]

The success of such a promotional effort reflected the latent impulse of the majority of urban Americans to claim the insignia of prestige. Although the demand for pianos was not universal, the instrument was commonly considered to be an important part of the refined home. On the basis of a detailed study of two hundred wage-earning families on the lower East Side of New York City from 1903 to 1905, Louise More concluded that "the most common ambition" of mothers was to have a piano, whether or not their children possessed musical talent.[22] To exemplify the social aspirations of the people she studied, More told of an Irish-American mother who had recently moved her family of nine to a better apartment, one that had five rooms and a bath for seventeen dollars a month. Complementing the move, she bought a secondhand piano, out of the desire that her children "have a home they can be proud of."[23] Based on a similar, though much smaller, study of New York families during the same years, Elsa Herzfeld pointed out the tendency of unskilled laborers to buy pianos, not only for the pleasure they provided, but also for the prospect of increasing the social prestige of their children.[24]

Once immigrants decided to settle in America, many appeared to view the piano as a highly desirable feature of the home. Slavic immigrants from central and eastern Europe showed a particular interest in obtaining instruments that would allow them to maintain strong musical traditions. In an extensive study of Slavic immigrants to America which was published in 1910, Emily Balch observed Slavic homes in the mining and steel towns of Pennsylvania that had no parlor yet included a piano, which was often fit between beds in the bedroom.[25]

Arriving in the United States with a clear intention to establish themselves, Jews quickly apprehended the importance of the piano to the American home. Although the basic musical instrument of the shtetl was probably the fiddle, which often appeared in Marc Chagall's dreamlike paintings of Jewish life in eastern Europe, the piano became the pride and joy of Jewish homes in America. When the *New York Tribune* noted in 1899 that "Happy East Side Homes" frequently contained pianos, it was recognizing the cultural influence of Jewish newcomers on the area.[26] During the first years of the great immigration from eastern Europe, first-rate pianos were unfamiliar to the residents of the Lower East Side. In 1886, when Joseph Spector founded what would be a thriving piano business on the corner of Grand and Orchard Streets, virtually no stores in the area sold high quality, brand-name pianos. Yet, within a few years, Jewish consumers came to be familiar with the names of Steinway, Chickering, Knabe, Kruger, Ellington, and other leading manufacturers whose instruments were sold by a number of local merchants in emulation of Spector's policy of offering fine products at reasonable prices and on the installment plan.[27]

Giving an indication of the popularity of pianos among Jewish newcomers around the turn of the century, the bold advertisements of piano dealers seemed at times to leap off the pages of Yiddish newspapers. An eye-catching advertisement of Wing and Son, a firm with a large showroom and factory at the corner of Ninth Avenue and 13th Street, proclaimed in Yiddish to "Mr. Piano Customer" that "19 CENTS A DAY Pays for a Piano in the Closing of our SENSATIONAL FACTORY TO CUSTOMER SALE." To emphasize the pecuniary advantage of buying directly from the warehouse, the advertisement pictured a larger-than-life, well-dressed merchant with an enormous pair of scissors cutting through a piano, from which a mass of paper money fell.[28] With cute aphorisms such as "One can dance only as well as the music is played," and "What is a Home without a Piano?" Yiddish advertisements for the many retailers of pianos in New York City embraced the popular enthusiam of Jewish newcomers for the grand product.[29]

The rhetorical question "What is a Home without a Piano?" registered an important attitude in Jewish neighborhoods, where the piano was often considered integral to the refined household. Sociologist Max Weber interpreted the piano as a characteristic product of the bourgeoisie of northern Europe. In contrast to the more public social life of Italy, Weber argued, the home-centeredness of the affluent middle class in the colder regions of Europe gave rise to the demand for a versatile instrument well-suited to home entertainment.[30]

The domesticity of Jewish life may have been conducive to the adoption of the piano. Among most other ethnic groups, the pub competed with the home as the center of social life. The separation of men and women at leisure restricted the opportunity for unifying the family around such a product. Some newcomers, most notably the Germans, whose traditional culture approved the manufacture and sale of liquor, established respectable family-oriented saloons to serve the social, economic, and political needs of German-America. In this saloon-centered world, the family could remain together and listen to a piano player, but the piano itself would not become a focus of private life.[31]

Unlike other European immigrants, Jews were culturally biased against excessive drinking, and they developed no "saloon culture" to vie with the home as haven from the world of work. Although cafés and restaurants, in addition to music halls and theaters, accommodated the strong social impulses of Jews, these leisure places lacked the addictive quality of the pub. They supplemented the home, which remained solidly at the center of Jewish life. Contrasting the domestic condition of Jews with that of Germans and Irish in urban America, Philadelphia social worker Charles Bernheimer observed in 1905 that "poor as he is," the Jewish immigrant "strives to live like a civilized man, and the money which another workman perhaps might spend on drink and sport he devotes to the improvement of his home and the education of his children."[32]

The intensity of the Jews' domestic focus was reflected in the vast popularity of sheet music for the piano. In a veiled reference to the overwhelming Jewish presence on Tin Pan Alley, the popular music center of America that was located around 28th Street and Broadway, a chronicler noted that, in the 1890s, "songs which were once the result of inspiration" became "products of industry, like trousers, or cloaks, and suits."[33] Producing an endless supply of sheet music for the latest popular songs, some of which sold over a million copies, the music firms of Tin Pan Alley stimulated the growth of a number of publishing companies specializing in Yiddish-American folios.

At the turn of the century, the Hebrew Publishing Company, a large downtown publisher of religious books, secular works, and paraphernalia for Yiddish-speaking Jews, began to print an extensive catalogue of "Jewish music for piano and song." In the late 1890s and early 1900s, many smaller Jewish publishers arose to meet the burgeoning demand for sheet music that recorded the scores of current Yiddish plays and operas, as well as individual songs that were "plugged" enthusiastically in music halls by aspiring Jewish singers. The Jewish market was extended by the concern of "American" companies, like the partnership of Irving Berlin and Ted Snyder, for reaching an audience that would appreciate popular tunes heavily spiced with Yiddishisms. Intent on learning English quickly, most Jewish immigrants became consumers of both Tin Pan Alley's music and the Yiddish song sheets of downtown firms.[34]

The overwhelming presence of Jewish composers on Tin Pan Alley, and the powerful response of Jewish newcomers to their creations, suggested that Jewish adaptation to America was facilitated through the production and consumption of popular music.[35] Many of the most popular and enduring American songs between the 1890s and World War I were produced by Jewish singer-songwriters, the most prominent being Charles Harris, Harry von Tilzer, Jerome Kern, and Irving Berlin. Not only had Jewish publishers established the foundation of Tin Pan Alley, but the American Jewish milieu turned out singers and composers like Al Jolson, Eddie Cantor, Sophie Tucker, George Gershwin, Lorenz Hart, Richard Rodgers, and Oscar Hammerstein II.[36] The rise of these stars on the American horizon inspired countless young Jews to see the piano as a key to success.

As an instrument of cultural adaptation, the piano attained unique qualities when used to play sheet music. Like the Yiddish theater, the large body of Jewish sheet music arranged for piano articulated the central themes of Jewish acculturation in urban America—from the reconciliation of traditional values with new circumstances to the celebration of American Jewish heroes.[37] As a result, the piano figured in the cultural assimilation of Jews not only by being the crowning piece of the American-style parlor but also by making the home, as well as the theater and the music hall, a forum for reconciling new and old attitudes. It became a private stage for the articulation of American Jewish identity.

Although the growth of a rich Jewish musical life in urban America underlay the enthusiasm of newcomers for the piano, Jews perceived the product to have other uplifting features that were social rather than artistic. As one of the purposes of building a refined home was to impart a taste for culture to the young, piano playing came to be seen as a staple for the upbringing of Jewish children, particularly girls. Alert to the prospects of improving their daughters' social position through marriage, the multitude of immigrants turned the piano into a fountain of American-style yikhes, the appearance of gentility that had become so important a social factor in the American city. Recalling that "a plain-looking young lady who played the piano had an edge, in the matrimonial market, over those who didn't," musician Samuel Chotzinoff pointed out that piano-playing was marked down as an "asset" in the making of Jewish matches.[38] The experience of Elizabeth Stern typified that of many young newcomers. When she was thirteen, Stern's mother signed her up for piano lessons in the expectation that this type of training would prepare the girl "for the life of an American lady."[39]

The perception of the piano as a preeminent symbol of prestige crossed the ethnic lines that separated Jews. Within New York's small group of Sephardic Jews, those of Spanish and Portuguese origin, skill at the piano was ranked with the ability to speak pure Castilian Spanish as a badge of gentility for young women.[40]

The social aspirations behind the use of this product were sufficiently plain to be satirized in the Yiddish press. In its ongoing criticism of the "allrightnik," the stereotype of the economically successful and rapidly assimilated Jew, the New York *Forward* delighted in caricaturing the extraordinary emphasis on the piano as a social as well as a musical instrument. A 1914 cartoon, with the caption "Play, Play, Dear Gussie," pictured a newly married couple. As the young wife plays happily at the piano, her mate, seated behind her, compliments his bride's musical flare as he holds his fingers in his ears and grimaces.[41]

In an equally vivid cartoon of 1907, the *Forward* betrayed an attitude of condescension toward the poorly educated multitude of which it was the self-appointed defender. Called "Mrs. Kremzel's Daughter Plays Piano," the cartoon mocks the inability of a mother to understand her daughter's effort to play pianissimo, as her teacher has instructed. Supposedly too uncultured to appreciate the instrument that she has strived to obtain, Mrs. Kremzel hires a different instructor who has her daughter banging the keys until "the walls shook." Delighted, the older woman exclaims, "Now that is what you call playing!"[42] The comedy of the *Forward*'s satire derived from the fervor with which many newcomers strove for prestige that had once been entirely out of reach.

In the city, the acquisition of a piano became a social event. The spectacle of the noble instrument being carted down the street to a tenement house attracted onlookers. When it was carried up the stairs of the building, neighbors would open their doors to watch its progress and to find out who had purchased it. In the view or earshot of these spectators, the new owners directed the movers to the entrance of their apartment, appreciating the social distinction that accompanied the shining piano.[43]

A means of entertainment, an instrument for expressing feelings about America, a sign of refinement and status, the piano also emerged as a symbol of domestic tranquillity. During the late nineteenth century, as the popularity of the piano grew, the parlor organ also gained a large market, particularly in American villages and towns. Embodying the religious associations of the church, and possessing an elaborate vertical body with shelves, brackets, and niches that doubled as a mantel for the living room, the organ had a link to tradition and a physical dominance that made it the center of family life. Advertisements of the organ tended to depict the stately product as a symbol of domestic harmony and stability.[44]

Though lacking the height and religious aspect of the organ, the piano was equally imposing within the confines of the tenement. In the Jewish parlor, which was perceived as a secular sanctuary, the piano held out the promise of family unity amid the strains of immigrant life in urban America. The act of immigration strained the bonds of marriage, frequently requiring the separation of husband and wife for months or even years. Marital stress was compounded by the varying response of husband and wife to American life, and by the breakdown of traditional attitudes toward the proper "place" of men and women. The gap between parents and children widened as young people became more thoroughly American in habit than their elders, and thus rarely deigned to defer to fathers and mothers as tradition commanded. Added to these specifically familial tensions, the difficulties of making a living bore down hard on the family.

The parlor piano could evince a sense of security and serenity that contrasted sharply with the insecurity and anxiety of city life. A vignette published in the *Forward* in 1910 brought to the surface the undercurrents of emotion that tied newcomers to this distinctive product. Entitled

"Little Bits from Life," the story focused on the family of an insurance agent who had spent a miserable childhood in a shtetl. The man's primary joy was to spend time at home after work. Through careful budgeting, his wife had beautifully furnished their apartment, which included a parlor with a Turkish carpet and a fine piano. In the evenings, the couple would sit peacefully while their daughter played the piano.[45] As a focus for entertainment, the piano in the parlor was uniquely suited to unite individuals into a more cohesive family. It evoked parental pride in the accomplishments of children, and it gave youngsters a way to make their parents' life more comfortable. Offering a soothing contrast to the seemingly interminable whir of sewing machines in the sweatshop or to the constant noise of people at the office or store, the instrument transported immigrants into another dimension of life, where the stress of the outside world could be momentarily allayed and the bonds of the inner family strengthened.

Much as the traditional Sabbath had done, the piano and the parlor liberated the home from the pervasive presence of work. Within a more refined domestic atmosphere, the individual was dignified. Thus, in a secular way, these elements of the American standard of living expressed the traditional Jewish perception of luxury as a sanctifying force. Although not every home had a piano, the popularity of the instrument, and the near universality of the parlor, suggested the social value and cultural importance of these things in the world of Jewish newcomers.

Another dimension of American mass consumption, the institution of advertising, also raised the status of the urban American as a consumer, and, in responding to it, Jewish newcomers would again blend old tendencies with a new point of view.

PART IV

The Culture of Advertising

ᘒᘓᘔᓏ 9 ᖶᘺᓏᓍᓍ

American Advertising in the
Yiddish Press

One of the most dynamic institutions to arise from the immigra-
tion of eastern European Jews to America, the Yiddish press quickly
developed into an attractive medium for American advertisers. By adapting the dominant trends in American journalism and advertising, leading
Yiddish newspapers cultivated a large, faithful, and commercially recep-
tive readership that represented a potentially lucrative market for local
and national firms. After the depression of the 1890s, increasing numbers
of major American corporations identified this body of consumers and
began to advertise in Yiddish. The receptivity of the immigrant press to
American advertising quickened the response of newcomers to important
new products, and heightened the significance of advertisements for the
cultural assimilation of Jews.

From the moment of disembarkation in American cities, newcomers
were exposed to a fascinating array of promotional words and images.
The primary destination of eastern European Jews, New York City,
appeared to be literally covered with advertisements. In the 1890s, passengers of ships approaching the harbor of Manhattan watched an enormous sign for H-O oatmeal come boldly into their view, and they stepped
down to a city that was "plastered and painted and papered with adver-

tisements."[1] In 1912, when New York had nearly five thousand billboards in addition to a large number of "sky-signs" that reached illegally to the height of forty feet above the rooftops on which they were perched, a municipal commission noted with chagrin that the city had "gone to greater lengths in the outdoor advertising business than any other city in existence."[2]

Even those Jews who had passed through the metropolis of Berlin, where street posters were neatly presented on kiosks, marveled at the license given to advertising in urban America. A multiplicity of names representing retail stores and famous products appealed to consumers from the walls of buildings, the overhead panels of street cars, the sides of fences, the umbrellas of pushcarts, and the ceilings of barber shops. After 1904, advertising also extended underground, decorating the passageways of the city's new subway system.[3]

Whereas Americans took advertisements for granted, newcomers found in the billboard and the store sign a challenge to mastering the basic vocabulary of city life. Benjamin Gordon, a *shoykhet*, or kosher slaughterer, from Lithuania who came to New York in the 1890s, recalled that he began to learn the English alphabet and vocabulary by studying the words on retail signs and billboard advertisements as he walked along Grand and Canal Streets. The similarity of some Yiddish and English words, such as milk, coffee, shoes, water, glasses, books, and bakery helped Gordon to gain a sense of stability amid the array of strange notations.[4]

Before Jewish newcomers had had time to acquaint themselves fully with American advertising, they were exposed to the aura of superiority in which the products of the modern city were shrouded. Luxury items were identified almost exclusively by their English names. "In America," Marcus Ravage discovered soon after coming to New York City from Rumania in 1900, "it was against the rules of good breeding to call things by their right names." Whether he was speaking Yiddish or Rumanian, Ravage learned that "certain articles must always be referred to in English."[5] Pressured to revise the language that defined objects, newcomers quickly learned that the products of the urban American were no trifling matter.

As a result of this chauvinistic attitude toward commodities, the development of "Yinglish," which incorporated American words into Yiddish speech, accompanied the growth of Yiddish advertising. In *The American Language*, an encyclopedic text that appeared in 1919, H. L. Mencken noted that words describing the most ordinary objects and concerns, such as the rooms of the house and the names of meals and occupations, were

The superstructure of the Second Avenue Elevated train gave the shops of Division Street the look of a shopping mall, 1905. [Courtesy of the New York Historical Society, New York City]

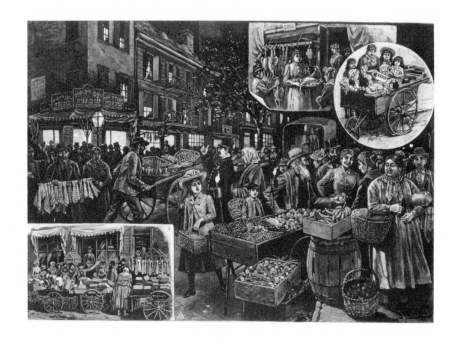

"Market night in the Jewish quarter," 1891. [From *Frank Leslie's Illustrated Weekly* (September 12, 1891)]

Referring to Hester Street in 1884 as a "Polish trading post in New York," *Harper's Weekly* remarked that young Jewish pack peddlers based in the Lower East Side would "warm their parents' hearts with tales of successful bargains and instances of the triumph of Semitic persuasive powers over Christian parsimony." [May 3, 1884]

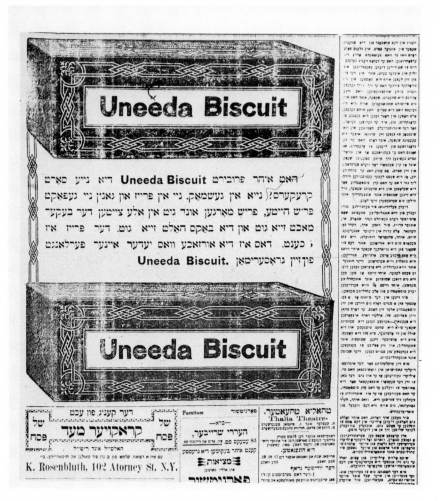

The Yiddish Uneeda Biscuit, March 15, 1899. [From the New York *Yiddishes Tageblatt;* translation appears on page 166]

Caricature of an immigrant Jewish merchant in New York City:
  "*Cholly: But how can you afford to sell genuine patent-leather shoes for that price?*"
  "*Solomon Isaacson: I vill dell you a segred, mine frendt: — der batent vos exbired.*"
[*From Puck* magazine, July 15, 1896. Courtesy of the American Jewish Archives]

Woman inspecting a pitcher at a pushcart, 1904. [Courtesy of the New York Public Library, Division of Local History]

A peddler arranging his pushcart, 1904. [Courtesy of the New York Public Library, Division of Local History]

View from the balcony of an elaborate movie theater that Marcus Loew built before 1914 on the site where he was born, 5th Street and Avenue B, New York City. [From Robert Grau, *The Theatre of Science* (1914)]

the most likely to be incorporated into Yiddish.[6] A forum of everyday items, advertising quickly submitted to the domination of English words rendered in the Hebrew script of Yiddish. The Yiddish words for clothing, suits, cloaks, shawls, jackets, dresses, skirts, pants, hats, gloves, handkerchiefs, hosiery, shoes, jewelry, watches, clocks, cutlery, table linen, napkins, oilcloth, embroidery, ribbons, lace curtains, dry goods, quilts, bedspreads, wallpaper, carpets, paint, furniture, chiffoniers, parlor sets, hardware, house furnishings, stoves, ranges, toys, presents, and baby carriages, as well as the names of foodstuffs, were often replaced by their English equivalents, as were commercial terms like "strictly one price," "spring styles," "bargains," and "sale."

For Jewish immigrants, as for native-born Americans, the urban press emerged as the primary medium through which consumers established an enduring relationship with advertisers. In a valuable study of the immigrant press of the United States, published in 1922, sociologist Robert E. Park explained that American advertising attracted the foreign-born reader out of all proportion to the space it occupied in ethnic newspapers. Newcomers often failed to make much of a distinction between news, editorials, and advertisements, and they thus tended to pay equal attention to each type of material. Advertising was actually preferred by many readers because it contained larger, more readable type and bore a close relation to daily concerns. Moreover, the news and editorials of many foreign-language newspapers were carelessly prepared, whereas American advertisers submitted skillfully designed copy that was likely to engage the average reader.[7]

More than other ethnic newspapers of the period, the Yiddish press managed to harness the receptivity of newcomers and to create an avid audience for American-style advertising. "In the Yiddish press the foreign-language newspaper may be said to have achieved form," Robert Park contended. The impulse to embrace both the trend of American journalism and the sensibility of a distinct ethnic group, inchoate in other foreign publications, was "outstanding and manifest" in the Yiddish press. "No other foreign-language press," Park concluded, "succeeded in reflecting so much of the intimate life of the people which it represents, or reacted so powerfully upon the opinion, thought, and aspiration of the public for which it exists."[8]

The catalyst for the rise of a buoyant press was the highly concentrated, spiritually uprooted community of Jews in New York City, a group in need of an institution through which unforeseen situations could be interpreted and understood. Spurred by the keen intuition of publishers and editors in search of a reading public, the Yiddish press adapted

149

itself well to the style of journalism that had made American newspapers an essential feature of urban life. The use of emphatic, sometimes sensational headlines, the attention to skillful editing, the emphasis on human interest stories, and the responsiveness of editors to popular taste—all emerged as prominent aspects of the leading Yiddish newspapers in the early twentieth century. This unique press virtually created a generation of readers who depended on it for psychological as well as intellectual support in the new world.[9]

Among the scores of Yiddish publications that rose and fell in New York between 1880 and 1914, two newspapers attained a position of broad authority. The first to emerge was the *Yiddishes Tageblatt*. Founded in 1885, the *Tageblatt* represented the second successful undertaking of Kasriel Hersch Sarasohn, an enterprising and resilient Polish Jew who settled in America in 1874, quickly attained his goal of becoming an Orthodox rabbi, and, in the same year, started the weekly *Yiddishes Gazetten*, the first Yiddish publication to prosper in the competitive marketplace of American journalism. In the *Tageblatt*, Sarasohn realized more fully his hope of reaching the growing Yiddish community in New York City. By the middle of the 1890s, the newspaper had become the leading Yiddish daily in the United States.

Oriented toward the majority of Jews who were politically moderate and emotionally bound to the Jewish way of life, the *Tageblatt* contrasted sharply with the variety of Yiddish newspapers produced by socialists and anarchists during the late 1880s and the 1890s. Of these, the socialist *Forverts (Forward)*, founded in 1897, would become the pacesetter of American ethnic journalism. With the return of the newspaper's original editor, Abraham Cahan, to the top post of the *Forward* in 1902, the publication began a phenomenal rise to power over the Yiddish-speaking people of the United States. Thriving off of Cahan's intimate knowledge of the American Jewish scene and impelled by his great literary skills, the *Forward* combined the exciting style of American journalism with a sense of concern for the perplexing situation of the Jewish newcomer. In 1900, the paper's relative obscurity was reflected in a reported circulation of 19,502, compared to the *Tageblatt*'s 40,000. Under the editorship of Cahan, however it leaped forward, achieving an estimated circulation of 122,532 in 1911, compared to 69,000 for Sarasohn's publication. In less than a decade, Cahan had created the most popular foreign-language newspaper in the United States.[10]

By establishing a style similar to that of the metropolitan press in America, prominent Jewish newspapers such as the *Yiddishes Tageblatt* and the *Forward* of New York City managed to become effective purveyors of advertising. In the last decades of the nineteenth century, the rise of large-scale advertising hinged on the ability of American newspapers and magazines to captivate the public. Advertising in the United States was inextricably tied to the popular press, as it would later be to broadcasting, because the media of mass communication in America forged a bond with the public, without which the appeals of advertisers would have been relatively ineffectual.

Between 1870 and 1910, the mutual rise of large-scale advertising and a far-reaching press gave America the reputation of being the home of modern advertising. In 1867, the total volume of advertising in the United States was estimated to be about 50,000,000 dollars. Thirteen years later, in 1880, the amount had quadrupled to 200,000,000 dollars, in spite of the deflation of the 1870s. By 1909, the estimated investment in advertising exceeded 1,000,000,000 dollars. In forty years, the volume had multiplied twentyfold.[11]

Although outdoor advertising remained an important medium, the upsurge in spending centered increasingly on the press. The personalized relationship of the metropolitan press to the consuming public was the critical characteristic that made it an excellent medium for advertising. In the creation of the human interest story, the essential difference between American and European journalism was spelled out. Urban newspapers in Europe tended to revolve around political divisions within the population, appealing to class-conscious laborers with reports and editorials that emphasized a particular ideology. The metropolitan press in the United States, however, appealed to a vast audience of heterogenous people based on the common concerns of city living. In light of this goal, the human interest story arose as the defining trait of American journalism. By probing and publicizing the lives of all sorts of city dwellers, newspapers created a sympathetic audience, and they came to be viewed as the definitive source of information and advice on how to survive in the American city.[12]

Serving as a type of social advisor, the metropolitan dailies had begun to address women disinctly as consumers by the 1880s, offering advice on how to prepare meals, how to dress, and how to furnish the home. Advertisements of products thus blended evenly into the texture of American newspapers, which viewed the urban lifestyle as being no less newsworthy than the dramatic and tragic events of the day.

The personal note that was injected into the urban newspaper also accounted for the sudden rise of the mass-circulation woman's magazine, which became an arbiter of consumption by virtue of its intimate rapport with readers. During the editorship of the Dutch immigrant Edward

William Bok, from 1889 to 1919, the *Ladies' Home Journal* exemplified the role of the magazine as a personal advisor. Bok instituted an immediately successful column for young women called "Side Talks with Girls" that drew almost 160,000 letters over a period of sixteen years. Another column, "Heart to Heart," was soon set up to deal with "the spiritual needs of the mature woman." This, too, was an instant success. In 1903, the *Journal* became the first good-quality magazine to attain a circulation of 1,000,000 readers. Eventually, Bok built up a staff of thirty-five editors whose task was to give a warm and helpful response to letters from readers, which amounted to nearly one million per year by 1917. The extreme personalism of Bok's column "At Home with the Editor" radiated the extraordinary concern of this immigrant for giving American women "comprehensive personal service." As a result of the "firm and unique hold" that the *Ladies' Home Journal* had on its readers, the wide-ranging advice it gave on matters of personal and domestic consumption carried a special authority. The magazine was thus a boon to advertisers.[13]

Blending the intimacy of an ethnic enterprise with the human interest style of journalism, the Yiddish press cultivated the personalized style that had turned the American newspaper and the woman's magazine into first-rate purveyors of advertising. The comforting sense of familiarity generated by the *Yiddishkeyt*, or Jewishness, of the press was recalled by an immigrant in a letter to the editor of the *Tageblatt*. "When I landed in the United States in 1886," the man recalled a decade later, "the *Jewish Gazette* was the first Jewish paper that met my eyes, and to be candid and without flattery . . . I fell in love with it at first sight." This devoted reader explained further that he and his family had since become subscribers to various American newspapers and magazines, but they "would not think of parting with the dear *Jewish Gazette*."[14]

The depth of the rapport between the people of the press and their public was demonstrated when Kasriel Sarasohn, the founder of the *Gazette* and the *Yiddish Tageblatt*, died of pneumonia in January 1905 at the age of 70. Sarasohn's funeral procession attracted a crowd large enough to draw the supervision of three hundred policemen. Jews struggled to enter the synagogue prior to the march to the cemetery in Brooklyn, and several thousand mourners followed twenty cars over the Brooklyn Bridge. The outpouring of souls was compared to that which marked the death of Jacob Joseph, the Chief Rabbi of New York, three years earlier. Kasriel Sarasohn was buried next to him.[15]

The magnetism of the *Forward* was fully manifested in the "Bintel Brief," the "bundle of letters" that editor Abraham Cahan instituted as a regular column in 1906. Soon evolving into a trademark of the newspaper, the "Bintel Brief" generated a flood of emotional letters to the editor from Jews needing advice and consolation in order to maintain their sanity and dignity in the face of unforeseen and often agonizing problems with spouses, children, lovers, neighbors, bosses, and landlords. During the first years of the column's existence, Cahan answered the letters himself, finding in this space of the daily newspaper a rare opportunity to establish an intimate relationship with the diverse Jewish immigrants of New York and other cities as well.[16]

The combination of literary spirit and social conscience that motivated Abraham Cahan to institute the "Bintel Brief" led him as well to transpose the human interest story onto the pages of the Yiddish newspaper. Between 1897 and 1901, Cahan had gained invaluable experience as a reporter for the *New York Sun* and the *New York Evening Post*, as well as for the *New York Commercial Advertiser*, the paper for which he had done the bulk of his writing on the vicissitudes of life in the Jewish quarter of New York City. Taking command of the *Forward* in 1902, Cahan captivated the Yiddish public with his refined talent for composing the human interest story.[17]

The personalized tone and the human interest reporting of the Yiddish press attracted readers to the medium of print and enhanced the image of the newspaper as an authority on urban living. As a prospective vehicle for advertising, the Yiddish paper gained even greater value through its coverage of consumers as a topic of interest. Typical of this type of writing was an article that appeared in the *Forward* in September 1905, with the title "New Season, New Hats." Mindful of the criticism that was customarily levelled at the newspaper's casual, down-to-earth style by socialists who valued ideological purity instead of popular journalism, Cahan's paper justified its focus on Jewish stylishness with the following discourse: "Perhaps it can be said that women's hats is not such an important topic to be worthwhile to write about in a newspaper. Not at all! It absolutely is an important topic. If it does not touch the heart, it does touch the pocket, and how far is the distance nowadays from the pocket to the heart?"[18]

The Yiddish press emerged as a dynamic promotional medium not only because it had an attractive text but also because it skillfully adapted the prevailing American style of advertising. In the industrializing nations of Europe as well as in the United States, advertising underwent profound changes in form between 1880 and 1910. The size of individual advertisements increased dramatically, often occupying from a quarter to a half of a page. Cramped rows of textlike print that strained the eye gave way to spacious white backgrounds that served to highlight terser messages in bolder typefaces. Improvements in printing made for more graphic and realistic illustrations and permitted sympathetic human characters, such as the happy Quaker of Quaker Oats and the statuesque Phoebe Snow of the Delaware, Lackawanna, and Western Railroad, to become popular trademarks. In magazines, the use of color gave advertisements a novel aesthetic effect. Improvements in the visual dimension of advertising were common to the urban newspapers of Europe and America. In the United States, however, a uniquely captivating verbal technique emerged, one defined by an informal, conversational tone.

During the late nineteenth century, the advertising of Philadelphia department store owner John Wanamaker provided a model of the American style. Contrasting with the principle of caveat emptor—let the buyer beware—that had customarily governed retail commerce, a sense of interest in the consumer formed the cornerstone of Wanamaker's advertising. Joseph Appel, a longtime advertising manager for Wanamaker's stores, described the new style as being "plain, sincere, intimate," and as having the qualities necessary to "establish confidence and goodwill between buyer and seller."[19] Unlike the grandiose pronouncements which P. T. Barnum had modeled for nineteenth-century advertisers, the tone of the neighborly chat allowed modern advertising to establish a context of believability for the hearty self-endorsements of emerging national advertisers.

The magnetic power of this promotional technique was exemplified by the rise of the pioneering mail-order firm of Sears, Roebuck (1893), whose success in creating a national clientele depended utterly upon the effectiveness of the printed word. The Sears, Roebuck catalogue was a perfect blend of sincerity and superlatives. Running over a thousand pages and containing well-illustrated descriptions of virtually every product desired by the public, the catalogue was spoken of as a rival to the family Bible in rural American homes. The book began with a persuasive, plainspoken letter from Sears that opened with the greeting, "Kind Friend," and closed with "Yours very truly." In the preface that followed, Sears appealed to the egalitarian bias of the American consumer, by stating, "if you favor us with your patronage, we will do everything in our power to merit your trade, and no matter how small your order may be, it will receive the same prompt and careful attention as if it were ever so large."[20] Generously interspersed among the pages of down-to-earth promotional conversation were profuse assurances that every type of product sold by Sears was of unsurpassable quality.

Inspiring and dignifying the ordinary consumer, the personalized format was characteristically American. In Europe the nature of advertising was influenced by the presence of a comparatively rigid social hierarchy, in which businessmen had customarily assumed that laborers had tastes and attitudes different from their own.[21] To varying degrees, the changes in the appearance of advertisements in the 1880s and 1890s were reflected in British, French, and German newspapers. Yet, the vivacious involvement of American advertisers with the public, apparent since the days of P. T. Barnum, was foreign to the socially conservative approach of many European entrepreneurs.[22] Deeply rooted social traditions encouraged businessmen not to abandon in their advertisements the air of propriety that was designed to separate them from the multitude of laboring people. The comparative lack of a popular, conversational style in European advertising was observed in 1913 by a German advertising agent, who explained that the personalism of American copy would not appeal to German consumers, who were used to a more dignified kind of promotion.[23]

Consistent with both the egalitarian leanings and the rhetorical exuberance that characterized traditional Jewish culture, the American style of advertising was given room to develop in the Yiddish press, where it was flavored with distinctly Jewish types of expression. By virtue of this method of promotion, Yiddish advertising developed a special dynamism that increased the receptivity of newcomers to fashionable American products.

From the beginning, the Yiddish newspaper tried to keep abreast of the latest developments in advertising. Kasriel Sarasohn's *Yiddishes Tageblatt* was not shy about soliciting advertisements, and it persistently preached to local merchants about the necessity of advertising in the modern commercial setting. In the context of an article on the heady competition among the large retail stores of Grand Street in 1889, the point was made that in New York City "one cannot advertise through a beadle as in the little Polish *shtetlach*." In a competitive marketplace, it was not enough to possess a large stock of merchandise. Merchants had to learn to "advertise through the newspapers . . . and bring the customers into the business."[24] A decade later, the name of John Wanamaker was invoked to persuade Jewish advertisers of the necessity of steady promotion. The *Tageblatt* stated that Wanamaker "would as soon think of shutting up his shutters as quit advertising in the newspapers."[25]

The seriousness with which Sarasohn took his own advice was illustrated by a letter he had written in the summer of 1900 to the editor of *Printer's Ink*, the leading trade journal of American advertising. Seeking to assert the superiority of his own daily paper in the eyes of potential advertisers, Sarasohn questioned the accuracy of the circulation figures ascribed to two competitors, the *New Yorker Yiddishe Abendpost* (1899–1905) and the *Teglikher Herold* (1891–1904), in the *American Newspaper Directory*, which was the primary national catalogue used by advertisers to determine the relative popularity of American newspapers.[26]

In his hope to enter the lanes of modern advertising, Sarasohn was encouraged by the alacrity of upcoming Jewish merchants on the Lower East Side. When the *Tageblatt* was an infant publication, Yiddish advertisers had already displayed a tendency toward the eye-catching advertisement. In the autumn of 1888, the Canal Street clothing firm of H. Silberman and Son, located near the intersection with Allen Street, struck Jewish newcomers with the picture of a large knife carrying the word "prices" that was set against the even larger, ornamental script of the word "CUT." These two words were printed in English, on the assumption that even Jews fresh off the boat had already learned the motto of retail competition in New York City. The rest of the advertisement, written in Yiddish, resorted to the popular American technique of explaining to customers why the store was able to sell at a great discount. "Because we're splitting up a partnership," Silberman and Son related, "our whole line of fall and winter clothing will be sold at very low prices until the first of January, 1889." Reliable customers, it was added, were entitled to a sixty-day credit.[27]

In the first decade of the twentieth century, building on the use of better visual effects and fashionably dressed models, Jewish clothing merchants spearheaded the drive toward the creation of a dynamic advertising that was not commonly found in ethnic newspapers. Retailers in other fields, such as pianos, eyeglasses, cigarettes, beauty cream, and tea and coffee, also adapted the innovations of American advertising, but, if only by force of numbers, merchants of garments, hats, and shoes formed a core of promotional energy. Experimenting with a variety of typefaces, illustrations, and borders for their advertisements, some of which resembled gilt-framed pictures featuring an array of garments or a procession of elegantly dressed people, these advertisers gave substance to the declaration made by the *Tageblatt* in 1899: "The best advertisement is the new advertisement. New in language. New in composition. New in content."[28]

The aesthetic potential of the clothing advertisement was realized most completely in the development of the fashion model. At the turn of the century, American advertising found its first model in the "Gibson look" that had been generated in the mid-1890s by Charles Dana Gibson's sketches of the leisure class for *Life* magazine. Exuding an air of supreme

self-confidence, Gibson's well-sculpted men and women fired the imagination of the public. They came to compose "the models for the manners
of a whole generation of Americans," journalist Mark Sullivan recalled in
his vivid history of the opening decades of the twentieth century, "their
dress, their pose, their attitude toward life."[29] The exploitation of the
Gibson look by advertisers was perfected in artist J. C. Leyendecker's
depiction of the Arrow shirt man for Cluett, Peabody, and Company. In
1912, this virile, beautifully tailored model of the American man, poised
in a sitting position as he gently but firmly gripped a wooden-headed golf
club, appeared in the Yiddish as well as the American press.[30] Yet the
introduction of the Arrow man was prefaced by the appearance of Gib-
sonesque models in the advertising of the successful clothing firm of Moe
Levy. Emerging in honor of the High Holidays and Passover, Levy's
advertisements installed the aristocratic, masculine model squarely in the
Jewish context, giving the god of American fashion a place among the
servants of the Lord.[31]

As Yiddish advertisers had adapted dominant visual forms, they also
imbued the conversational style of American advertising with Jewish
qualities. In respect to ebullient rhetoric, Moe Levy was one of many
merchants to engage consumers by emphasizing the common bond of
Jews. "We wish all Jews a good year and good clothing," Levy declared
at the High Holidays of 1904, "a good year is in God's hands and good
clothing is in our stores."[32] In the American press, the personalized New
Year's greeting from merchant to customer had been used to good effect
by Adolphus Busch, president of the Anheuser-Busch Brewing Association, whose "telegram" on the eve of 1900 thanking customers for their
support entered the annals of that era.[33] Yiddish advertisers deftly employed the technique in the context of the Jewish New Year, Rosh
Hoshanah. In 1911, the *Tageblatt* included two pages of special advertisements under the banner of the traditional Hebrew greeting, "L'Shanah
Tovah Tikat'vu," "may you be inscribed [in God's book] for a good year."
The pages were divided up into a total of thirty-nine greeting "cards"
from merchants and bankers wishing to express their thanks and good
wishes to a devoted clientele. Recognizing the value of the intimate
holiday advertisement, Borden's Condensed Milk Company appropriated
the traditional Jewish greetings for its own "card" to Yiddish-speaking
customers.[34]

As the intimate and down-to-earth conversation of John Wanamaker
and Richard Warren Sears worked to raise the dignity of the ordinary
consumer, the sprinkling of Talmudic-style aphorisms and parables
throughout Yiddish advertising tapped the democratic currents in Jewish

culture. Reminiscent of the Talmudic references in the day-to-day conversation of Sholom Aleichem's character, Tevye the dairyman, the language of Yiddish advertising affirmed the common dignity of Jews based
on a modicum of scholarship. Louis Minsky, a prominent merchant tailor
of Grand Street and a pioneer of the full-page advertisement in the
Yiddish press, injected a great vitality into the conversational style of
Jewish advertising. In October 1900, Minsky shared an anecdote from
the Midrash, the massive collection of biblically inspired homilies that
constitutes a major source of Jewish folklore. The lesson focused on a
scholar who was asked which songs he could recognize if he should hear
them sung or played. The scholar, having no ear for music, answered
that he knew only two songs, one being "Kol Nidre," the solemn melody
of the Day of Atonement, and the other being all that is not "Kol Nidre."
"The same saying is said by thousands of customers of the world-re-
nowned store of Louis Minsky," the advertiser added, playing the itinerant preacher whose purpose was to interpret Midrashic tales for the
public—"That is, they know only of Minsky and not Minsky." [35]

Combining folksy talk and exaggerated self-endorsement, Louis Minsky demonstrated the way in which the American style of advertising was
given a distinctly Jewish twist. The sharing of conversation rooted in the
tradition of Jewish scholarship attracted Jews from all strata of society.
Creating a bridge between the streams of ethnic identity and American
consumption, the personalized style flattered the Jew as a consumer, by
acknowledging that the merchant cared for the business of every customer. While it conformed to the egalitarian trend of American retailing,
this approach sprang wholly from traditional Jewish culture. In the old
world, social divisions between rich and poor had been bridged by the
common love for Torah and Talmud. In America, these sources provided
the natural pretext for advertisers seeking to develop a large market for
their goods.

The apparent effectiveness of Yiddish advertising swiftly won the
attention of prominent American firms. In the late 1880s and early 1890s,
the patent medicine companies which had been the trailblazers of large-
scale advertising in the American press similarly comprised the primary
national advertisers to buy space in the *Tageblatt*. Products such as Warner's Safe Cure, Ayer's Sarsaparilla, Beecham's pills, Mrs. Winslow's
Soothing Syrup, Ripan's Pills, and the more reputable Fletcher's Castoria
were interspersed among the relatively simple announcements of local
dry goods and furniture dealers, kosher food vendors, steam bath propri-
etors, jewelers, booksellers, pawnbrokers, dentists, and druggists.

After the depression of the 1890s, the general growth of American advertising manifested itself in a crescendo of major brand names appearing in Yiddish typeface. Fleisher's yarn, Columbia bicycles, Waltham and Ingersoll watches, Uneeda Biscuit, Quaker Oats, Borden's condensed milk, Gold Dust washing powder, and Cuticura soap had become regular advertisers by 1902. Within the next four years, Baker's cocoa, Postum, Sozodont tooth polish, Arrow shirt collars, Elgin watches, Singer sewing machines, Rogers Brothers' "1847" silverware, Mennen's talcum powder, Welsbach lamps, Edison phonographs, Regal Shoes, Salada tea, Grape Nuts, Bell Telephone, Fels Naptha soap, and Metropolitan Life Insurance became prominent advertisers in Yiddish.

The relative speed with which national advertisers identified Jewish immigrants as potential customers stands in comparison to the advertising section of *Il Progresso Italo-Americano*, the most important newspaper of the massive Italian community that had immigrated to New York in the decades after 1880. Reflecting the diffidence of most Italians in relation to the new urban society, the advertising in *Il Progresso Italo-Americano* was virtually devoid of major American brands as late as 1905. Italian advertisements were dominated by local merchants selling pasta, olive oil, cheese, and wine, and of Italian doctors, dentists, bankers, and undertakers. Also missing in comparison to the Yiddish press was the boldface, well-illustrated, eye-catching announcement to which Jewish newcomers had become accustomed during the 1890s. By 1914, the adaptation of New York's Italians to American city life was reflected in the emergence of some prominent American brands and in the appearance of local merchants selling expensive furnishings, such as pianos.

Yet, where Italians waded gently into the waters of American consumption, Jews seemed to dive in with all their might. Between 1910 and 1914, the Yiddish press acquired an impressive number of outstanding national advertisers, including Ivory Soap, Pabst's Blue Ribbon Beer, Coca-Cola, Gold Medal Flour, Ex-Lax, H. J. Heinz's beans and soups, Colgate's talcum powder, Vaseline, and the brands of the three major cigarette manufacturers to emerge from the breakup of the American tobacco trust in 1911. The sensitivity of the Yiddish press to national trends was illustrated as well by the presence of landmark advertising campaigns, such as that for Procter and Gamble's Crisco shortening in 1911 and that for R. J. Reynold's Camel cigarettes in 1914, both of which initiated new trends in modern marketing.[36]

The rate at which major American products entered the Yiddish press was remarkable even by comparison with the well-established German press. Germans constituted one of the largest ethnic groups in New York City, and the largest German-language daily newspaper was the New

The Culture of Advertising

York *Staats-Zeitung und Herold*, founded in 1834. By 1895, when the eastern European Jews had just attained a true daily newspaper, the *Staats-Zeitung* already resembled a metropolitan daily in most respects, including the character of advertising.[37] Possessing a Sunday edition of twenty-eight pages, the publication attracted the business of large local department stores, dry goods and furniture stores, and a number of national advertisers, such as Sapolio and Pearline soaps, Quaker Oats, Royal Baking Powder, Fleisher's woolen goods, and the Gorham Manufacturing Company, a producer of tableware.

Within the next decade, when national advertisers began flocking to the Yiddish press, the advertising pages of New York's principal German paper underwent only mild change, adding a few important local retailers and a limited number of brands. The advertisements tended to be inconspicuously designed. By 1914, with the exception of some automobile advertising, the bulk of nationally known products that were promoted in the *Staats-Zeitung* had already been added to the list of the principal Yiddish newspapers, which appeared to outpace their physically larger German counterpart in the relative volume of this type of advertising.

The unique attractiveness of newspapers like the *Tageblatt* and the *Forward* to American advertisers stemmed to a great extent from the fresh, buoyant spirit with which these enterprises captured the sympathies and the imagination of the multitude of newcomers, a body of people bent on finding a way into American society. The intimacy of the text and the personality of the advertising, which made the Yiddish press an attractive medium for American advertisers, were the products of eastern European Jewish life in the American city.

By virtue of the distinctive characteristics of the Yiddish press, Jewish newcomers were exposed comparatively quickly to a wide range of nationally known products. Acceptance of these things, and of the American perspective that supported them, would depend on the compatability of traditional Jewish concerns with the qualities that modern corporations ascribed to their products.

ഏⱥ 10 ⱦⱨ

"American Bluff":
The Exaltation of
American Products

In September 1910, the New York *Yiddishes Tageblatt* carried an advertisement for Ivory Soap, the product on which the Cincinnati-based firm of Procter and Gamble had been building a national reputation since the early 1880s:[1]

> **Don't the Americans make the best locomotives, the best cutlery, the best cotton in the whole world?**
> **Why should they not make the best soap?**
> **They make it.**
> **Ivory Soap.**

Typifying the tone and content of American advertising, which relied on a congenial style of conversation to suggest the superiority of American commodities, the announcement was imbued with the quality that Jewish newcomers referred to as "American bluff."

An unwieldy tendency toward exaggeration seemed to be characteristic of both Jews and Americans, in the view of the great Yiddish satirist Sholom Aleichem, who had visited the United States in 1907–1908 and lived in New York City from 1914 until his death in 1916. In a sketch titled "On America," Sholom Aleichem described the impulse to embroi-

161

der dull facts with lofty rhetoric, through the character Berel-Ayzik. A resident of the fictional shtetl of Kasrielevke, Berel-Ayzik was a man whose enthusiastic oratory proved the fact that "America can't even shine Kasrielevke's shoes when it comes to bluffing."

After a visit to the United States, Berel-Ayzik's formidable talents reached their zenith: America was a place where people made money left and right, where beggars used two hands, where the buildings were so high that, standing on the roof of one, Berel-Ayzik felt a strangely smooth and cold sensation on his left cheek which, he discovered by turning to his left, was nothing other than the moon itself. The men were as strong as steel, the bitter herbs for Passover were produced in a factory by thousands upon thousands of workers, and when people died in America, they dropped dead by the streetful. Whole cities were swallowed up as was Korah in the Bible. America, in short, was "nothing to sneeze at."[2]

Whatever nuances of culture had imparted a love of grandiloquence to Jews and Americans, the comparatively rapid acceptance of American advertising by the Yiddish press indicated in black and white that this form of communication could serve as a bridge between the two cultures. Through advertising, Jews familiarized themselves with the American belief in the cultural importance of successful brand-named merchandise. Just as the penetration of American advertising depended upon specific qualities of the leading Yiddish newspapers, the responsiveness of Jewish immigrants to nationally advertised products stemmed from specifically Jewish values and concerns. The cosmopolitan outlook, customary interest in festive luxury, and special dietary code of Jews motivated them to favor some of the latest products of American corporations, which adapted their advertising to suit the Jewish market. American pride over brand-named goods was absorbed through the filter of traditional attitudes.

Advertising has been referred to as a typically American institution because it arose out of the condition of economic abundance that prevailed in the United States in the late nineteenth century. As American manufacturers commanded the ability to produce a perpetual surplus of merchandise, they needed a powerful device to stimulate the desire of consumers on a broad scale.[3] Yet the institution had a more precise relation to the character of American society. It gave a concrete form of expression to the perspective of abundance. Reiterating high praise for the great harvest of mass production, advertising nourished the faith of the people in their outstanding ability to create luxuries for themselves, a trait that was viewed as an anchor of American democracy and a contribution to Western civilization.

Although Americans paid homage to Europe about the creation of fine art, the citizens of the newer nation quickly realized a potential to produce the luxuries on which modern urban living was based. During the first half of the nineteenth century, European manufacturers, particularly those of Great Britain, had set the standard of desirable merchandise in the United States. Yet, as the American system of mechanized mass production and the American drive toward large-scale marketing gathered momentum, the flow of commerce shifted dramatically. Between the Civil War and World War I, when American retailers pioneered in mail-order selling and brought the department store to its fullest development, American manufacturers won an international reputation for the marketing of popular products. As early as 1880, British, German, and Austro-Hungarian companies had begun to face an "invasion" of merchandise from America that impelled them to imitate American products and to label domestically made items "American."[4]

Two decades later, the upsurge of inexpensive American luxuries in Europe had become overwhelming, as was made apparent by *The American Invaders*, an exposé that appeared in England in 1902. "In the domestic life we have got to this," the author explained, "the average man rises in the morning from his New England sheets, he shaves with 'Williams' soap and a Yankee safety razor, pulls on his Boston boots over his socks from North Carolina, fastens his Connecticut braces, slips his Waltham or Waterbury watch in his pocket, and sits down to breakfast." At the table, the narrative continued, the Englishman ate bread and meat from the great mills and meat-packing companies of St. Louis, Chicago, and Minneapolis, pickles from the H. J. Heinz Company of Pittsburgh, and canned oysters and peaches from the canneries of Baltimore, as his children enjoyed a portion of Quaker Oats, which originated in Ravenna, Ohio.[5]

Within the United States, the nationally advertised product came to be perceived as a standard of excellence. In *A Hazard of New Fortunes*, a novel that appeared in 1889, William Dean Howells satirized the American tendency to exaggerate the value of brand-named merchandise. Describing a meeting of characters involved in the production of a new magazine, Howells has one of the collaborators evaluate the periodical's prospects in terms of the success achieved by several brand-named commodities: "It's the talk of the clubs and the dinner-tables; children cry for it; it's the Castoria of literature, and the Pearline of art, the Won't-be-happy-till-he-gets-it of every enlightened man, woman, and child in this vast city."[6] By inverting the cultural hierarchy, in which common objects were subordinate to artistic works, Howells stressed the great reputation that had been achieved by successful American products.

In 1914, Christine Frederick, a prominent home economist, made the same point by juxtaposing the social effect of nationally advertised products with the influence of sophisticated social planners.

> Architects may think they have developed the distinctive American home, but such things as Morgan doors, Standard Sanitary outfits and the Dutch Boy Painter have been the most active agents in creating and spreading standards of home building. Health boards may think they are responsible for the aseptic attitude of the modern housekeeper, but Platt's Chlorides, Vacuum cleaners, and dustless dusters did it. Pure food champions and pure food laws have told us what to avoid to keep out of an early grave, but Heinz, Beechnut, National Biscuit, and other honest manufacturers, through advertising, have told us what is pure food and how and where we can get it.[7]

As Jews from eastern Europe made contact with the world of American advertising, they encountered a point of view that held mass-marketed products to be the pillar of modern urban life and a transcendent feature of American culture. In the aftermath of World War I, a time of intense anxiety about the effect of ethnic differences upon the moral constitution of the nation, the trade journal *Advertising and Selling* suggested that the preference for American products supported the appreciation of American values. "Practical Americanization," the magazine contended, was defined by "the use of American things." Once immigrants adopted these products, they would ideally learn "to like them and prefer them to other things."[8]

The arrival of Jewish newcomers on the scene of American advertising was heralded by the campaign for the Uneeda Biscuit, an item that was built on the American desire to exalt the mundane products of their industrial system. Launched by one of the most influential promotional efforts in the history of American advertising, the first product of the National Biscuit Company had attained a volume of sales exceeding ten million packages per month within the first year of its existence.[9] The product announcement appeared in the *New York World*, a leading American newspaper, on March 10, 1899. Five days later, it debuted in the *Yiddishes Tageblatt*. The rapid emergence of a Yiddish Uneeda Biscuit indicated the degree to which eastern European Jews had come to be identified as a strong market for American products. Through an acquaintance with this product, newcomers began to appreciate the decisive influence of marketing upon the American view of their material world.

The phenomenal success of the Uneeda Biscuit was underscored by the fact that the product was marketed by a huge corporation at a time of public antagonism to big business. The offspring of a large consolidation of bakeries that stretched from Maine to Louisiana to Colorado, the National Biscuit Company emerged in the winter of 1898. In harmony with the trend toward oligopoly in some sectors of the American economy, the corporation was one of fifty-three mighty industrial combinations that came into being between 1898 and 1900 with a capital of over $10,000,000 each. Many of these firms controlled at least 50 percent of the production in their respective fields.[10]

In light of rising reservations about big business, the creation of a unique name for the fledgling product of the National Biscuit Company turned out to be essential to winning over the American public. The name "Uneeda Biscuit" resulted from the painstaking collaboration of Adolphus Green, the chairman of the board of directors of Nabisco, and Henry McKinney, an agent for the prominent advertising firm of N. W. Ayer and Son. Contrary to McKinney's initial idea, Adolphus Green decided that the generic name of the item should be "biscuit" rather than "cracker." Perhaps considering his own advancement from average origins to commercial success, Green sensed that the public might appreciate the connotation of quality attached to the word "biscuit."

An accomplished copywriter, Henry McKinney knew how to harmonize the tone of gentility with the vernacular sound that Americans were accustomed to. Having experimented with "Taka Cracker," "Hava Cracker," "Usa Cracker," "Wanta Cracker," and many other possibilities, McKinney finally brought his conversational style into focus by adding "U" to the persuasive "Needa" and wedding the contraction to Green's "biscuit."[11] Together, the entrepreneur and the copywriter had created a name that was full of democratic connotations. Condensing into two words the down-to-earth conversationalism of American advertising and the egalitarian attitude toward luxury, the Uneeda Biscuit initiated the conversion of National Biscuit Company from an intimidating corporate title into a familiar and friendly brand name.

When the Uneeda Biscuit entered the Yiddish newspaper, the American style of advertising was displayed in its most basic form, deliberately stripped of vocabulary and context that might confuse the foreign-born reader. The large, well-designed advertisement, framing its text at top and bottom with identical pictures of the Uneeda Biscuit package, addressed the Jewish newcomer in extremely simple Yiddish, mixed with Yinglish:

> Have you tried Uneeda Biscuit, the new kind of crackers? New in taste. New in price and entirely new in package. Fresh now, fresh tomorrow, and good all the time. The baker makes them good and the box keeps them good. The price is 5 cents. That is the reason that everyone is ordering from their groceryman, Uneeda Biscuit.[12]

The effort of the National Biscuit Company to reach Jewish consumers appears to have been rewarded. When the marketing of the Uneeda Biscuit began in January 1899, two months prior to the start of newspaper advertising in New York City, there were already signs of interest among the eastern Europeans. Anticipating a strong public response to the luxuriously packaged new cracker, the United Jewish Cracker Dealers of New York issued a warning to Jewish grocery dealers not to carry the products of the "biscuit trust."[13] By the following year, the Uneeda Biscuit had become part of the vocabulary of the Lower East Side. In one instance, a Broome Street pharmacist was inspired to market the Uwanta Pill (pronounced "you-vant-eh"), which he called "the king of all cathartics."[14] Reflecting the apparent popularity of the Uneeda Biscuit among Jewish immigrants, the National Biscuit Company continued to promote the cracker regularly in Yiddish and, in 1902, the company added two more of its products to the advertising section of the *Yiddishes Tageblatt*, Kennedy's Oysterettes and ZuZu ginger snaps.

The core of the advertising campaign for the Uneeda Biscuit was composed of the package, as well as the name, of the new product. This feature, which marked a change in the nature of food marketing, may have had a pronounced effect on Jewish newcomers. To turn a simple cracker into an item of luxury, it was imperative to overcome the principal defects of cracker-barrel marketing—the inevitability of staleness and the exposure to dirt and germs. Determined to meet the challenge, Adolphus Green supervised the development of the "In-er-Seal" package, which hinged on the ingenious idea of enclosing the product in an airtight, inner compartment of waxed paper. The package of the Uneeda Biscuit proved to be an enduring focal point for Green's advertising campaigns. When the product was introduced in 1899, consumers were assured that the In-er-Seal package kept the crackers "as crisp, tender and delicious as when fresh from the oven."[15]

By raising the reputation of the most ordinary type of commodity to an almost unbelievable height, the Uneeda Biscuit package culminated an important trend of American marketing in the late nineteenth century. At the Philadelphia Centennial Exposition of 1876, where the exhibits of consumer products looked "like retail stores," the attractive manner in which American manufacturers packaged their products was a point of distinction noted by foreign businessmen.[16] Subsequent progress in the development of appealing packages was marked by the comment of a prominent New York City grocer, who stated in 1895 that the "skill and taste" invested by American manufacturers in the packaging of their products had "transformed the retailer's store into a sightly and attractive showroom."[17]

Crowning the accomplishments of the past and inspiring the efforts of the future, the Uneeda Biscuit appeared appropriately at the dawn of the new century. In August 1900, the primary trade journal of the advertising world, *Printer's Ink*, confidently pronounced "The Package" to be "the very keystone of modern advertising." To exemplify the argument, the magazine had only to point to the Uneeda Biscuit, the successful promotion of which depended not on the "intrinsic excellence" of the product, but on the "identification in the public mind of that peculiar package with goods of a high quality."[18] In the first authoritative history of American advertising, published in 1929, Frank Presbrey, whose own career in the business began in the late 1890s, explained that the significance of the Uneeda Biscuit lay in its having "shown that even the lowly soda cracker could be rescued from the barrel and made into something with position and prestige in the world."[19]

Through the Uneeda Biscuit, Jews discovered that the value of a commodity might depend almost completely on the ingenuity involved in its presentation. Having emerged out of the chaos of the cracker barrel, the Uneeda Biscuit represented the triumph of order in an area of daily life that newcomers had never considered to be worth much fuss. Descended from a world in which packaging had little physical and psychological basis, Jews in the American city soon learned that lunch was supposed to have the sharply defined contours of a Talmudic interpretation. In 1903, a roving reporter for the *Tageblatt* recounted an episode observed on the elevated railway that seemed to warrant the title "A Poor Lunch." The focus of the article was a young woman fresh from the old country, whose lunch of bread and fruit, wrapped clumsily in a newspaper, spilled all over the floor of the car. The young women seated nearby laughed at the sight, causing the newcomer great embarrassment.[20]

Upon entering the public schools, youngsters immediately recognized how much different the lunches of Americans appeared in comparison to their own. Whereas Jewish mothers were used to wrapping odds and ends of food in a clump of newspaper, the schoolteachers and the American students had precisely packaged meals—neat, regular-sized sandwiches, square paper napkins, and lunch boxes. Elizabeth Stern, whose family came to New York City from Poland in 1891, remembered vividly "the embarrassing moment" when she first opened her lunch parcel in a new high school. In contrast to the neat geometry of the other students' lunches, her meal consisted of a mass of fried potatoes and a crushed tomato wrapped in newspaper. Even though she like the food her mother prepared for her, the criticism of her peers shamed her into throwing her lunches away.[21]

The Uneeda Biscuit bore more than an incidental relationship to the encounter of newcomers with the American way of presenting meals in public. From the beginning of its career, the package in which the crackers came was recommended to consumers as an excellent lunch box for schoolchildren. A fifty-year retrospective of American advertising published in 1938 testified to the popularity of the idea, stating that "those who took their lunch to school thirty or thirty-five years ago may remember its being packed in a Uneeda package."[22]

The symbolism of the common commodity being elevated through a package to the status of a luxury was not lost on Jewish newcomers. Having worked as a servant in a wealthy Viennese household, a young Austrian woman who came to the United States just after World War I had already been exposed to American products such as Hecker's flour, Nestlé's cocoa, and Carnation evaporated milk. These items were treated by her former employers as genuine luxuries, to be locked in the closet and kept from the servants. "I saved all the labels," the immigrant commented years later, recalling her feeling that Americans must have had "everything so good if they pack everything so good."[23]

Lacking a prior exposure to American brands of merchandise, with the exception of the Singer sewing machine, the multitude of Jews from eastern Europe depended on advertising, which was inextricably linked to packaging, for an education in the conceits that came with American products. In the Uneeda Biscuit campaign, newcomers were fully exposed to the transcendent aspect with which American things were endowed. They came face to face with the idea that a mundane commodity could embody the powerful strivings of a people to fulfill their own sense of the civilized life.

Because the documents of city life at the turn of the century told very little about the use of advertised products by urban Americans, the popularity of these items must be inferred from the huge volume of sales they achieved and from the extent and focus of their advertising. Among eastern European Jews, the Uneeda Biscuit clearly attained the role of a symbol by virtue of consistent Yiddish advertising, and as an item to be consumed, it appears to have circulated among significant numbers of people. The prominent features of the product—its origin in a huge corporation, its appeal as a luxury for the masses, its guarantee of physical purity—suggested some of the cultural leanings that predisposed Jewish newcomers to respond to nationally advertised products in general. Working in conjunction with each other, the comparatively cosmopolitan attitude of the Jews, the traditional belief in the power of luxuries to dignify the ordinary person, and the inordinate concern for purity that derived from the Jewish dietary code, all encouraged the belief that the large American corporation, which was personalized through modern advertising, had the ability to provide outstanding products for consumers.

Helping to dissolve initial suspicions of new and unfamiliar things, Jewish cosmopolitanism was best demonstrated in the acceptance of the modern life insurance policy. An intangible commodity that involved the sensitive, private affairs of the family, the life insurance policy of the American corporation seemed to be full of disadvantages for immigrants, who were prone to create mutual aid societies in response to the need for some form of medical, unemployment, and life insurance. The disposition of eastern European Jews toward this more congenial type of organization was reflected in the statistics gathered by the Jewish Communal Register of 1917–1918, which located 1,016 mutual aid societies in Greater New York and estimated a membership in excess of 100,000 Jews.[24] Yet, while these informal organizations enabled newcomers from the same regions of eastern Europe to congregate and to support each other in times of sickness and unemployment, they lacked an efficient procedure for handling death benefits. Failing to make use of actuarial tables, the Jewish Orders, as they were called, usually determined rates for life insurance in an arbitrary manner, and members paid the same premiums regardless of age, a practice that ultimately drove out younger people and left the elderly with an unmanageable burden of dues.[25]

This sort of problem undoubtedly plagued the fraternal organizations of other ethnic groups as well, but Jews seemed likely to turn to American insurance companies as an alternative. "The Jew is the easiest man to sell life insurance to," sociologist Edward A. Ross stated in 1914, "for he catches the idea sooner than any other immigrant."[26] The receptivity of eastern European Jews to the idea of buying life insurance from an impersonal corporation was manifested in the course of a battle between the New York Life Insurance Company and the Equitable Life Insurance Company that took place at the turn of the century. In January 1900, large advertisements for these two powerful firms appeared in the *Yiddishes Tageblatt*. By February, the competition over what appeared to be a formidable network of Jewish agents and consumers had prompted New York Life to charge that a mass of Jewish agents had defected to the Equitable. In defending the image of the eastern European Jews against the derogatory tone with which the accusation was made, the newspaper acknowleged that this community of newcomers had furnished the life insurance companies of the city not only with a substantial number of agents and managers, but also with an impressive number of policy holders.[27]

Willing to entrust their money to American corporations, Jewish immigrants showed themselves to be relatively free from the suspicions of the huge, unfamiliar corporate enterprise that were harbored by many American workers, as well as by provincial immigrants from the European countryside. Until the end of the nineteenth century, rumors about the life insurance business fed the fears of people who had been accustomed to the local burial association. Actual defects, such as the failure to act promptly and generously on claims, policies that stipulated the forfeiture of premium reserves in the event of lapsed payments, "Tontine" plans that enabled some policyholders to profit from the death or forfeiture of others, and mercenary agents who made exaggerated claims about their firms' insurance in order to win inflated commissions, combined with unsubstantiated, often sensational accusations in the press, such as the suggestion that policies taken out on the children of wage earners promoted infanticide, to create an atmosphere of distrust. In the 1880s, when the new "industrial" insurance policies geared to people with small incomes had just recently emerged, the prejudices of urban wage earners against life insurance were "too numerous to mention," as one of the first salesman of industrial insurance for Metropolitan Life recalled in 1896.[28]

As American companies began to seek a mass market for life insurance, Jews were attracted by the egalitarian air of social service that the more innovative sellers of insurance tried to foment. The Metropolitan Life Insurance Company, in particular, appealed to the traditional Jewish concern for creating efficient institutions to meet the needs of the poor. Having begun to seek the mass market for low cost policies in 1879, Metropolitan Life was identified during the early years of the century as "The Company of the People, By the People, For the People."[29]

Around 1909, the company instituted a welfare department with an eye to the large market of Jewish consumers in New York. Lee Frankel, the former head of the United Hebrew Charities, was chosen to supervise the department, which included an innovative visiting nurse service conceived by Jewish settlement worker Lillian Wald. The public response to Metropolitan's bold departure in the marketing of insurance was expressed by a flood of approving letters from needy policy holders.[30] The Yiddish advertising placed by the firm at this time similarly emphasized Metropolitan's interest in meeting the needs of wage earners and small business people, carefully explaining the features of a commodity that would at first strike newcomers as being utterly foreign to their experience.[31]

Fostered by the habitual uprootedness and by the supranational identity of the Jews, a cosmopolitan outlook helped newcomers to accept the product of the large-scale, modern corporation as a basic part of American urban life. Preference for the life insurance policy, instead of the death benefit of the mutual aid society, exemplified the willingness of Jews to take the broad view, while large sectors of the public continued to be suspicious of a product that derived from a statistical chart in a remote corporate office.

By virtue of the traditional Jewish conception of luxuries, which had been secularized in the American city, newcomers were able to see other mass-marketed commodities in a favorable light. Even though the products of the old world smith surpassed those of the mechanized factory in terms of the time and effort required to make them, prominent American brands of tableware and watches, the primary types of metalware to be advertised nationally, nonetheless came to occupy a seat of honor in the world of Jewish immigrants.

Out of the desire to cater to a broad base of consumers, American craftsmen had broken with the European tradition of providing the affluent with expensive, hand-crafted articles. At the beginning of the 1830s, Alexis de Tocqueville observed how American artisans concentrated on creating products, such as imitation jewelry, that cost relatively little but looked expensive, in order to satisfy the great demand of the masses for the appearance of luxury.[32] Based on the striving of the people for objects associated with a high station, American manufacturers pioneered in techniques for the standardization of luxuries. The result of their effort was a genre of products that was, as the official catalogue of the London Crystal Palace Exhibition of 1851 noted, "distinct from that of many other countries."[33]

Stimulated by the desire to create first-rate facsimiles of hand-crafted tableware, American manufacturers readily exploited technical innovations in order to appeal to a large market of consumers. In the opening years of the nineteenth century, the tinsmiths of New England, who had already established a nationwide commerce through adept marketing, adopted the new process of plating sheet iron with tin in order to provide housewares that shimmered like the more expensive metal yet cost relatively little. In the 1830s, the whitesmiths of that region began working with Brittania, a white alloy of tin, copper, and antimony, to create popularly priced tableware that looked like silver. After the process of "electroplating" metals with real silver was patented in England in 1840, a handful of silver manufacturers, most notably Rogers Brothers and Meriden Britannia of Connecticut and Reed and Barton of Massachusetts, began to cultivate a large market for the comparatively inexpensive tableware that resembled sterling silver. The Philadelphia Centennial Exposition of 1876, which exposed ten million people to the latest types of products for the consumer, made the possible rewards of aggressive marketing too obvious to be ignored, and the leading manufacturers of tableware escalated the effort to reach a national public.[34]

The American attempt to standardize the elegant luxuries of the old world through the application of new industrial methods culminated in the production of inexpensive watches during the 1870s and 1880s. Clocks had been mass-marketed since the beginning of the nineteenth century, but the delicate construction of watches had seemingly defied the effort to introduce machinery into the craft. Yet, by 1876, the treasurer of the Waltham Watch Company could proclaim that the firm's experiments with mass production had realized the "dreams of really cheap goods and successful competition with the great producers of Switzerland" whose craftsmanship had traditionally dominated the market for timepieces.[35] In the 1880s, the Waterbury Watch Company introduced the dollar watch, which enabled virtually every consumer to enjoy the luxury of a portable timepiece.

Nationally advertised silverware and watches were perceived by Jewish newcomers in terms of their traditional concept of luxuries as an instrument for sanctifying the home and dignifying the individual. In the past, Passover had provided the ideal occasion for enjoying the hand-crafted, silver wine goblets and tableware that had been kept in storage the entire year. Bearing the individual stamp of the Jewish artisan, these vessels and utensils were cherished as heirlooms. They served generations of Jews as a shining, tangible link to each other and to the faith in God's immanent splendor. In the American city, where everything swayed and buckled to the pressure of change, heirlooms coexisted with the latest objects of mass production. The quiet, inherent dignity of the relic paled before the loud reputation of the successful, nationally advertised product.

At the turn of the century, the best known brand of silver-covered tableware in America, Rogers Brothers' "1847" silverware, which was marketed by a large conglomerate under the direction of the Meriden Britannia Company, started to be advertised in the Yiddish press. While the mass-marketed product itself hardly compared to the hand-made utensils that the affluent could possess, the reputation and the affordable price of the item made the Rogers Brothers' brand extremely suitable for the majority of Jewish newcomers seeking to prepare a fine table on Passover. Consequently, it tended to be recommended as a luxury "in honor of Passover." In March 1900, Sam Zirinski, a Grand Street jeweler, urged his prospective customers—with boldface type—to buy this prestigious brand of silver-coated utensils for use at their Passover seders. Two days later, I. Greenspan, a jeweler from across the street, went one step better by identifying Rogers Brothers' tableware as an important part of his selection of silver *kley koydesh*, the special Yiddish word for Passover utensils that derived from the Hebrew phrase "holy instruments."[36] Although immigrants learned in the city that American goods had to be described with American words, at Passover, the queen of the holidays, the prestige of the American brand was magnified by the ancient tongue of the Jews.

Whereas mass-marketed silverware strove for parity with the hand-crafted heirlooms of Jewish families, the inexpensive timepiece was without precedent as a luxury for the majority of people. Having been sold, since the 1880s, at a price that could be afforded by virtually everybody, Waltham and Waterbury watches turned out to be among the earliest nationally advertised products in the Yiddish press. Yet, in addition to the exotic appeal of the gold-plated timepiece for immigrants accustomed to rudimentary kinds of personal adornment, these low-priced luxuries were perfect embodiments of the striving for time-efficient self-regulation on which success in America seemed to depend. Possession of a watch implied the possibility of managing one's daily life with the singleminded determination to succeed that was celebrated in immigrant guidebooks. As an item for the average consumer, the timepiece silently suggested that the challenge of self-determination was open to all. Sensing the symbolic potential of the product, the *Forward* celebrated the achievement of the leading American manufacturers and cited the Waltham Watch Company and the Waterbury Watch Company as examples. With prices dropping as low as sixty-nine cents apiece for watches that lasted a few years, these exemplars of the replaceable luxury had brought about a state of affairs in which even "a pauper" could not "get along without a watch."[37]

In accepting successful brands like Rogers Brothers' silverware and

Waltham and Waterbury watches, eastern European Jews were inspired by their traditional culture, which had interwoven the enjoyment of luxuries with the dignity of the ordinary person. The regularity with which leading manufacturers of prepared foods advertised in the Yiddish press suggested that another customary feature of Jewish life, the code of dietary purity, contributed to an appreciation of the staples of urban living in the United States.

The search for pure foods in the modern marketplace was a pursuit that native-born Americans and incoming Jews had in common. As the preparation of food waned in the urban household and passed into the domain of the factory system, anxieties about quality naturally arose. Stemming more from the fear of the unknown than from an epidemic of defective products, a tone of dire warning had marked the crusade for "pure" food in the United States since the 1820s, when the graphic phrase "there is death in the pot," accompanied by an illustration of a skull, serpent, and pot, appeared in the English translation of *A Treatise on Adulterations*, written by the German pharmacist and chemist Frederick Accum.[38]

Yet, as Harvey W. Wiley, chief chemist of the United States Department of Agriculture and principal advocate for federal legislation of food and drugs at the turn of the century, explained to the Senate Committee on Manufactures in 1899, the major problem with faulty goods was misrepresentation rather than unhealthfulness. Products like honey cheapened with glucose or coffee mixed with inert matter typified "adulterated" foods. Furthermore, harmless food colorings such as turmeric had been classified as adulterants even though they ultimately proved acceptable. According to Wiley, whose investigations anticipated the Pure Food and Drug Act of 1906, only about 5 percent of commercial foods were adulterated.[39]

Nonetheless, public concern induced the emerging advertisers of prepared foods and beverages, and also of soaps, dentifrices, and cosmetics to emphasize the purity of their merchandise. The outstanding need for advertising that assuaged the fear of consumers was pointed out in 1893 by Dr. I. W. Lyons, a prominent manufacturer of tooth powder, who attributed the success of his business to the public belief in its wholesomeness. Lyons claimed that it was "unquestionably the best policy" to promote the physical purity of any product that applied to the human body.[40] Because foods, beverages, soaps, and cosmetic items dominated American advertising in the decades prior to 1910, the theme of purity resonated throughout the medium. By the opening of the twentieth century, the word "pure" had been reiterated so monotonously, advertising writer Claude Hopkins recalled, that it "made about as much impression on people as water makes on a duck."[41]

Promotional campaigns for purity, however, did affect Jewish newcomers whose strict dietary code seemed to be disintegrating in the environment of the modern city. Breaches of the Jewish code of kashruth, "ritual fitness," had been documented for centuries in the Jewish communities of central and eastern Europe, but the utter lack of rabbinical control over economic competition in the big cities of the United States had created a problem of grave proportions. As a reporter for the New York *Commercial Advertiser* in 1900, Abraham Cahan interviewed a rabbi who had come to the Lower East Side in 1884. At that time, the scholar remembered, "the chosen people had been living abominably," because of the flagrant disregard of "kosher" slaughterhouses for Jewish law.[42]

Moses Weinberger, another rabbi who arrived in New York in the mid-1880s, left a scathing indictment of dietary practices in the city. The newcomer, Weinberger noted, did not anticipate the great difference between the new situation and that of the shtetl, where the shoykhet, the ritual slaughterer, knew the condition of his animals exactly, and where "people knew everything that was done and said, even behind closed doors." In the old world, "not even the stupidest butcher" could transgress, because "every stone had seven eyes," whereas, in New York City, corruption was impossible to check—"Who could force [a butcher] to show what was out back in the icehouse? Who could inspect what was hidden in holes and crevices?"[43] After Jacob Joseph arrived from Europe to fill the post of Chief Rabbi of New York in 1888, supervision of kosher slaughtering improved somewhat, but violations continued to be reported. Abetting the problem, many Jewish restaurants and saloons freely added unkosher foods to their menus and often misleadingly advertised kosher fare.[44]

In 1899, a Yiddish advertisement for the Attorney Street firm of Rotweil and Litoyer, retailers of cooking oil, summarized the ambiguous circumstances into which the traditional Jewish dietary code had fallen. Under the title, "Is There a Kosher Butcher?" the advertisement commented that this was the most common question of Jewish consumers. Indicating the inherent difficulties of maintaining kashruth in the system of long-distance marketing, Rotweil and Litoyer informed Jews of a less publicized defect in their consumption of food—the purchase of baked goods containing cooking oil that had been made in distilleries handling nonkosher oils or shipped in barrels that had previously been used to hold these liquids.[45]

In a setting so unfavorable to the inherited sensibility of Jewish immigrants, advertising acquired the special role of having to assure the legitimacy of products. Thus, the rabbinical seal emerged as an auxiliary trademark of various Jewish goods. These symbols, such as that of the rabbi of the First Hungarian Congregation Oheb Zedek (Love of Righteousness) which appeared in the advertising of the Hebrew National Kosher Sausage Factory, certified the reliability of a manufacturer.[46]

Recognizing the psychological value of the religious mark, advertisers of American products began to adopt either the seals themselves or a similar sign of approbation. In 1901, the advertising of Agate Nickel-Steel Ware, a brand of cooking utensils that was actively marketed to downtown Jews, appealed to the Jewish concern for certifying the fitness of objects. Announcing that Agate ware was pure and safe, the advertisement added in bold print that the product was "bashtetigen"—confirmed —by a chemist's certificate, which was intended to be a credible surrogate for the rabbinical seal. By the end of the first decade of the new century, nationally known brands, like Quaker Oats and Babbitt's cleanser, were starting to carry the religious seals themselves. In an advertisement of 1912, Old Dutch Cleanser was promoted in Yiddish with a rabbinical memo and with the guarantee that the product was "strictly kosher."[47]

In the landmark campaign for Crisco vegetable shortening that was carried out through 1911 and 1912, the firm of Procter and Gamble showed a keen awareness that the theme of purity was full of meaning for consumers reared in the shtetls of eastern Europe. By combining an innovative product, the first shortening made from hydrogenated vegetable oil, with an effective advertising campaign, Procter and Gamble sustained the reputation for adept marketing that it had established with Ivory Soap in the 1880s. In seeking the patronage of Jewish newcomers, the company emphasized the novel quality of the product and used the intimate style of advertising to good effect.

Opening with large advertisements and follow-up articles in the Yiddish press, the campaign heralded the advent of "A Completely New Product" in December 1911. Much of the descriptive information about Crisco focused on the suitability of a purely vegetable shortening for Jews, whose dietary code prohibited the mixture of dairy and meat products in a meal. In support of this argument, Jews were informed that two rabbis, one from New York City and one from Cincinnati, which was the home of Procter and Gamble and the center of midwestern Jewry, had inspected the factory in which Crisco was produced and had deemed the product both kosher and pareve, "neutral," or suitable for serving with milk products. In a subsequent announcement, the manufacturer engaged Yiddish readers with the intimate style of advertising that had long distinguished the promotion of Ivory Soap. Inviting Jews to correspond with the makers of the vegetable shortening, the advertisement was headed, "Have You Any Questions to Ask about Crisco?" In reiterating the virtue of a cooking item free from animal fat, Procter and Gamble displayed a strong interest in the Jewish consumer—"for Jews it is especially a great invention."[48]

As the Crisco campaign indicated, a wedding was taking place in the Yiddish press between American and Jewish concepts of purity. In the effort to quell the apprehension of the American public about foods made in distant factories using new techniques of production, national advertisers strove to guarantee the quality of their products. The evolution of modern, sanitary methods of preparing food for mass consumption occurred at the moment when eastern European Jews were experiencing a crisis of confidence in the quality of commercial foods. Into the vacuum created by the loss of traditional rabbinical supervision in large cities, leading American firms saw fit to enter. Hoping to capture the loyalty of a ripe market of Jewish consumers, advertisers executed the coup de grace of equating the modern standard of efficient manufacture with the traditional standard of kashruth. In 1910, Borden's Condensed Milk Company, which had been a regular advertiser in the Yiddish press for a decade, identified the old and the new with fine simplicity: "Pure Means Kosher—Kosher Means Pure."[49]

From the first glimpse of the H-O Oats sign that presided over Manhattan harbor to the casual consumption of Borden's condensed milk, newcomers had made a trek that was relatively short in time but impressively long in psychological distance. They had come from a world where clever packages were virtually nonexistent and where famous brand names were barely known. They entered a society that defined itself in no small measure by the abundance of these things. Traditional Jewish attitudes played a key role in bridging the chasm between old and new. Certain cultural traits that thrived in the world of Yiddish translated well into the exalted language of American products.

With the knowledge that Americans identified successful, mass-marketed items as a sign of cultural progress, eastern European Jews were well equipped to focus their commercial skills on the enrichment of American urban culture.

PART V

The Culture of Marketing

Jewish Commerce and American Culture

In the late 1930s, historian Cecil Roth tried to assess the economic contribution of the Jews to western civilization over the course of his lifetime. Bolstered by a great commercial tradition, the group had assisted in bringing about what Roth termed the "great peaceful revolution" of the age, the delivery of luxuries to the multitude of people who had been used to a meager standard of living. At the turn of the century, he observed, "the rift between the rich and the poor was more profound by far" than it was at the time he was writing. The seemingly immutable separation of the haves from the have-nots was the social fact that defined "the real importance" of the Jews in the economy of the West.[1]

The validity of Roth's argument was obvious in the United States. In the massive striving of city people for a more refined material life, Jews found an aspect of American society that their traditional culture had prepared them to understand and address. Nourished by American conditions and values, Jewish merchants were able to make a profound impact on American society in the era before World War I. In the areas of street marketing and film marketing, they would completely change the prevalent mode of operation, thereby demonstrating that Jewish adaptation in America entailed the creation as well as the reception of new forms of consumption. The rise of entrepreneurship in these two fields, however, would be based on the general encounter of the Jewish commercial tradition with American mass consumption. In commerce, Jews found an effective medium for realizing the powerful desire to contribute to the society that had accepted them.

The persistent activity of entrepreneurs in many fields of business had been the precondition for American abundance in the industrial age. The growth of mass consumption depended on the creative response of merchants and manufacturers to popular demand for affordable merchandise. Whereas some outstanding entrepreneurs, like Richard Warren Sears and Aaron Montgomery Ward, succeeded by assessing and meeting the needs of the rural population of consumers, the focus of American economic growth during the late nineteenth century was the urban market. The responsiveness of astute businessmen to the demands of city people constituted the dynamic force behind that growth.[2] In Andrew Carnegie's perception that the future of the steel industry would lay more in the construction of elevated railways and skyscrapers for the city than in railroads across the countryside, in James B. Duke's recognition that a latent demand among urbanites for cigarettes would justify the application of new machinery of mass production to an old industry, in C. W. Post's sense that a fast-paced society would learn to like cold cereal in the morning—in these and many other cases, entrepreneurial insight yielded new products or more effective ways to market old ones. The rapid development of the American urban lifestyle around the turn of the century depended upon such innovations.

Entrepreneurship in consumer-oriented businesses was defined by the ability to provide a large body of consumers with products that had formerly been either unavailable or difficult to obtain. In discovering ways to create or distribute merchandise, enterprising businessmen replaced a situation of want with one of plenty. Thus, the condition of abundance derived from the entrepreneurial awareness of *potential* resources that had been overlooked. Only by assessing the marketplace in a novel way were merchants or manufacturers able to carve out new areas of mass consumption.[3]

By this definition, many anonymous Jewish street merchants and a more limited number of famous Jewish film merchants would fill the role of entrepreneurs in the American system of mass consumption during the era of the great migration. By envisioning and implementing a better way to sell products to urban consumers, they would transform their respective fields of business. On the level of individual contributions, Jewish immigrants and their children would act as innovators in other industries as well, particularly in the clothing industry that housed so many of them.[4] These innovations, however, represented advances in a well-established trade rather than a dramatic change in the character of the industry. The considerable impact of Jewish entrepreneurs upon the American city was integral to Jewish acculturation, but it also fit a general pattern in which immigrants reshaped the urban way of life in the United States.

During the nineteenth century, immigrants decisively influenced the growth of mass consumption in the American city. From its birth in the 1820s and 1830s to its decline in the 1910s and 1920s, when the automobile promoted individualism at the expense of an urban community, the modern city in America represented a point of convergence for a diverse population of migrants from the countryside and immigrants from abroad. The common quest of the native-born and the newcomer for a more comfortable urban existence manifested itself in the birth of the American department store, which served as a magnificent house for the ideal of spreading luxury across a large spectrum of people. The monument to democratic consumption was first conceived and executed between 1846 and 1862 by Alexander Turney Stewart, a Scotch-Irish immigrant who arrived in New York City from Belfast in 1825. Thriving on an ability to dignify the shoppers of New York City as he offered them service and bargains, Stewart crowned his merchandising effort with a superb emporium on the block surrounded by Broadway and Fourth Avenue, 9th and 10th Streets that mirrored his reputation as the country's leading retailer until his death in 1876.[5]

The extensive network of department stores founded by Jews from Germany illustrated even more fully the fluid relationship between immigration and urban consumption in America. Drawing on a rich commercial tradition developed in central Europe, German Jews responded to the opportunity of conducting wholesale and retail trade in the United States.[6] Often starting out as pack peddlers, and frequently heading toward the commercially needy settlements of the South and West, these enterprising newcomers established specialty and department stores during the last decades of the nineteenth century that quickly gained a regional reputation for the Filenes of Boston, the Strauses of New York (who bought Macy's in 1887), the Kaufmanns of Pittsburgh, the Lazaruses of Columbus, the Goldsmiths of Memphis, the Sangers of Dallas, the Spiegelbergs of New Mexico, the Goldwaters of Arizona, and the Meiers of Portland.[7]

The contribution of German Jews was set within the larger context of German impact upon the patterns of urban consumption in America. During the nineteenth century, more American immigrants came from

German-speaking parts of central Europe than from any other region. The tide of German immigration, moreover, was at its fullest between 1850 and 1890, a span of years that witnessed the rise of mass-marketed products and the elaboration of urban entertainment for the American consumer. Among the nearly four million Germans who came at this time, traditions of social entertainment and craftsmanship overflowed the boundaries of urban ethnic neighborhoods, leaving a conspicuous legacy to the American consumer.

Contrasting sharply with the reserved demeanor of native-born Americans, the German love of song, sport, and celebration endowed city life with beer gardens and bowling alleys, as well as musical, literary, dramatic, and gymnastic clubs that transplanted German culture to America. In opposition to the Sabbatarian movement of American Protestants, Germans instituted the custom of Sunday picnicking. The efforts of commercially adept brewers and artisans made for a German presence in the mass-marketing of beer, furniture, pianos, lithographs, and eyeglasses. By the end of the nineteenth century, the names of Pabst, Anheuser-Busch, Steinway, Prang, and Bausch and Lomb, among others, were widely known.[8]

When the eastern European Jews arrived in mass during the last decades of the nineteenth century and the beginning of the twentieth century, the weighty demand of urban Americans for more refined merchandise stimulated the deeply rooted commercial impulses of these newcomers. The flowering of Jewish retail commerce in the United States culminated a tradition of trading in products for widespread consumption. Thriving on international connections, Jewish merchants had helped to introduce European society to sugar, coffee, tobacco, spices, and diamonds from the continents of Asia, Africa, and the Americas during the sixteenth and seventeenth centuries. In the same epoch, small-scale Jewish merchants and craftsmen, forced by law and custom out of the lucrative domain of urban trade, increasingly turned to the rural masses as a potential market. Exchanging manufactured products and imported luxuries for surpluses of grain, flax, wool, and livestock, Jews figured prominently in the commercial development of the European countryside by stimulating the desire of the peasantry for more refined merchandise.[9]

In the lands of western Russia, Poland, Galicia, and Rumania, the rapid growth and steady urbanization of the Jewish population between the eighteenth century and the early twentieth century produced a staggering record of Jewish activity in trade. In 1897, when the nearly five million Jews of the Russian Pale of Settlement constituted about 11 percent of that region's population, they amounted to 52 percent of the urban population in Lithuania and Byelorussia. Of the one hundred and ten cities in Russian Poland, fifty-seven had populations that were at least 50 percent Jewish. Statistics gathered shortly after 1900 for Galicia and Rumania showed the same tendency to congregate in cities. In the forty Galician towns with populations above five thousand, more than 37 percent of the residents were Jewish, and in nine of these towns, Jews amounted to a majority. One-fifth of the people in the provincial capitals of Rumania was Jewish. In some of these cities, such as Jassy, Jews were a majority.

Urbanized by history and tradition, the Jews of eastern Europe concentrated in commerce and in the skilled trades, nearly monopolizing the production of clothing and footwear. During the first decade of the twentieth century, more than three-quarters of the merchants in the Pale were Jewish, and in heavily Jewish provinces such as Grodno and Minsk, Jews constituted from 88 to 96 percent of the merchant population. The commercial dominance of Jews in Galicia was particularly evident. Compared to the figure of 75 percent in the Russian Pale at the turn of the century, approximately 92 percent of the merchants in eastern Galicia and about 82 percent of those in western Galicia were Jewish.[10]

Until the late nineteenth century, many of the most prosperous Jews had been economically entrenched in the estates of the Russian nobility, from whom they received the privilege of marketing timber, grain, furs, and hides, and of producing and selling liquor. Yet the upper echelon of retail commerce had customarily been dominated by Gentiles, and the anti-Semitic restrictions of the 1880s and the 1890s, which ruined many well-to-do merchants, intensified the prevailing form of Jewish commerce in eastern Europe—petty trade. Large numbers of people strove to make a living by compiling a small inventory of goods that posed pathetically as a store. "No bigger than a yawn," was the way the Yiddish writer I. J. Singer recalled one of these shops, which was located in the Polish town of Bilgoraj in the early twentieth century and was stocked solely with pumpkin seeds, cod liver oil, and a few sacks of spices, bay leaves, and capers.[11] The rudimentary state of consumption in eastern Europe had set natural limits to the retail commerce of Jewish peddlers and shopkeepers, whose humble business with local peasants typically revolved around the exchange of a few manufactured items for a handful of animal and vegetable products.

In urban America, the drift of Jewish commerce was strengthened by the persistent demand of city people for luxurious merchandise. Escaping from the tyranny of anti-Semitic restrictions on economic enterprise, eastern Europeans discovered that their aspirations to create and to sell products for the consumer were favored by the reign of fashion and commercial leisure in the American city. Although the political equality and social freedom gained by immigration were in themselves valuable, the lush economic environment that resulted from these conditions was viewed as the most immediate and conspicuous benefit of the decision to leave Europe for the new world. Thus, in 1892, the New York *Yiddishes Tageblatt* focused an article entitled "No Anti-Semitism in America" on the changed economic circumstances of the immigrants. Persecution in eastern Europe had pauperized the Jews and created a setting in which "business pulled itself, crawling on the ground," the newspaper explained, whereas the climate in America seemed to ignite the aspirations of Jewish merchants.[12]

From the earliest years of the great immigration, the rapid adaptation of eastern European Jews to the pace of the American economy struck a number of observers as a phenomenon. Matthew Hale Smith's chronicle of New York City in the late 1870s focused on the bustling sale of clothing, jewelry, and furniture conducted in the Bowery by the "children of Israel."[13] A few years later, in 1883, the *New York Tribune* referred to the Lower East Side as a "Hebrew Hive of Industry," in which the harmony of individual efforts in the manufacture and sale of food, wine and liquor, gold and jewelry, artificial flowers, feathers, clothing, and dry goods proved beyond a doubt that these newcomers knew how to develop "the industries necessary for the comfort of their quarter."[14] The accumulation of successful enterprises during the next two decades prompted the *Tribune*, a newspaper that kept a close and sympathetic eye on the eastern European Jews, to conclude that the "remarkable rise" of this once-impoverished people to a position of importance in the commerce of New York seemed to show that "the Jew is wonderfully apt in adapting himself to American conditions."[15]

After four decades of heavy immigration, New York had acquired a Jewish presence resembling that of Warsaw, Odessa, and a number of smaller cities in eastern Europe. By 1915, when the nearly 1,400,000 Jews of New York constituted about 28 percent of the city's population, Jews had attained a formidable position in the marketing of food, clothing, jewelry, and dry goods. A study published in 1888 pointed out that the transformation of the city's business since the early 1870s was marked by two events: the transfer of the retail center to uptown neighborhoods and the proliferation of Jewish firms. According to this account, of the four hundred buildings on Broadway between Canal Street and Union Square, the vast majority were occupied by Jews. Between them, the central and the eastern Europeans operated 1,000 wholesale firms out of a total of 1,200, ran 234 out of 241 companies engaged in the manufacture of clothing, and predominated in the manufacture and sale of cigars and leaf tobacco as well as in the distribution of diamonds, watches, and jewelry.[16]

The retail environment of the Lower East Side was so dense that some streets virtually specialized in various types of merchandise. By 1892, no fewer than 149 dry goods stores, 138 watch and jewelry shops, 136 diamond shops, 129 shoe stores, 94 clothiers and 94 hat stores, 84 furniture (new) stores, 73 home furnishing (chinaware, glassware, etc.) stores, and 22 furriers were doing business in or next to the Jewish district of lower Manhattan. The Bowery, which ran north and south at the western end of the Lower East Side, excelled as a site for furniture stores, clothiers, and millinery shops, and also included a good number of stores in other lines. Grand Street, the district's main thoroughfare, held the largest number of dry goods stores, including traditional houses like Lord and Taylor's and Ridley's as well as the host of newer Jewish enterprises. Watch and jewelry stores, shoe stores, and millinery shops also thrived on Grand Street. One block below Grand, another east-west artery, Hester Street, competed as a home for dry goods, and, with Ludlow Street, it dominated the trade in home furnishings. A number of furriers clustered at the lower end of Clinton Street, and a multitude of diamond and jewelry stores huddled together on Maiden Lane, a small street that lay a few blocks southwest of the Lower East Side. Without predominating in a particular type of merchandise, streets like Canal, Delancey, Spring, Rivington, Stanton, East Houston, and Division all did a brisk retail business.[17]

The ubiquitous commercial energy of immigrant Jews in New York City could not be completely captured by the statistics of the local business directory. This spirit of enterprise was rendered clearly by Jacob Riis, the Danish immigrant whose photography and journalism of downtown Manhattan gave many Americans their first glimpse of the region in the late 1880s and 1890s. In the Jewish quarter, Riis reported, "the very hallways [have] been made into shops." Hopeful newcomers fit themselves into spaces three feet wide and four feet deep, set up their wares on boards hung across the hall entrances, and thus made potential customers out of pedestrians on the sidewalk before them.[18]

Because New York was a center of trade and finance, Jewish merchants found an unparalleled opportunity to extend their activities. Consequently, the Lower East Side attained considerable importance in regional and interregional commerce. In the 1850s and 1860s, a number of early arrivals from the Russian Pale set up successful businesses that served as depots for peddlers who fanned out beyond the metropolitan area. Exemplifying the expansion of Jewish commerce from downtown New York was the highly successful enterprise of Newman Cowen, formerly Nehemiah Lipinski, a Talmudic scholar and glazier from the town of Lipno in western Poland. Cowen immigrated to the Lower East Side in the early 1850s and became one of the most prosperous retailers of glass. From a store on Canal Street, he launched the careers of a number of relatives and acquaintances by giving them consignments of glass on the condition that they cover a territory not already taken by his current peddlers.[19] Granting a fairly long period of credit to newly arrived salesmen, the merchants of the Lower East Side developed a system that both benefited their countrymen and increased the size of their American clientele.

With the rise of the department store in the 1860s, which permitted consumers from outlying areas to buy the same type of merchandise at lower prices, the Jewish merchants of the Lower East Side gradually ceased dealing directly with these customers through a network of peddlers. Yet they continued to forge links with retailers in other parts of the country. In 1898, a trade journal of the furniture business commented on the ability of East Side furniture dealers to appeal to a far-flung clientele. Observing that the spokes of Jewish trade extended not only to New England but also to the West and South, the periodical considered it "a rare thing for the average furniture store to enjoy much more than a local trade," but the Jewish retailers of downtown Manhattan proved to be "the exception to this rule."[20]

The intense evolution of Jewish commerce was based on the distinctive character of consumption in the American city. Traditional commercial skills guided but did not determine the economic destiny of newcomers. Equally important was the destination to which they had traveled. In Buenos Aires, the principal urban settlement of eastern European Jews in Latin America, immigrants pursued similar lines of work as in the United States, but to a different effect. Prior to 1920, the Jews of Buenos Aires, numbering in the tens of thousands, became important purveyors of clothing, jewelry, and furniture. But the stunted progress of mass consumption in Argentina restricted these merchants to the sale of low-grade merchandise for the poor. Having yet to develop strong domestic industries to meet the needs of consumers, Argentina was bound to a double standard of consumption, in which the affluent enjoyed foreign products of good quality and the majority of poorer people put up with shoddy clothes and furnishings. Much as they had done in eastern Europe, Jews fit into the lower tier of Argentine society, serving a populace that had little cause to demand sophisticated merchandise.[21]

The economic prospects of Jewish immigrants were shaped not only by the level of consumption existing at the point of destination but, moreover, by the flexibility of the society into which they had moved. In London, which attracted well over one hundred thousand Jews from eastern Europe between 1880 and 1914, newcomers were able to reap the benefits of an advanced industrial system. They entered the garment trades, operated pushcarts, and manufactured and sold furniture and other consumer goods, as they did in American cities. Yet, because English society was not as open and fluid, the eastern Europeans were more reclusive than in the United States, and the entrepreneurs among them generally did not introduce major innovations into the larger world of business, as was the case in America.[22]

Along with a comparatively high degree of social freedom, the love of business in America sparked the potential of Jewish merchants. In Europe and Latin America, where aristocratic traditions had perpetuated the social prestige of land ownership, military skill, and intellectual and artistic refinement, a career in business was far from being considered the height of accomplishment. Circumstances in North America differed. Although land retained great economic and cultural value in the United States, many leading citizens had achieved success through industry and commerce. Consequently, the world of business was exalted. Americans might question the ways in which magnates used their fortunes, but they agreed on the importance of making money, which was most efficiently done in the market. Basking in public affection, American businessmen often viewed themselves as missionaries and their products as hallmarks of civilization.[23]

The American view of business sharpened the aspirations of Jewish newcomers who wanted to contribute to the society that had welcomed them. Though not the only means of fitting into American society, commerce opened up the most accessible avenue for the majority of ambitious yet unschooled immigrants. Jews raised in America, and the handful of older immigrants who managed to master the English language, would illustrate the validity of the *Tageblatt's* statement that the group had "a great spiritual wealth [and] a long intellectual development" with which to enrich American life.[24] But the multitude of unlettered immigrants relied on the Jewish commercial tradition to provide a way of communicating and interacting with the larger society. The silent language of exchange would open up a broader relationship to American society than the sophisticated idiom of the artists and intellectuals who rose from the crowded quarters of the eastern European Jews.

In an address on the occasion of the Jewish New Year 5665, which occurred in September 1904, Rabbi Henry Pereira Mendes of New York City's venerable congregation Shearith Israel made a point that helped to explain the enthusiasm with which so many Jewish newcomers dedicated their skills to American urban society. "The Hebrew does not stand on the stage of history for his own profit or glory," the spiritual leader declared, "he is there to benefit the world at large, or, to quote the Bible phraseology, 'to be a blessing' to all mankind."[25]

The social and economic freedom granted at least to Europeans in the American city lifted Jewish commercial activity to a higher plane than it had occupied in Europe, where Jews had been socially isolated. Inspired by the prospect of acceptance and by the special status of business in America, commercially able newcomers conducted their affairs in the spirit of a democratic crusade. Having inherited from their traditional culture a rich sense of the dignifying power of luxuries, Jewish merchants were all the more prepared to accept the American belief in mass consumption as the bulwark of civilization.

The inspiration of these newcomers was conveyed eloquently by Louis Borgenicht, a Galician Jew who established a successful business in children's clothing in New York City during the 1890s. Of the thousands of newcomers to enter the garment trade, Borgenicht was one of the few to record impressions of his life and to voice some of the rarely expressed motivations of the Jewish businessman cutting a path from poverty to prestige. Published in 1942, when news about the atrocities of the German occupation of Poland was being broadcast throughout the West, Borgenicht's autobiography did not fail to stress the connection between the spreading of luxuries and the prospect of creating a more humane existence on earth. "There is nothing sinful about spreading material goods around to the greatest number," Borgenicht argued, with the critics of "American materialism" in mind, "my life has been devoted to that work." The manufacturer's aspiration was "to see everybody have all the gadgets in the world," and all the basic comforts. Then, the fear of scarcity would no longer motivate nations to wage war with each other, and human energies could be devoted to "human and not jungle-beast activities."[26]

In America, the messianic spirit of the Jews resounded in the revolutionary rhetoric of transplanted socialists and anarchists, but it surfaced as well in the unarticulated striving of merchants and manufacturers. The field of commerce gave widest play to the Jewish drive for integration into American society. A focus of contact between the two cultures, trade provided the only way for unsophisticated newcomers to alter the urban American lifestyle. Almost imperceptibly, this was what an army of pushcart peddlers would do in New York City.

Anonymous Entrepreneurs: Jewish Street Merchants

Fostered in the social atmosphere of the United States, the commercial idealism of eastern European Jews was initially conveyed by the push-carts of New York City. Street marketing was the first and most sponta-neous form of commerce for incoming Jews, the activity that posed fewest obstacles to the impoverished greenhorn. Entrusted by relatives or friends with a few dollars for the purchase of a small stock of wares, newcomers embarked on a career in American business. As a result of the ease of entering the occupation, peddling attracted thousands of Jews, whose collective energies turned a primitive form of retailing into a forum for mass consumption. By introducing a wide range of affordable luxuries and a degree of service that had formerly been alien to outdoor marketing, Jewish newcomers bolstered the power and the prestige of ordinary consumers and aided many newcomers in their search for an American lifestyle.

Rootless and vulnerable, canvassing the rural areas of Poland and America, surviving by means of quick wits, verbal finesse, and sheer stamina, the peddler had been for centuries a symbol of Jewish life in the diaspora. By the early twentieth century, the massive immigration of eastern European Jews into New York City had created the basis for a new kind of peddler, one who functioned as part of a sizable commercial network within a well-defined urban area. Yet, subtle changes in the economic character of peddling were masked by the symbolic appeal of these lone and humble merchants.

To contemporaries who observed the strains and humiliations characterizing the life of peddlers, the curbside merchant seemed to embody the rootlessness and desolation of modern life. In a 1902 poem, Morris Rosenfeld, the celebrated Yiddish poet of Jewish life in the American city, eulogized "The Greenhorn Peddler." The man who had been the intellectual light of his peers in the old country was compelled by conditions in America to live out an undistinguished life at the helm of a pushcart. "Oy, how pitifully he goes around, knocking on strange doors!" Rosenfeld wrote, "such is the way a beautiful flower withers, that would have adorned a people."[1]

Reinforcing the literary image of the Jewish street peddler, the New York *Yiddishes Tageblatt*, the popular daily newspaper which published "The Greenhorn Peddler," printed the melancholy description of streetside trade written in 1903 by Rose Pastor, a young Polish Jew who was the paper's assistant editor. Pastor focused on a poor, elderly woman, a relatively recent arrival in America, who scraped together a living by selling Sabbath candles. Her features paled by exhaustion and her body covered by a coarse jacket and shawl, the woman momentarily set her basket down in front of a store in order to make change for one of her few customers. Immediately, the storekeeper came out and kicked the basket into the street. Distraught, she could do nothing but give thanks to God that the road was dry and that the candles were not ruined. Concluding her careful description of this downtrodden peddler, Pastor commented on the sadness of a world in which "so much pain and sorrow, so much poverty and suffering" was heaped upon those who were "God's best beloved."[2]

Provoked by what they considered to be the pathetic condition of pushcart peddlers, Rosenfeld and Pastor discovered a literary vehicle for exposing the trauma of immigration and the purported evils of capitalism. Particularly during the earliest years of the great migration from eastern Europe, the lot of the Jewish peddler could be a miserable one. Door-to-door vendors suffered the most abuse, having to roam through strange neighborhoods, where they might be humiliated by rude or bigoted New Yorkers who viewed peddling as little better than begging.[3] After the mid-1880s, when permanent pushcart markets began to appear, street merchants achieved greater physical security and occupational legitimacy. While individual instances of mistreatment would naturally continue to occur, and while some Jews would never rise out of poverty through the pushcart, the emergence of the busy street merchant as an established city type made the humble pack-peddler into a relic of the past.

Though the image of the old-fashioned, bedraggled vendor contained a germ of truth, it obscured the commercial significance of Jewish peddlers from eastern Europe. The old-world flavor of street marketing also could disguise the entrepreneurial features of these merchants. Seemingly more reminiscent of the shtetl than the metropolis, the strange "yaaik, yaaik" calls of the milk vendors which served as an alarm clock for many East Siders, the sad cries of the old orthodox glass peddlers, the blaring percussion of the tin and copper men banging their pots as they shouted for buyers, and the verbal blasts of the fish sellers filled the air of the Jewish quarter.[4] Yet, while the whirl of life on the crowded city streets seemed to suggest nothing but confusion, anonymous merchants were at work transforming the character of outdoor marketing.

The maturation of street marketing at the turn of the century depended on the determination of immigrants, as consumers, to increase their purchasing power. Emerging as a conspicuous part of city life during the massive Irish and German immigration of the 1840s and 1850s, street marketing in New York City appears to have originated in the need of poor people for inexpensive produce.[5] Until the arrival of the eastern and southern Europeans, however, this form of selling was a slow-moving tributary of the city's rapidly flowing trade. In 1870, the streetside vendor of Manhattan was observed to have "much leisure to spend in cloudy revery, in tranquil chat with a neighbor, in poring over a book or paper, in smoking a pipe, or in dozing," his existence appearing to be a "monotonous and uneventful round."[6]

During the last decades of the century, the growth of the urban population and of the marketing system produced a congestion in the retail trade of New York City that a new ethnic army of street merchants would help to relieve. After the Civil War, when railroads came to dominate the transport of foodstuffs, shippers and buyers tended more than ever to concentrate their business in the downtown markets that had formerly thrived on water-borne commerce. The presence of a centralized market enabled distant shippers to increase the likelihood that their goods would find buyers, and it gave buyers the opportunity to inspect the quality and quantity of incoming foods with a minimum of effort.

The bulk of produce arriving in the metropolitan area was collected at the Washington Market, a depot that eventually occupied nearly fifty-six acres on the lower West Side between West and Hudson streets below Fulton Street. The primary point of distribution for the city's unusual variety of fish, which came not only from fisheries in the Northeast but also from California and England, was the Fulton Market on the Lower East Side, situated several blocks below the Brooklyn Bridge. In the early 1880s, when the Fulton Fish Market, equipped with enormous refrigeration units, was handling well over fifty million pounds of fish each year, the downtown wholesale centers of Manhattan had already attained a phenomenal scale of business. By 1914, over six billion pounds of fruit, vegetables, dairy products, and fish entered the city through these areas.[7]

The distance of the downtown wholesale markets from the northeastward center of the city's population, in addition to the frequency of gluts accompanying the concentration of trade, posed a distinct problem for consumers interested in obtaining perishable items as quickly as possible. In this commercial situation, newcomers to New York City, particularly Jews, Italians, and Greeks, recognized an opportunity to make a living by means of the pushcart. This type of selling was well suited to the city's need for a more extensive network of merchants and it was tailor-made for poor immigrants. With operating expenses limited to tens cents a day for the rental of a wagon and a few dollars per year for a license—an expense that many peddlers probably avoided—street merchants efficiently met the needs of immigrants like themselves, who sought low prices and accepted imperfect goods.

The density of Jewish and Italian neighborhoods in the city supported the transition of street marketing from an occupation restricted to a small number of itinerant peddlers to an established retail institution. During the middle and late 1880s, pushcart peddlers began to station themselves on certain streets of the Lower East Side, where they developed a steady clientele of housewives. Within the next two decades, Hester Street, Grand Street, Orchard Street, and Rivington Street, along with most of the other streets of the Jewish quarter, had virtually become marketplaces. Throughout the day and well into the evening, these streets were filled on both sides with continuous lines of pushcarts that extended from block to block. In the Italian areas surrounding Mulberry, Elizabeth, and Mott streets to the west of the Bowery, in Italian Harlem, situated roughly along First Avenue between 106th and 116th Streets and along Third Avenue between 116th and 125th Streets, and in several other parts of the city, large clusters of street merchants also appeared.

After 1899, as immigration from Jewish eastern Europe accelerated, the influence of immigrants over street marketing came to a peak. In 1906, a municipal commission conservatively estimated the number of pushcart peddlers in Manhattan to be about five thousand, of which 97 percent were reportedly foreigners. Fourteen percent were Greek, 22 percent were Italian, and 61 percent were Jewish.[8] The body of customers served by the pushcarts grew proportionately. In 1923, an official survey reckoned that one-and-a-half million New Yorkers patronized the street merchants. The majority of these consumers appeared to be Jews and Italians.[9]

Contrary to the image of the street peddler as a rootless, elderly, downtrodden outcast, peddling had quickly developed into a legitimate occupation. Most vendors were between twenty and sixty years old, and their income in 1906 reportedly averaged between fifteen dollars and eighteen dollars per week, a figure that compared well to the wages and salaries obtained in many other occupations. Far from being inescapably bound to the pushcart by poverty, Jews tended to treat peddling as a stepping stone to a more substantial business. They usually spent about five or six years on the streets and then invested their savings in an enterprise of their own.[10] In 1913, a municipal commission on the state of the pushcart industry in New York gave a fair portrayal of the business when it described the peddlers as "self-respecting merchants."[11]

As a source of inexpensive yet good-quality foods for a large number of city people, street marketing had evolved into a vital retail institution. By virtue of the location of New York's primary wholesale markets for produce and fish on the lower West and the Lower East Side, residents of the lower portion of the city were able to buy food at prices considerably lower than those available to shoppers in other districts. In the early 1880s, before pushcart peddlers had begun to congregate on particular streets, many residents of lower Manhattan used to buy produce at outdoor markets that operated on Saturday nights and Sunday mornings. By dusk on Saturday, the streets that bordered these markets would be piled high with all sorts of fruits and vegetables and the air would ring with the shouts of hawkers. Here, at "the great green grocer's shop of economical buyers," as a reporter for the *New York Times* referred to one of the sites, shoppers could "get more for their money" than they could anywhere else in town.[12]

The advent of large-scale street marketing made these advantages available on a daily basis. In the summer of 1893, a survey of produce prices at the street markets of lower Manhattan was reported by Maria Parloa, a well-known lecturer on cooking and home economics. Parloa stated that items of similar quality were less expensive on pushcarts than they were in local stores.[13] Abetted by the negligible costs of operating a pushcart, street merchants specialized in a single type of commodity, which enabled them both to know the market more thoroughly than a general merchant and to gain economies of scale denied to small shopkeepers. "Perhaps no other class of buyers . . . comb the market as do the push cart vendors in search of bargains," stated the most authoritative government report on this type of retailing, published in 1925; "nothing in the way of produce capable of a quick turnover, at prices reasonable to insure a profit, escapes their observation."[14]

Prior to the 1920s, street marketing offered consumers bargains unsurpassed by other forms of retailing. The chain store also originated in New York City, when the Great American Tea Company, which evolved into the Great Atlantic and Pacific Tea Company (A & P), was founded on Vesey Street in 1859. The grocery chain had set up nearly five hundred units by 1912, when it launched the concept of the large-volume, rapid-turnover, cash-and-carry "economy store." Yet, for at least another decade, the prices of the A & P stores seem to have been, at best, slightly lower than those of smaller grocery shops. The greatest bargains were found on the streets, and, consequently, people who lived near the principal pushcart markets were found to spend much less of their income for the staples of daily life than did shoppers who depended upon stores.[15]

As a source of inexpensive food, large-scale street marketing was a vital economic resource, but the outstanding social consequence of the institution came with the expansion of the curbside inventories into other types of merchandise. The flowering of products and of retail techniques on the streets of New York City was a boon to consumers of modest means. By reducing the prices of a seemingly unlimited variety of products and by refining the image of shopping on the streets, peddlers mimicked some of the essential features of the department store and raised the prestige of ordinary shoppers. The transformation of street marketing into a socially valuable institution was directed by eastern European Jews.

The influx of eastern and southern Europeans after the 1870s virtually produced an ethnic division of labor in the industry of street marketing. Italians and, to a lesser extent, Greeks played a large role in the expansion of the fruit and vegetable selection available to street shoppers. In addition to carrying the products of the region, such as cabbages, turnips, cauliflower, squash, corn, lettuce, tomatoes, apples, pears, and peaches, they peddled bananas, pineapples, coconuts, grapes, oranges, lemons, limes, dates, figs, and mangoes, foods that most eastern Europeans regarded as true luxuries.[16]

Jews, who constituted a majority of the peddlers in Manhattan, also participated in the food trade. Yet they practically monopolized the sale of clothing and fabric, furs, shoes, hats, jewelry, eyeglasses, cosmetics, bedding, curtains, stationery and books, crockery, glassware, kitchen utensils and hardware, toys, and miscellaneous items. In 1906, an observer of the bustling curbside commerce of Manhattan recognized the impact of ethnicity upon the business. "The Americans sell lunches, the Greeks fruit and ice cream, almost exclusively, while the Italians widen the list by adding vegetables," he stated, "but the Jewish peddlers sell practically every conceivable thing."[17] The general impression that Jews were broadening the horizon of street marketing was confirmed a decade and a half later by a statistical survey of peddling in New York City. Of over seven hundred vendors selling merchandise other than food, 95 percent were Jews.[18]

Lower Manhattan was not only the distribution point for food, but it also accommodated many small factories producing dry goods, clothing, cosmetic items, and household furnishings. By the end of the 1880s, Jewish peddlers had begun to tap these nearby sources of merchandise. Their enterprise was manifested in the startling variety of products for sale on the Lower East Side, where the streets were steadily turning into an emporium for shoppers. Arriving in New York from Hungary in 1889, Louis Borgenicht was startled by the booming trade that was conducted out-of-doors. He had rarely seen a peddler in his homeland, where, except for the days of the annual trading fair, retail trade had been slow. Yet, "in one single street" of New York City, Borgenicht observed "more people offering wares than in the largest Jahrmarket, and more different items than in a hundred Jahrmarkets."[19] By the late 1890s, the refinement of street marketing had progressed so steadily that a woman who had tried in vain to match her draperies at the finest uptown stores was able to do so at the pushcart of a peddler on Hester Street. The woman's story, told in the *New York Tribune* in 1898, was accompanied by the statement of an alleged authority that "what cannot be bought in the pushcart market cannot easily be bought in New York."[20]

In the city, eastern Europeans sustained a tradition in which Jewish peddlers performed the important function of catering to consumers who had been excluded from the burgeoning retail trade of America. During the middle decades of the nineteenth century, prior to the age of the railroads, thousands of German Jews spanned the country peddling urban products to consumers whose migration had carried them beyond the centers of trade. In 1860, when there were probably around 20,000 peddlers in the United States, a large proportion of these petty retailers appear to have been Jews.[21] By the close of the nineteenth century, the focus of American economic growth had shifted. The bulk of consumer demand rested not in the west-bound settlements, but in the burgeoning population of city people. Accordingly, the chief challenge facing itinerant entrepreneurs was no longer how to link remote consumers to the urban source of luxuries but, instead, how to sell these items at more affordable prices.

As the pioneers of the department store had done in the 1860s and 1870s, Jewish street merchants set to the task of furnishing the public with good-quality merchandise at lower prices than were usually found in retail stores. The activity of these street-side entrepreneurs helped to turn the Lower East Side into a haven for consumers. The urban "ghettos" that emerged in the late nineteenth century have typically been interpreted as places in which consumers were burdened with inferior merchandise and inflated prices.[22] In actuality, the commercial vitality of the crowded Jewish neighborhoods of New York city produced a retail setting that was unusually advantageous to shoppers of modest means.

Into the domain of street selling, the eastern Europeans infused traditional Jewish concepts of quality and price. Acknowledging the importance of commerce in Jewish life, the Talmud had set forth a series of injunctions to maintain a high standard of conduct while allowing for competition in retail trade. Drawing on passages in Leviticus (19:35, 25:14) and Deuteronomy (25:13–15), the revered texts of Jewish law insisted on honest representation of merchandise and on generosity toward consumers. In addition, merchants were specifically permitted to sell goods below the market price in order to attract customers.[23]

Like all precepts, these points of commerce would not be unanimously upheld, but they shaped the method of Jewish merchants in both Europe and America. Inordinately dependent upon the ability to succeed in trade, Jews had been compelled by circumstances to attract consumers by retailing products at competitive prices. In the Russian Pale, the success of Jewish commerce was based on the tendency to sell for cash at a low margin of profit in order to achieve a rapid turnover of merchandise. Russian merchants, by contrast, were attached to the time-honored principle of maintaining prices and granting long credits.[24] The transplantation of the Jewish style of selling to the fertile territory of the American city prompted economist Isaac M. Rubinow to declare, in 1907, that "nowhere in the United States are the prices of general merchandise, whether it be dry goods, clothing, or groceries of well-known make and supposedly fixed prices, so low in price as they are on the east side of New York City."[25]

The ability to sell at a competitive price enabled Jewish retailers to usurp the position of American department and dry-goods stores on the Lower East Side during the 1880s. According to a chronicle of the development of the Lower East Side between 1885 and 1910, eastern

European Jews had outpaced the three large department stores that had been previously established on Grand Street, by upholding the policy of giving "more 'money's worth.' "[26] By 1906, the Jewish district of the Lower East Side was reported to have at least fifty large dry-goods stores whose stocks of silks, woolens, and other fine fabrics offered competition to the city's major retail firms. On account of the low profit margins they operated with, these stores sold merchandise at prices that attracted women from uptown as well as from outlying areas of New York City. [27]

The competitive approach of Jewish vendors accentuated the endemic tendency of street marketing toward lower prices, attracted large clienteles, and stimulated retail business in general. As the president of the New York City Board of Police noted in 1897, the coming of the pushcart markets in the 1880s had initiated vast improvements in the social milieu of Jewish streets, some of which, like Hester Street, had formerly been a refuge for criminals. [28] By virtue of their competitive advantages, street merchants quickly came to be identified as a magnet of commerce to which shopkeepers were strongly attracted. The arrival of a cluster of peddlers on a street was reputed to cause a boom in business and in the value of real estate on the block. Streets outside the perimeter of the outdoor marketplaces were often strikingly slow in business compared to those within, and the course of trade on one side of a street often appeared to be linked to the presence or absence of a line of pushcarts. [29]

The positive effect of street merchants on surrounding businesses was discussed by a Jewish peddler called to testify in 1906 before a mayoral commission on pushcarts in New York City. The witness explained how the owner of a men's clothing store on Fulton Street had asked a number of peddlers to locate on his side of the street. After the shift had occurred, the proprietor claimed to be making much more money on account of the crowds of shoppers who had entered his sphere. [30]

The key to the popularity of the pushcarts was not only the competitive sale of desirable products but also the effective use of the latest techniques of display. By concentrating on the aesthetic presentation of specialized lines of merchandise, street merchants distinguished themselves entirely from the pack peddlers of the recent past. Although some vendors continued to pile wares carelessly on their carts, many made sure that their mobile stores were "so beautifully arranged" as to "attract and hold the attention" of shoppers. [31] Foods were segregated and mounted in neat stacks, which were sometimes interspersed with fresh greenery. Dishes and utensils were compartmentalized. Fabrics and oilcloth were juxtaposed according to color and pattern. A visitor to the street markets of the uptown "Little Italy" on the East Side of the city in the spring of

1914 saw fit to comment on a pushcart that contained roughly sixty rolls of oilcloth, commonly used as table covers, which displayed a "multitude of different patterns [that] resulted in good business for the owner."[32]

The refinement of display enriched the atmosphere of street shopping. The large-wheeled wooden carts that were housed each night in stables throughout the city were transformed by day into attractive couriers that literally put merchandise at the fingertips of urban consumers. Some merchants built auxiliary compartments onto their wagons in order to show off surplus wares, increasing the image of abundance to which the city's newcomers were exposed. Through the discreet use of modern techniques of specialization and decoration, peddlers created the illusion of streets paved, not with gold, but with a panorama of luxuries.

At Christmas time, the momentum of outdoor marketing reached a peak. Jewish wholesalers stocked up on holiday candies and Christmas tree decorations that would effectively reach Italian neighborhoods by the pushcart.[33] Competition for space became so intense that peddlers camped out overnight in their favorite spots, establishing "a sort of squatter sovereignty on the premises."[34] During the holidays, conventional effects like glass showcases and oilcloth canopies were augmented, as pushcarts were adorned with bunting, edged with colored paper, and furnished with sprays of holly and Christmas bells. A Serbian Jew who grew up on the Upper East Side fondly reminisced about the eye-catching rows of pushcarts on First Avenue after the turn of the century. "The pushcarts held the most marvelous, exciting promise of things to buy," she stressed, adding that "for us a need was filled at Christmas time by the gaily decorated wares spread out by the street merchants."[35]

As skillful displays introduced an aesthetic into the world of street marketing, retail devices for the pleasure of customers injected an element of convenience and service that had not previously belonged to outdoor shopping. Peddlers of clothing and shoes made use of mannequins, folding chairs, carpets, and mirrors, so that customers could survey the items for sale, sit down to try on shoes and garments, take a walk to test for comfort, and make a final judgment of how the new things looked. A successful shoe salesman in Little Italy, whose stand was well stocked with shoes, rubbers, and slippers in a large variety of sizes astonished a reporter with his ability to serve customers despite the apparent difficulties of finding a good fit on the street. In order to guarantee reliable service to his customers during busy times, the merchant kept a messenger to replenish the stock as it diminished during the day.[36] The effort to serve the public, rather than simply to sell, represented an important innovation in street marketing. Through service, merchants refined the character of outdoor selling and elevated the dignity of the street shopper, who received respectable products in a respectable manner.

The sophistication of urban peddling allowed city people of modest means to strike a balance between need and desire. The families of immigrants that comprised the majority of street shoppers discovered just beyond their doorsteps a method of obtaining all types of products at affordable prices. They found also a degree of refinement that had not traditionally been part of the peddler's repertoire of techniques. The activity of street merchants, dominated by eastern European Jews, helped consumers to harmonize the press of finances with the flight of expectations.

In the modern city, entrepreneurial opportunities were pervasive, appearing on the dusty streets as well as in the marble palaces of high-class retailers. On Grand Street, the retail center of the Lower East Side, the jutting rows of richly endowed pushcarts formed a sinuous, wooden monument to the special accomplishments of Jewish street peddlers. In December 1903, a columnist for a popular Yiddish newspaper observed the extent to which the inventories and the retail methods of the vendors on Grand Street approached the standard of modern selling. Cognizant of the fine furs that were sprinkled among the wares to be had in the outdoor emporium, the writer keenly remarked that Grand Street looked like "a great department store on wheels."[37]

As street merchants, eastern European Jews moved with the tides of trade in the city. They sensed the momentum toward social democracy in the urban marketplace, where city people restlessly looked for luxuries that would once have seemed out of place on the rough pavement of the tenement districts. The defining urge of the consumer-minded entrepreneur, that of finding novel ways to bring products to market, was expressed in an elemental form by Jewish peddlers who saw in the most common of settings, the city street, an appropriate outlet for refined merchandise and retail techniques.

Taken as a whole, the practices of thousands of anonymous street merchants gave the first indication of how the Jewish commercial tradition might alter the geography of urban consumption and transform the lives of consumers. The most illustrious exhibition of Jewish commercial impact would take place in the moving picture world.

᠊ᠥᢀ 13 ᢀ᠊ᠥ

A Jewish Monument to the Masses: Marketing the American Film

Mirroring the profound impact of mass consumption upon newcomers, Jewish commerce left its own indelible mark on American society by transforming the moving picture industry. Nourished by the dense atmosphere of Jewish leisure in urban America, a number of bold merchants responded to the latent demand of city people for a more elaborate cinema. The vision of creating an unsurpassed medium of public entertainment induced Jewish merchants to take command of a stagnant system of movie marketing that limited the experience of consumers. Although they were not the sole commercial innovators in the bustling young industry, Jews demonstrated a superior awareness of the fact that film had to be packaged differently in order to generate a high level of enthusiasm among the public. Consequently, they pioneered in marketing the American film as a long-playing feature production, as a vehicle for charming screen personalities, as the legitimate heir of the high-class theater, and as the exclusive focus of an elaborately staged show. On account of their efforts, the decade preceding World War I witnessed the swift conversion of a crude type of entertainment into the monument of mass leisure.

Jewish influence upon film marketing was analogous to that in the pushcart trade, insofar as a rudimentary economic activity was refined to a level of quality that was much more satisfactory to consumers. Yet the potential of film marketing to transform daily life in the city far surpassed that of street marketing. Extensive street marketing was largely relegated to the immigrant generation. Flourishing from the scrappy resourcefulness of men and women who started out with little money and with limited understanding of their new society, the outdoor industry was outmoded by administrative decree in the 1930s, when mayor Fiorello LaGuardia began to move the peddlers indoors.[1] The trade in moving pictures, however, was neither relegated to newcomers nor confined to a brief span of decades.

Including a few outstanding individuals who had immigrated as young adults but consisting primarily of Jews raised in America, the most successful of the Jewish merchants in the moving picture industry entered the field only after they had seasoned themselves and acquired capital in other trades, particularly the garment business. Equal in importance to this commercial experience was the potential richness of urban entertainment in the United States. Watchful of opportunities to tap a mass market, these entrepreneurs perceived the destiny of the American film at a time "when everyone else was blind," as a Harvard symposium on cinema concluded in 1926.[2]

The vision of rising entrepreneurs was clarified and sharpened in the rich environment of commercial leisure—the network of theaters, arcades, dance halls, cafés, and vaudeville houses—that existed among the eastern European Jews in the American city. Like the pushcarts, many of the first movie theaters were established in Jewish and Italian areas of New York City. In June 1905, when two showmen in Pittsburgh opened a "nickleodeon," a small, but well decorated, five-cent theater devoted exclusively to moving pictures, the response of the public was such that similar store-front enterprises sprouted up in cities across the country. In Manhattan, at least one hundred twenty-three of these small movie houses, which normally seated two to three hundred people, had appeared by 1908. Forty-two of these were located on or adjacent to the Lower East Side, and ten were in the uptown area identified as Jewish Harlem. In addition, nineteen nickel theaters were spread out along the Second and Third Avenue streetcar lines of the East Side, which spanned the area to which many Jews were migrating from the lower part of the city. The uptown district of Little Italy contained thirteen nickleodeons. Newcomers appeared to compose a significant proportion of the early moviegoing population in New York, and Jews stood out as an audience for the new art form.[3]

The enthusiasm of Jewish immigrants for moving pictures was exemplified by the fact that in 1907, just one year before the Jewish masses of New York erupted in indignation over the unfounded statement of the city's Police Commissioner that Jews were inclined to be criminals, a film with a similar message was being received with open arms.[4] Released by the Edison Company in 1904, *Cohen's Fire Sale* was one of the earliest American films about Jews. Unlike some of the short films of the day that portrayed the new Americans sympathetically, *Cohen's Fire Sale* perpetuated the popular stereotype of the Jew as a short, large-nosed, scheming merchant. In the film, the owner of a millinery store suffers a loss when a large stock of new hats is accidentally carried off by the trash collector. Cohen manages to recover the merchandise, but it has been damaged and will not sell. Frustrated, Cohen checks his insurance policy, sets up a fire in his store, and, afterward, advertises a great reduction sale.[5]

A brief controversy over the presentation of *Cohen's Fire Sale* on the Lower East Side demonstrated the magnetic effect of the movies upon Jewish audiences. At a showing of the film in the summer of 1907, in a theater that was owned and patronized by Jews, a young Zionist protested to the theater owner about the anti-Semitic connotations of the picture. As the debate between the two men developed, other members of the audience began to take an active interest. In apparent unanimity, they rallied to the side of the owner, declaring that the protestor did not have to attend shows that he disliked. The lure of the moving picture medium seemed more potent than the meanness of particular messages that might be conveyed on the screen.[6]

The powerful support of the Jewish public for the new kind of urban entertainment inspired the early efforts of Jewish entrepreneurs who would take command of the movie business during the second decade of the twentieth century. Stirred by the uncommon appeal the movies held for the hard-working people among whom they had lived and prospered, these young Jewish men—some of them immigrants, others Americans, most of eastern European descent, but a few of German background— were well grounded in the domesticity of Jewish leisure, which influenced them to provide a respectable brand of entertainment that would attract a large audience of families, rather than one dominated by solitary men.[7]

Moreover, the profound anticipation of the multitude for relief from the burdens of existence in congested urban neighborhoods excited an awareness of the latent demand for a style of moviegoing that would rival the sophistication of the opera-going elite. A. J. Balaban, who co-founded the extensive and widely respected Balaban and Katz theater chain in the Chicago region between 1917 and 1923, had originally been inspired by the audiences that attended his first small-time shows in the immigrant districts of Chicago around 1907. The moments of happiness enjoyed by people in the semidarkness of the movie house compelled the young showman to strive "to make people live in a fairyland and to make them forget their troubles."[8]

The drive to create a cinema capable of transporting moviegoers into another world entailed dramatic changes in the method of marketing film during the first decade and a half of the century. In complete opposition to the reigning mode of presenting a series of short films in small theaters that were, at best, modestly decorated, Jewish merchants moved confidently into the vanguard of modern presentation, which defined the moving picture show as consisting of one central film oriented around screen stars, housed in an elegant picture "palace," and complemented by well-orchestrated music, sound effects, and occasional visual props.

The original leaders of the American movie industry failed to perceive the readiness of the public for pictures that would constitute the basis of a self-sufficient and sophisticated form of entertainment. Once the profitability of showing moving pictures in the United States had been demonstrated in 1896, all kinds of prospective businessmen were attracted to the industry. Yet, by 1909, the numerous rank and file of small-scale manufacturers had been overshadowed by seven American companies— Edison, Biograph, Vitagraph, Selig, Essanay, Lubin, and Kalem—and two French companies—Méliès and Pathé—that had created the most useful machinery for making and projecting films. In January of that year, these manufacturers, in addition to one large-scale distributor, announced the formation of the Motion Picture Patents Company (MPPC), a trust that sought to control both the production and the distribution of all films in the United States through the exercise of patent rights. Without the permission of the MPPC, independent producers could not legally use the standard equipment for making movies, and exhibitors were compelled to pay an extortionate licensing fee in order to obtain the Company's pictures.

The domination of the MPPC thwarted the development of the long-playing feature film which was already emerging in Europe and which was essential to the refinement of film marketing. Having created an efficient system of mass production based on the short, one-reel film, the big manufacturers were able to standardize all aspects of the business, from the cost of shooting and the wages of actors to the price paid for each film and the amount of time it would be exhibited. As European filmmakers ventured into the production of exciting long-playing films of four and more reels, the American industry fell into a state of inertia. Confined by a schedule of production that virtually prohibited a film from being more than two reels, or approximately thirty minutes in length, the American movie could not aspire to provide viewers with more than a flicker of entertainment.[9]

The dominant marketing system strictly limited the nature of the final product that was consumed by movie audiences, as was illustrated by the unfortunate fragmentation of one of the first long-playing films made in America, D. W. Griffith's *Judith of Bethulia.* The most talented director of the prewar era, David Wark Griffith was stimulated by the arrival of spectacular long-playing films from Europe in 1912 and 1913 to make a four-reel feature of his own. His screen adaptation of the story of Judith, the young Jewish woman who beheaded a Babylonian general and thus saved the Jews of Palestine, included the type of flamboyant mass scene, such as the storming of the fortress of Bethulia and the fiery destruction of the Assyrians' camp, that had contributed to the success of the imported Italian spectacle of the Roman Empire, *Quo Vadis?* in 1913. Despite the high cinematic quality of Griffith's film, the Biograph Company did not release the picture until almost a year after its completion. When it was distributed to exhibitors, it was marketed not as a long-playing, feature film worthy of an extravagant promotional campaign, but, in accordance with the emphasis of the MPPC on the short picture, as a series to be presented one reel at a time. The frustration of Griffith's venture indicated that, in the film business, the final product received by consumers was shaped by the prevailing mode of marketing.[10]

From their superior awareness of public taste, Jewish merchants of film promoted a new marketing strategy that redefined the mode of production. The existing barrier between producer and consumer was bridged by the principle that movie goers would prefer a long film presented as a whole, not as a series of parts, and centered on lavishly publicized stars. By 1915, four outstanding Jewish immigrants had laid the foundation for powerful movie enterprises by capitalizing on this double-sided approach to film marketing: Adolph Zukor and William Fox, who came from Hungarian shtetls in the 1880s to become the leaders of Paramount Pictures and Fox Pictures, Carl Laemmle, who immigrated from southern Germany in 1884 and founded the Universal studio in 1912, and Samuel Goldwyn, formerly Goldfish, a Warsaw native who came to America around 1895 and emerged as one of the most successful producers in the business after 1913. The desire of these Jewish merchants to sell a more captivating type of product led them almost inevitably to move into control over production. The path taken by Adolph Zukor, in particular, served as a model of the transition from marketing to producing.

To an uncanny degree, Zukor displayed the attentiveness to popular taste which characterized the new approach to marketing. Born in 1873 and orphaned shortly thereafter, Zukor came from a family of small shopkeepers in Ricse, a shtetl that was nestled into the foothills of the Carpathian mountains in eastern Hungary. He arrived at Castle Garden in 1888, learned how to work with fur, and established a successful career as a furrier in Chicago. In 1903, searching for a ripe area of investment, he and a partner from Chicago set up a penny arcade in Manhattan at East 14th Street and Broadway, in the heart of the old entertainment district. Soon after opening the arcade, Zukor sensed that there was enough demand for moving pictures to justify starting two five-cent theaters in the same building. In the new theaters, the young merchant developed a characteristic habit that seemed to epitomize the entrepreneurial impulse to decipher the unarticulated feelings of the consuming public. He would take a seat in the front rows in order to observe the responses of the movie audience, which he believed to be especially sensitive to the images appearing on the screen. "I spent a good deal of time watching the faces of the audience," Zukor recalled, as he made the observation that "with a little experience I could see, hear and 'feel' the reaction to each melodrama and comedy."[11]

Sensing the urge of American urban consumers for a more sophisticated product, Zukor burst into the vanguard of the business by defining a perspective on film marketing that had been only dimly perceived by others. Contrary to the prevailing belief that audiences would not sit through longer movies, Zukor's rapport with city people led him to the conclusion that the public was tiring of the short films on which the American industry was based. He knew prominent theater owners who had begun to curtail the role of moving pictures within the programs of entertainment they presented. Convinced that people would enjoy stories with more elaborate plots and artistic flavor, Zukor began to import longer-playing, high-quality features from Europe. In the summer of 1912, he initiated the concept of presenting audiences with "Famous Players in Famous Plays" as he prepared to introduce the four-reel French film *Queen Elizabeth*. Starring the world-famous, French Jewish actress Sarah Bernhardt, the film broke through the barrier that kept prominent stage actors from performing in movies, which had always been considered an inferior medium.

The innovation underlying the Famous Players Film Company, which planned to set up a rigorous schedule for the production of pictures featuring stage stars, was immediately acclaimed. Declaring that "the famous theatrical stars of both America and Europe have entered the film end of the theatrical business," *The Billboard*, a journal of show business, emphasized that the goal of Adolph Zukor, who was until that time relatively unknown, was to make long-playing pictures that were "strictly first-class and on a higher plane than pictures have ever been put before."[12]

From his experience in the American film marketplace, Zukor understood that his desire to market films of a wholly new caliber would be fulfilled only if he supervised their production. Concerned about the availability of such pictures, and eager to fulfill personally the expectations of the American public, the merchant became a manufacturer. The success of *The Prisoner of Zenda*, the first film made and released by Famous Players, in the winter of 1913, suggested that the American feature film would be the mainstay of a moviegoing public that was quickly becoming conscious of its own importance. Enriched by the involvement of pioneering director Edwin S. Porter, stage star James K. Hackett, and respected theater agent Daniel Frohman, the film elicited from one reviewer the announcement that "with this four-act drama the producers have leaped to the pinnacle of moving picture fame at one gigantic bound."[13]

Soon after the plan to make first-rate films based on the standards of the theater was launched, it became apparent to Zukor that the stars of the stage did not necessarily make the best players on the screen. Consequently, he began to redefine cinematic quality in terms of the preference of moviegoers for charismatic screen personalities. Unlike the old guard of filmmakers, which bridled at the thought of the soaring expense of productions and salaries that would derive from the unleashed torrent of popular demand, the emerging Jewish producers saw the exaltation of movie stars as the key to the future. The discovery that films would sell better once they were identified with fresh screen personalities had been made by Carl Laemmle. Laemmle initiated the star system in movies in the winter of 1910, when he staged a fantastic stunt designed to familiarize the public with the identity of Florence Lawrence, the extremely popular actress who had formerly been known anonymously as "The Biograph Girl." Whereas the well-established Biograph Company, a member of the Motion Picture Patents Company, failed to perceive the eagerness of fans to form cults around their favorite characters, Laemmle understood that the name of the performer, not that of the company for whom she performed, was the monument for which the public, and he himself, was willing to pay extraordinary sums of money. [14]

Recognizing that the presence of stars made the American film highly marketable, Adolph Zukor rushed to exploit the promotional value of movie actors. In 1914, the producer launched a campaign to dominate the marketing of movie stars by hiring Mary Pickford, one of the first stars of the silent screen, for the outlandish salary of 104,000 dollars a year, double what she had been earning at the time. [15] By 1916, having merged with the successful film company of Jesse Lasky and Samuel Goldwyn, Zukor had managed to assemble a dazzling "stable" of film stars, which could be advertised as "the greatest aggregation of celebrated stage and screen favorites ever assembled in the history of the motion picture." [16] The promotional use of movie stars partly resembled that of brand names, insofar as the famous personalities attracted a loyal market of consumers and signified the desirability of the product they embellished.

The rapid evolution of Zukor from merchant to manufacturer suggested that the definition of the American film as a product was determined as much by the commercial vision of street-wise merchants as it was by the artistic perspective and technical expertise of directors and cameramen. In a brief span of years prior to World War I, Jewish entrepreneurs leaped into the breach that had grown between the fluid expectations of movie consumers and the stodgy marketing system of the major producers. As they sought to meet the emerging taste of the public, these individuals took the lead in establishing the full-story length and the screen star as essential attributes of the American film.

The drive to market a more refined product not only entailed the production of star-studded feature films but also determined the mode of exhibition, which represented the "packaging" of the product. Convinced that moving pictures had the potential to be the most luxurious form of mass entertainment in America, Jewish merchants were virtually bound to envision a more elegant cinematic setting than the ordinary nickleodeon could provide. They perceived the physical and sensual context in which films appeared as critical to the moviegoing experience they wanted to provide for consumers.

As had been the case with the innovation of feature films and movie stars, Jews were not alone in transforming the style of moving picture exhibition but they clearly occupied the vanguard of the movement. Already prominent in American show business at the turn of the century, Jews in large cities like New York, Chicago, and Philadelphia, and in smaller cities throughout the country, moved rapidly into the ownership and management of chains of movie houses, which attracted millions of customers who had stayed away from theaters in the past. During the first decade of the century, amid the competition for the nickels and dimes of enthusiastic moviegoers, the owners of storefront theaters and vaudeville houses in cities across the nation vied with each other to refine the methods of showing movies. Month by month, improvements were registered by a host of exhibitors. By the end of the decade, however, the most effective and ambitious merchants of film often turned out to be Jews, and by 1914 the most prestigious movie theaters stood in New York City.

The emergence of the picture palace culminated a developing awareness that the response of consumers was subtly related to the structure in which film was "consumed." As early as 1904, when Adolph Zukor opened his first nickel theater, it was evident that the most ambitious Jewish entrepreneurs imagined the showplace and the picture as an indivisible whole. In contrast to the dingy halls of the day, Zukor's modest theater, situated on the floor above his penny arcade, was approached by ascending a glass staircase beneath which water cascaded over lights of changing colors.[17] Aesthetic improvements expanded the scope of moviegoing, by increasing the importance of the setting to the satisfaction of the audience.

Although the refinement of the nickelodeon represented a significant step in altering the mode of exhibition, the concept of the picture palace was rooted in the awareness that movies could be legitimately marketed through conventional theaters. When Zukor arranged the premiere of *Queen Elizabeth* to take place at Manhattan's prestigious Lyceum Theatre, he was adhering to a trend that had been developing for years, most conspicuously through the ventures of two theater owners raised on the Lower East Side. William Fox, the son of a Hungarian shopkeeper turned machinist in New York City, had been brought as an infant to America from the village of Tulchva, Hungary in 1880. Marcus Loew, the son of an Austrian waiter and a German widow, was born in 1870 into a tenement household on 4th Street near Avenue B. Between 1906 and 1913, Fox and Loew, whose names were to become synonymous with the picture palace of the 1920s, acquired, in the metropolitan area, sizable chains of theaters whose refinement placed these merchants on the cutting edge of movie exhibition. The success of William Fox and Marcus Loew reflected the desire of the public to receive film in a first-rate package, ensconced in the setting of luxury that had been provided for the respectable stage.

The upbringing of these men in the multifaceted leisure environment ⟵

211

of the Lower East Side, which was created purely from the aspirations of hard-working, often barely educated people like themselves, liberated them from preconceptions about the superiority of the stage over the screen. Although Marcus Loew was slower than his good friend Adolph Zukor to recognize the imminent domination of movies over vaudeville, he did not hesitate to place film on a par with stage shows in the high-class theater chain he erected during the nickleodeon era. It was to Loew's ultimate advantage that he had not become entrenched in the stage end of show business, which might have dulled his sensitivity to the rising demand for the refinement of cinema. Instead, he, like Zukor, moved from the fur business into the world of the penny arcade, and he considered himself to have moved up when he began converting these arcades into small movie theaters during the autumn on 1905.

Approaching the entertainment market from the bottom and looking up, Loew was able to sense the viability of renovating dilapidated playhouses in which moving pictures, along with vaudeville, could be marketed on "such a high plane" that the theaters "were not only looked up to but were patronized by the very best people."[18] By 1914, he had developed into an owner of "gold-laden temples of the silent drama" with a swiftness that inspired Robert Grau, one of the earliest chroniclers of the movie industry, to describe his career as "the most extraordinary in the history of the theatre."[19]

Once film began to be marketed in the more elegant structure of the traditional theater, with its majestic proscenium, plush auditorium, and box seats, movie consumers won the unique privilege of expecting first-class treatment at low prices. William Fox recalled that he had originally viewed the film trade as simply a novel way to make fast profits, but that he came to perceive the redeeming social value of providing the majority of people with good quality, low-cost entertainment.[20] In 1908, only five years after he left the garment business for show business, Fox's handling of customers at the newly acquired Dewey Theatre on East 14th Street was cited as "an admirable example of modern showmanship" in the new world of moving pictures.[21] At a price of ten cents for seating on the main floor and a nickel for a place in the gallery, audiences of up to 1,000 people were furnished with a lengthy, well-planned show of movies, vaudeville, and illustrated songs under the supervision of twelve ushers who were attractively outfitted in red uniforms. Integrated into the structure and format of the first-rate theater, film appeared to be the definitive luxury for the majority of urban consumers.

The final step in the redefinition of film marketing was taken by impresarios who envisioned the moving picture as a self-sufficient form of entertainment within the setting of the elegant theater. Outstanding among this group of innovative showmen was Samuel L. Rothapfel, the son of a German Jewish cobbler, who ushered in a distinctive way of "packaging" the feature film. Through the careful orchestration of musical accompaniment, and other aural and visual effects, Rothapfel showed how the silent film could be the sole basis for a spectacular show suited to the best theaters. Unlike the names of William Fox and Marcus Loew, who would be remembered as the heads of great studios in the 1920s, that of Samuel Rothapfel passed into relative obscurity after the silent era ended. Yet the impact of his method upon the first generation of movie consumers was profound.

From the beginning of his career, Rothapfel's unrelenting drive to provide moviegoers with a sophisticated brand of entertainment compelled him to find ways of transforming the silent picture into a full-fledged show. Like many of the other Jewish entrepreneurs in the business, the young showman's perspective on entertainment had been influenced by the milieu of the Lower East Side, where he moved with his family from Minnesota in 1894, at the age of twelve. At fourteen, he started out working as a clerk in a 14th Street department store, which may have implanted in the youngster an awareness of the sophisticated way in which the modern urban consumer had to be treated. In 1907, after spending several years in the Marines and then as a baseball player, the barely educated Rothapfel ended up in Forest City, Pennsylvania, where he started a nickel movie theater in the back room of the beer-and-frankfurter saloon of Julius Freedman, his prospective father-in-law.[22]

Within the remarkably short span of three years, "Roxy," as the young Rothapfel had been called since his days as a baseball player, had gained the reputation of being the model exhibitor of moving pictures. In the winter of 1910, when he was invited by the trade journal *Moving Picture World* to write an advice column on film exhibition, the prodigy declared under the title "Dignity of the Exhibitor's Profession" that "the day of the ignorant exhibitor with his side-show methods" was "a thing of the past." The destiny of the movie theater would lie with managers who knew how "to make the people forget" that they were paying only five or ten cents for their entertainment."[23]

Critical to Roxy's method of retailing film was the subtle addition of sound. The showman sensed the yearning of silent film audiences for an extra dimension of experience that blended with the images on the screen. Despite a lack of formal education in music, he was able to infuse a new aura of artistry and prestige into the movie theater by orchestrating musical and oratorical extravaganzas to enhance the films themselves. In doing so, he affirmed the idea that moving pictures were a self-sufficient form of entertainment that need not be intermingled with vaudeville routines. Within the impressive confines of large theaters that increasingly turned to the presentation of films, Rothapfel gave his audiences a standard of sophisticated showmanship for the price of a few coins.

During the autumn of 1911, when Roxy managed the 1,700-seat Lyric Theater in Minneapolis, the twenty-nine-year-old impresario demonstrated that the proper supplementation of special effects allowed the feature film to be sold as a self-sufficient type of entertainment, freed from the addition of vaudeville. The musical and dramatic effects staged at the Lyric were cited as the outstanding example of how to furnish moviegoers with a "straight-picture show," one that contained no vaudeville, and they earned Rothapfel the title "the Belasco of Motion Picture Presentations," after David Belasco, a Jewish theatrical manager from San Francisco who dominated the American stage at the time. [24]

The ingenious intermingling of music, light, and oratory that made for a successful season at the Lyric culminated in Roxy's presentation of *The Passion Play* at Christmas time. Heralded by the solemn tones of the theater's pipe organ and by the spraying of a light mist of perfume of lilies over the auditorium, the film began. A soft blue light was thrown over the fountain that was obscured by palms in the front of the theater. A chorus of twenty boys and several operatic soloists, all dressed in white vestments, appeared on the stage, which was strewn with dozens of roses. At appropriate points of the film, the staff of professional musicians and singers performed a variety of Christmas songs, concluding with the Hallelujah chorus of Handel's Messiah. The public response to Roxy's pageantry was overwhelming—the film, which was scheduled for a conventional four-day run, had to be held over for an additional week. [25]

Once the star-centered feature film had emerged as the focal point of a great show, the picture palace could be introduced as the model of luxury for the multitude. The indispensability of Roxy's marketing technique to the unique effect of the modern movie theater was proven at the opening of the Regent and the Strand in Manhattan, which heralded the era of the picture palace. These theaters furnished the multitude of city people with a forum for entertainment comparable to the opulent opera house that had been created for the wealthy during the late nineteenth century. Within them, the aim of Jewish entrepreneurs to market film as a luxury item was completed, and unified with the expectation of American consumers.

For several years, elegant playhouses had been featuring moving pictures, but the Regent, located at 116th Street and Seventh Avenue and reopened in November 1913 under the management of Rothapfel, has been considered the first deluxe theater designed explicitly for the showing of movies.[26] The building had a white and green Venetian-styled facade and a glass canopy that covered and illuminated the sidewalk with hundreds of electric lights. Inside, a brightly lit, richly carpeted lobby, paneled with mirrors, opened on each side to broad marble stairways with fine-quality green carpeting running along the center toward the auditorium, which was decorated with massive wood carvings and gold flourishes across the walls and ceiling. For ten and fifteen cents, moviegoers won the privilege of sitting in the plush environs of the Regent and experiencing what a "master builder" of film presentations could do with motion pictures.

The physical setting of the picture palace would have been hollow without a style of exhibition emphasizing the quality of romantic fantasy that was unique to cinema. On opening night, the standing-room-only crowd came under the influence of Roxy's "magic wand," as one observer described it. The arrangement of lighting around the fountain at the front of the auditorium and of the floral displays near the orchestra pit, the orchestration of a tasteful selection of musical pieces to conform to the various countries and themes portrayed in the films of the day, and the synchronization of visual and musical effects with the pace of the films evinced the feeling that the Regent might be called "the Theater of Realization," because it fulfilled the unexpressed desires of the audience for a mesmerizing show.[27]

Less than half a year later, the opening of the Regent was eclipsed by the opening of the Strand, where Roxy managed to identify the refinement of film exhibition as a foremost expression of the American national character. Crafted by Thomas Lamb, the architect who had remodeled the Regent, the Strand, located on Broadway and 47th Street, appears to have been the first deluxe theater built for the movies. Consequently, on opening night, April 11, 1914, the possibilities of the immense, 3,000-seat hall for transporting moviegoers to a dimension of utter luxury were immediately evident. Thousands of people crowded around the building, entranced by the artificial flash of lightning that alternated with the words THE STRAND on the huge electric sign overhead. To handle the vast public anticipating the opening of the Strand, Roxy had organized a "little army" of ushers and doorkeepers that was elegantly attired and extremely well behaved, as if it had been "trained in a school of Chesterfieldian principles."[28] Created to serve the ten-and-twenty-cent public with the type of dignity that had once been reserved for the affluent, the well-groomed staff personified the aim of the American movie house to become the palace of the average man and woman.

The Strand represented a deliberate effort to transcend whatever sense of democratic luxury had already been established in movie theaters. Whereas Roxy had organized a fifteen-person orchestra at the Regent, he boasted a symphony orchestra of fifty musicians at the Strand, in addition to a prodigious 40,000-dollar organ. To emphasize the commitment to total entertainment, the theater possessed a tango-restaurant that stayed open every night until one in the morning. As a suggestion of the house's capacity to serve the public in all respects, an emergency hospital was built into the premises. To encourage the notion of the movie palace as a home away from home for the multitude of city people, there was a cafeteria for "working girls" serving lunch to crowds of young women, as many as 1,500 each day during the first year of the Strand's life. These facilities helped to account for a daily attendance of unparalleled proportions: 10,000 each day of the week and 14,000 every Sunday.

Possessing "more Italian marble, Florentine mosaic, costly frescoing, velvet and cloth of gold than any so-called legitimate theatre in America," the palace displayed not only flamboyant highlights, such as mirrors framed in crystal and gold, but, moreover, several unusual artistic and architectural effects that expressed the essence of the American movie theater as a place of transcendence for the masses. The walls of the auditorium were decorated with murals representing the senses, as if the great hall itself could contain the manifold mysteries of human sensation. Above the proscenium, a spacious painting of "The Dreams of Life" justified the innermost desires of the audience to gain some relief from daily toil and anxiety. Finally, the mezzanine of the Strand was a rotunda opening into a great marble court, from which promenading moviegoers could look out over the expanse of the auditorium. The architecture of the theater not only allowed people to behold the spectacle of the modern moving picture show; it gave them an additional vantage point from which they could comprehend their own wonderment. From this position of superiority, individual moviegoers easily felt as if the palace had been designed exclusively for them.[29]

As the structure of the Strand strained to make people feel thoroughly at home in the luxury of the moving picture world, Roxy bent his formidable talents toward the same end. The extraordinary shows of America's leading movie manager had always been designed to accustom audiences to a higher standard of artistry than had been thought possible in connection with moving pictures. Focusing on the rigorous training of ushers, on the meticulous rehearsal of musical scores, and on the precise deployment of lighting and visual effects, Roxy's perfectionism aimed at creating a show of perfect synchrony and subtlety, one that allowed movie audiences untutored in luxury to feel comfortable. Every detail of the presentation was put in place, with the result that it seemed completely natural to have a setting of first-class entertainment for the viewing of moving pictures that had once been confined to dingy store-front theaters. The harmony of Roxy's ambitions with the design of the Strand, which was characterized as "a theater in which a master exhibitor like Rothapfel can do himself full justice," generated the unmistakable impression that "the ideal temple of the motion picture art" had emerged.[30]

On opening night, Roxy strove to demonstrate that the new style of presenting film was grounded in the heritage of America. Impulses of patriotism that had inspired the young man during his service with the Marines, and feelings of democratic comradery that had flowed from his experiences on the baseball field, now found ultimate expression in the movie house. The feature film of the evening, the summit toward which all of the manager's effects would have to move, was *The Spoilers*, a robust picture, over two hours in length, that told a story of the Alaskan gold rush of the late 1890s. Bound for a highly successful run, *The Spoilers* was "a red-blooded story, saturated through and through with the spirit of the 'Old West,' " in which the common man's "sense of elemental justice" on the frontier overcame "the semblance of law" erected by crooked politicians in Washington.[31] Blending with the motif of the upcoming film—the superiority of the common man as the root of American democracy—the atmosphere at the Strand on opening night was one in which ordinary people mixed with stars such as William Farnum, the hero of *The Spoilers*, and William N. Selig, the "self-made" movie magnate who produced the film.

Aware of the powerful undercurrent of emotion that would sweep the audience toward the focus of the night's show, Roxy hesitated until the crowd grew slightly restless, waiting in the semidarkness of the Strand for the action to begin. Then, suddenly, several loud bursts of sound, like the firing of heavy artillery, created an instantaneous stillness in the auditorium. After a few seconds had passed, the orchestra again surprised the crowd by starting to play "The Star Spangled Banner." In a few more moments, there appeared on the screen a succession of images from the War of 1812, on which the anthem was based. As the audience recognized "the happy inspiration of sending the new theater on its career to the strains of patriotic music with this rare glimpse of American glory," it rose as one to applaud Roxy's imagination, which had become its own.[32]

217

The Culture of Marketing

The customers at the Strand in April 1914 were hailing a type of show that would have been unimaginable ten, or even five, years earlier. Over the course of a decade, a whole new approach to the selling of the American film had been elaborated, principally through the vision of Jewish entrepreneurs seeking to cultivate the ultimate market for mass entertainment. In the marketing acumen of men like Adolph Zukor, Carl Laemmle, William Fox, Marcus Loew, Samuel Rothapfel, and other ambitious, idealistic entrepreneurs, Jewish and American aspirations toward a state of democratic luxury attained a high point of convergence. Beyond the goals of money, position, and power that motivated most businessmen, the cultural aim of Jewish commerce bound the individual producers and exhibitors of this unusual generation into a coherent whole. These entrepreneurs articulated through the marketplace of entertainment the persistent yearning for a higher style of life that Jewish newcomers generally shared and passed down to their children.

Carried by the great flow of Jewish immigration, entrepreneurs explored new ways of marketing the essential luxuries of modern city life. From pushcarts to picture palaces, they enriched American urban culture by extending the range of possibilities open to consumers. Through these individuals, including the nameless fur vendors who remained on Grand Street as well as the movie magnates who migrated to Hollywood, the striving of the average, hopeful immigrant was transmitted to the larger society, translated into the terms of daily trade, and transformed by the American pursuit of material abundance.

Epilogue

In moving from eastern Europe to America, Jews moved from a world of scarcity to a world of abundance. Like the vast majority of immigrants in the era before the First World War, they were deeply impressed by this stark contrast in material condition. As consumers, immigrants could possess things that only the affluent had in their native lands, and, once they decided to settle in America, they could gain a sense of social membership more quickly as consumers than as workers.

Unlike most other newcomers, Jews intended from the start to establish themselves in American society, and they soon recognized the prospect of identifying with Americans as consumers. They came to understand that a society of abundance required a special mode of behavior, one based on constant effort to raise the standard of living. In adapting to the new way of life, they inevitably acquired a new perspective, one defined by the awareness of abundance, the sense that surplus would govern the American future as it had the past.

The new attitude upset one of the bases of traditional Jewish culture, the distinction between the holy and the mundane that enabled Jews to preserve their relationship to God. In the common culture of the shtetls and ghettos of Poland, Russia, Galicia, and Rumania, the Sabbath and festive holidays had been reinforced by the selective use of luxuries. By virtue of the environment of material scarcity in which Jews lived, these special items of food, clothing, and houseware contrasted starkly with their day-to-day counterparts, and they therefore gave a rich physical dimension to the splendor that was to fill the holy days.

In urban America, where luxuries were routinely transformed into necessities, material objects ceased to serve this spiritual purpose. Moreover, the lure of consumption hastened the decline of traditional Judaism, which culminated in the conversion of the Sabbath into a shopping day. Yet Jews were able to integrate American and Jewish attitudes toward material luxury in the celebration of three important holidays, Sukkot, Chanukah, and Passover. The newcomers' awareness of abundance thus figured prominently in the expression of an American Jewish identity, which depended heavily on these occasions. In shifting their cultural identity from eastern Europe to America, Jews shifted their attitude toward the role of luxuries. Whereas before, these objects had elevated the dignity of the ordinary Jew as a partner in the divine covenant, afterward they raised the dignity of the ordinary Jew as an American consumer.

The most conspicuous symbol of the changed status of Jewish immigrants was the new suit of clothes. Jews adapted readily to American fashion because it communicated plainly their intention to fit into American society. Intensive involvement in the garment business and retail trade of New York City reinforced an interest in clothing, but Jewish sensitivity to American appearance stemmed from the pervasive desire for self-transformation, the willingness to seek a new identity instead of clinging to the old, that animated these immigrants.

Without the influence of Jewish women over domestic consumption, the impulse toward cultural assimilation would have been inhibited. Extending the traditional role of the *baleboste* in America, homemakers exerted control over the consumption habits of their families, taking the lead in urging newcomers to become more American through their capacity as consumers. Combining a sharp discrimination in regard to merchandise with an astute flexibility in relation to their children's desire for American ways, Jewish women expedited the search for an American identity.

The increasing influence of Jewish women propelled newcomers toward new American forms of leisure and encouraged them to adopt the habit of treating, which reflected the relatively carefree attitude toward spending money that derived from the perspective of abundance. The most striking change in Jewish leisure involved the practice of vacationing. As they created a distinctly Jewish version of the American vacation, eastern Europeans introduced the concept of the summer vacation as a convention for ordinary families. Although Jews turned out a large audience for dances, theater, vaudeville, and movies, the vacation outside of the city held special significance, addressing the vision of an earthly paradise that had been carried to America.

The attainment of a parlor and a piano marked the rising dignity of the ordinary person in America. These ideals of home furnishing provided a secular outlet for the traditional Jewish belief in dignifying the individual through the creation of a Sabbatical atmosphere in the home. Appropriate to the comparatively home-centered social life of Jewish newcomers, the piano enabled people to use popular music as a way of adapting their attitudes and values to American society, and it served also as an instrument of social refinement. The culminating object of the parlor, the piano endowed the unsettled immigrant family with moments of unity and stability in a disorienting urban world.

Advertising provided another medium of contact and convergence for Jewish and American attitudes. Aiming to embrace a wide audience of Jews, the Yiddish press in America rose to prominence and authority around the turn of the century. Quickly incorporating dominant trends in American journalism and advertising, the leading newspapers emerged as excellent media for national advertisers, who came to identify Jewish newcomers as a distinct market during the 1890s. These major corporations skillfully addressed Jewish concerns and adapted Jewish themes in their advertisements. In turn, Jews found that the products of some American businesses were suited to their own needs. The reconciliation of traditional Jewish attitudes with the values and images promoted by American advertisers quickened the integration of newcomers into the larger society. Through American advertising in the Yiddish press, Jews absorbed the belief that the products of the American corporation were a mark of national superiority.

The sensitivity to American marketing displayed by the Yiddish press appeared as well in the activity of Jewish merchants. Supported by a venerable commercial tradition, newcomers moved by the thousands into the streets of the American city, turning the vast potential of urban consumers into the reality of pushcart markets that became a true medium of mass consumption. By means of street marketing, immigrants unfamiliar with American ways were nonetheless able to make a strong impression on their environment. They turned streets that had once been mere produce outlets into emporia of merchandise that gave a touch of reality to the immigrants' expectations that the new world would be overflowing with goods. In the period before World War I, the most conspicuous achievement of Jewish merchants was the transformation of American film from a relatively crude entertainment into a sophisticated show housed in elaborate theaters. Movie entrepreneurs were steeped in the rich leisure environment created by Jewish newcomers, and their innovations in marketing film to urban Americans directly reflected the lessons and inspiration gained from that world.

Jewish commerce blossomed in America, not only in the fields of street and movie marketing, which were reshaped by Jews, but also in the clothing industry and the music business, because of the potential for mass consumption that characterized American abundance. The effect of this element of American society must be measured not only by the degree to which Jews adopted American modes of consumption but also by the extent to which they extended them. As the twentieth century unfolded, the involvement of Jews in consumer-oriented trade would only increase. Just as movie pioneers like Adolph Zukor had benefited from alliances with American Jews prominent in show business, they, and their colleagues in the newer fields of radio and subsequently television, would sponsor the creative efforts of many young Jewish performers, writers, directors, and producers. Entrepreneurship and artistry were intertwined in the growth of these media, giving Jewish commerce a cultural dimension. Far from a purely economic phenomenon, the Jewish commercial tradition in America played a basic role in the cultural adaptation of the group.

Because the American impact on Jews and the Jewish impact on America was pronounced in the area of mass consumption, a large chapter in the story of Jewish acculturation must be focused there.

The movement into a society of abundance affected immigrants of all backgrounds. Depending on their motivation to fit into American society, their comprehension of American modes of consumption, and their cultural tendencies, newcomers perceived American products differently and emulated American consumers to varying degrees. The specific response of groups other than the Jews remains to be studied.

Eastern European Jews possessed a number of traits that enabled them rapidly to identify themselves as Americans through consumption: the motivation to settle in America rather than repatriate, the transplantation of families rather than single men, comparative youthfulness and cosmopolitanism, the distinctive position of the Jewish homemaker, the comparative domesticity of Jewish social life, the dynamic evolution of the Yiddish press as an advertising medium, a rich commercial tradition, and, finally, running like a thread through the experience of cultural adaptation, a unique perspective on the inspirational capacity of material luxuries. The traditional, spiritual meaning of luxury ended in the secular environment of urban America, but Jews relied on their awareness of the symbolic potential of special products as they searched for a tangible American identity.

Creating elements of a new cultural identity with consumer goods, Jews showed great resourcefulness in overcoming the barrier of alienation that initially faced all immigrants. Their adaptation to American abundance illuminated the importance of the symbolic world of immigrants. Luxury items that had once symbolized the richness of holy days in the Jewish world, were turned into emblems of secular adjustment and progress in America. The components of the American standard of living—fashionable attire, the vacation, the parlor and piano, the nationally advertised product—satisfied not just the desire for a more comfortable and prestigious existence but also the psychological need of newcomers to express profound and subtle aspirations bound up with the ordeal of immigration and assimilation.

In the precarious world of newcomers, where the unknown loomed large and the familiar receded into the past, where tradition failed to support the eternal struggle with disorder, where nothing, not even one's name, seemed to escape the winds of change, the effort to create a meaningful life with new products must be recorded as an example of human creativity and inspiration.

Notes

Introduction. Consumption:
A Bridge Between Cultures

1. The results of recent research on this subject by Russell W. Belk, a scholar in the field of marketing, are most easily found in "My Possessions, Myself," *Psychology Today* (July–August 1988), 22:51–52. A more in-depth sense of the state of the art in the psychology of consumption, which contains citations of Belk's innovative work in the area, can be gotten from Melanie Wallendorf and Eric J. Arnould, " 'My Favorite Things': A Cross-Cultural Inquiry into Object Attachment, Possessiveness, and Social Linkage," *Journal of Consumer Research* (March 1988), 14:531–547. See also the papers given for a panel chaired by Belk at the 1987 Annual Conference of the Association for Consumer Research, investigating "The Deep Meaning of Possessions," *Advances in Consumer Research* (1988) 15:528–553.

2. Carl J. Friedrich, ed., *The Philosophy of Hegel* (New York, 1954), pp. 249–250. Hegel's discussion of consumption forms part of his *Philosophy of Right and Law*, which was published in 1821.

3. This definition of culture comes from the *International Encyclopedia of the Social Sciences*, 18 vols. (1968), 3:533, which cites Raymond W. Firth, *Elements of Social Organization* (New York, 1951), p. 27.

4. Mary Douglas and Baron Isherwood, *The World of Goods* (New York, 1979), p. 65.

5. James S. Duesenberry notes that concern about a rising standard of living

is a dominant aspect of American consumer behavior, *Income, Saving, and the Theory of Consumer Behavior* (Cambridge, Mass., 1949), p. 26.

6. See the essay, "The Significance of the Frontier in American History," in Frederick Jackson Turner, *The Frontier in American History* (New York, 1920).

7. David M. Potter, *People of Plenty: Economic Abundance and the American Character* (Chicago, 1966). This analysis of American culture first appeared in 1954.

8. Daniel J. Boorstin, *The Americans: The Democratic Experience* (New York, 1973); Gunther Barth, *City People: The Rise of Modern City Culture in Nineteenth-Century America* (New York, 1980).

9. Philip Gleason, "American Identity and Americanization," in Stephan Thernstrom, ed., *Harvard Encyclopedia of American Ethnic Groups* (Cambridge, Mass., 1980), p. 56.

10. The suggestion was first made by sociologist David Riesman in his introduction to Elliott E. Cohen, ed., *Commentary on the American Scene* (New York, 1953), pp. xvi–xvii. More recently, Elizabeth C. Hirschman has pointed out the lack of scholarly inquiry into the relationship between ethnicity and consumer behavior and has undertaken preliminary research which seems to confirm the hypothesis that Jews are innovative consumers, "American Jewish Ethnicity: Its Relationship to Some Selected Aspects of Consumer Behavior," *Journal of Marketing* (Summer, 1981), 45:102–110; also, "Religious Differences in Cognitions Regarding Novelty Seeking and Information Transfer," *Advances in Consumer Research* (1981) 9:228–233.

11. Daniel Miller, *Material Culture and Mass Consumption* (Oxford, 1987), pp. 3–4.

12. A few articles have focused on the aim of immigrants to adopt the American standard of living. Irish consumer behavior over several decades, as reflected in government studies of household budgets, is examined by John Modell, "Patterns of Consumption, Acculturation, and Family Income Strategies in Late Nineteenth-Century America," in Tamara K. Hareven and Maris A. Vinovskis, eds., *Family and Population in Nineteenth-Century America* (Princeton, N.J., 1978), pp. 206–240. Ewa Morawska discusses the attitude of peasants from Austria-Hungary and Poland toward new possessions in " 'For Bread with Butter': Life Worlds of Peasant Immigrants from East Central Europe, 1880–1914," *Journal of Social History* (Spring 1984) 17:387–404; Dorothee Schneider examines aspects of domestic consumption among Germans in New York City in the early 1880s in " 'For Whom Are All the Good Things in Life?' German-American Housewives Discuss Their Budgets," in Hartmut Keil and John B. Jentz, eds., *German Workers in Industrial Chicago, 1850–1910* (DeKalb, Ill., 1983); Lizabeth A. Cohen, "Embellishing a Life of Labor: An Interpretation of the Material Culture of American Working-Class Homes, 1885–1915," *Journal of American Culture* (Winter 1980), 3:752–775, does not focus on immigrants but does touch on the household furnishings of newcomers.

13. This view is taken by Elizabeth Ewen, *Immigrant Women in the Land of Dollars: Life and Culture on the Lower East Side, 1890–1925* (New York, 1985).

14. Alfred Gell, "Newcomers to the World of Goods: Consumption among the Muria Gonds," in Arjun Appadurai, ed., *The Social Life of Things: Commodities in Cultural Perspective* (Cambridge, England, 1986), p. 111.

15. Grant McCracken, *Culture and Consumption: New Approaches to the Symbolic Character of Consumer Goods and Activities* (Bloomington, Ind., 1988), p. 137.

16. Horace M. Kallen, "Democracy Versus the Melting-Pot: A Study of American Nationality," *Nation* (February 18, 1915), 100:192.

17. Robert E. Park and Herbert A. Miller, *Old World Traits Transplanted* (New York, 1921), pp. 43–44.

18. Milton Gordon, *Assimilation in American Life: The Role of Race, Religion, and National Origins* (New York, 1964), p. 79.

19. *Ibid.*, p. 77.

20. Park and Miller, *Old World Traits*, p. 276; C. Bezalel Sherman, *The Jew within American Society: A Study in Ethnic Individuality* (Detroit, 1965), p. 26. First published in 1960, this study derived from the Yiddish volume, *Yidn un Andere Etnische Grupes in di Fareynikte Shtatn (Jews and Other Ethnic Groups in the United States)* that appeared in 1948.

21. John E. Bodnar, *The Transplanted: A History of Immigrants in Urban America* (Bloomington, Ind., 1985), pp. 118, 169–183.

22. Stephan Thernstrom, *Poverty and Progress: Social Mobility in a Nineteenth Century City* (New York, 1974), p. 136, first published in 1964; Thomas Kessner, *The Golden Door: Italian and Jewish Immigrant Mobility in New York City, 1880–1915* (New York, 1977), p. 171. John J. Bukowczyk's recent study of Polish immigrants, *And My Children Did Not Know Me: A History of the Polish-Americans* (Bloomington, Ind., 1987) upholds the underconsumption thesis, although Ewa Morawska's work on Slavik immigrants in Pennsylvania recognizes the impact of the American standard of living on these newcomers. In addition to the article cited in note 12 above, see her full study of *For Bread With Butter: The Life-Worlds of East Central Europeans in Johnstown, Pennsylvania, 1890–1940* (Cambridge, 1985), pp. 115–116.

23. This argument was made in the influential article by Nathan Glazer, "Social Characteristics of American Jews, 1654–1954," *American Jewish Year Book* (1955) 56:30–32. See also Arkadius Kahan, "Economic Opportunities and Some Pilgrims' Progress: Jewish Immigrants from Eastern Europe in the U. S., 1890–1914," *Journal of Economic History* (March 1978), 38:250, which contends that Jewish immigrants saved money by maintaining "a largely pre-immigration consumption level" for several years after arrival.

24. Emphasis on the 1920s as the seedbed of modern mass consumption is widespread. A few general histories of the period to hold this view are George E. Mowry, ed., *The Twenties: Fords, Flappers, and Fanatics* (Englewood Cliffs, N.J., 1963); Robert Sklar, ed., *The Plastic Age, 1917–1930* (New York, 1970); James J. Flink, *The Car Culture* (Cambridge, Mass., 1982), p. 140; Robert S. McElvaine, *The Great Depression: America, 1929–1941* (n.p., 1984), pp. 40–41.

25. Harold G. Vatter, "Has There Been a Twentieth-Century Consumer Durable Revolution?" *Journal of Economic History* (March 1967), 27:9–10.

26. See the discussion of installment buying in chapter 1 of this study.

27. Rolla M. Tryon, *Household Manufactures in the United States 1640–1860* (Chicago, 1917), pp. 217, 225, 248; Albert S. Bolles, *Industrial History of the United States* (Norwich, Conn., 1889), p. 399, a detailed history of American manufactures originally published in 1878; F. J. Warne, "The Rise in the Standard of Living," *Good Housekeeping* (October 1910), 51:394; Arthur I. Judge, ed., *A History of the Canning Industry* (Baltimore, 1914); Elizabeth Bacon, "The Growth of Household Conveniences in the United States, 1865–1900" (Ph.D. thesis, Radcliffe, 1942); Margaret L. Brew, "American Clothing Consumption, 1879–1909" (Ph.D. thesis, University of Chicago, 1945).

28. "Ready Made Housekeeping," *Good Housekeeping* (October 1, 1887), 5:266.

29. Kenneth L. Ames, "Grand Rapids Furniture at the Time of the Centennial," *Winterthur Portfolio* (1975), 10:23–50; May N. Stone, "The Plumbing Paradox: American Attitudes Toward Late Nineteenth-Century Domestic Sanitary Arrangements," *Winterthur Portfolio* (Autumn 1979), 14:283–309.

30. See the increasing number of articles on the "Cost of Living" and "Standard of Living" that are listed in the *Readers' Guide to Periodical Literature*, vols. 1–3, covering the years 1900–1914.

31. Massachusetts Commission on the Cost of Living, *Report* (Boston, 1910), pp. 494–495.

32. Douglas, *World of Goods;* Miller, *Material Culture and Mass Consumption;* McCracken, *Culture and Consumption.*

33. In a summary of the field of consumer research, Elizabeth C. Hirschman has emphasized the lack of "an integrated framework for the analysis of symbolic consumption." See "Comprehending Symbolic Consumption: Three Theoretical Issues," in Elizabeth C. Hirschman and Morris B. Holbrook, eds., *Symbolic Consumer Behavior* (Ann Arbor, 1980), p. 4.

34. Arjun Appadurai, "Introduction: Commodities and the Politics of Value," in Appadurai, ed., *Social Life of Things*, p. 38; for a comprehensive review of the scholarly literature on consumption as a means of communication, see Rebecca H. Holman, "Product Use as Communication: A Fresh Appraisal of a Venerable Topic," in Ben M. Enis and Kenneth J. Roering, eds., *Review of Marketing, 1981* (Chicago, 1981), pp. 106–119.

35. McCracken discusses the tendency of consumers to create a relationship between products and thus to see them as fitting together in a whole, *Culture and Consumption*, pp. 119–129.

36. Moses Rischin, *The Promised City: New York's Jews, 1870–1914* (Cambridge, Mass., 1977), pp. 92–94. *The Promised City* appeared in 1962.

37. Daniel Horowitz, "Consumption and Its Discontents: Simon Patten, Thorstein Veblen, and George Gunton," *Journal of American History* (September 1980), 67:301–318; Daniel Horowitz, *The Morality of Spending: Attitudes Toward the Consumer Society in America, 1875–1940* (Baltimore, 1985). The critical response of American novelists to elite and mass consumption in the late 1800s and early 1900s is analyzed by Neil Harris, "The Drama of Consumer Desire," in Otto

1. Perspective of Abundance

Mayr and Robert C. Post, eds., *Yankee Enterprise: The Rise of the American System of Manufactures* (Washington, D.C., 1981), pp. 189–216.

38. José Ortega y Gasset, *La Rebelión de las Masas* (Madrid, 1981), p. 134. The original text was published in 1930.

39. Bernard Rosenberg and David Manning White, eds., *Mass Culture: The Popular Arts in America* (New York, 1964), p. 9. This anthology was first published in 1958.

40. Karl Marx, *Capital: A Critique of Political Economy*, 3 vols. (New York, 1974), 1:71–72. The first German edition of *Das Kapital*, vol. 1, was published in 1867. The English edition, edited by Frederick Engels, appeared in 1887, four years after the author's death.

41. One of the leading advocates of Marxist cultural history today is Raymond Williams. See his collection of essays, *Problems in Materialism and Culture* (London, 1980). Consumption in France has been interpreted by several scholars as a vehicle for asserting the dominance of "bourgeois" attitudes. See Roland Barthes, *Mythologies* (New York, 1972), which was first published in 1957; Rosalind H. Williams, *Dream Worlds: Mass Consumption in Late Nineteenth-Century France* (Berkeley, 1982); and Pierre Bourdieu, *Distinction: A Social Critique of the Judgement of Taste* (Cambridge, Mass., 1984). An orthodox Marxist analysis of consumption is found in Edmond Preteceille and Jean-Pierre Terrail, *Capitalism, Consumption, and Needs* (Oxford, 1985), which was first published in 1977. The influence of Marxist analysis on American studies may be seen in Richard W. Fox and T. Jackson Lears, eds., *The Culture of Consumption: Essays in American History, 1860–1960* (New York, 1983). Speculation about the relation of American consumption to immigrants and people abroad may be found in Stuart and Elizabeth Ewen, "Americanization and Consumption," *Telos* (Fall 1978) 37:42–51.

42. Meyer Levin, *The Old Bunch* (New York, 1937), p. 232.

43. Jacques Maritain, *Reflections on America* (New York, 1958), p. 33.

1. The Perspective of Abundance

1. The connection between advertising and an economy of surplus is noted by David Potter, *People of Plenty: Economic Abundance and the American Character* (Chicago, 1954), pp. 172–173.

2. Richard Goldthwaite, "An Economic Analysis of Luxury Demand in Renaissance Italy," a paper included in symposium "Medieval Workshop: Consumption and Economic Change," *Journal of Economic History* (June 1985), 45:447; Jan de Vries, *Economy of Europe in an Age of Crisis, 1600–1750* (New york, 1976), pp. 176–182; Joan Thirsk, *Economic Policy and Projects: The Development of a Consumer Society in Early Modern Europe* (Oxford, 1978), pp. 162–169, 178–179; see also Neil McKendrick, John Brewer, and J. H. Plumb, *The Birth of a Consumer Society: The Commercialization of Eighteenth-Century England* (Bloomington, Ind., 1982).

3. Quoted from Thirsk, *Economic Policy and Projects*, p. 175.

1. Perspective of Abundance

4. One of the early official reports on the condition of European workers in comparison to Americans is Edward Young, Chief of the United States Bureau of Statistics, *Labor in Europe and America* (Washington, D.C., 1876), pp. 403, 820; the extensive literature on the standard of living in nineteenth-century Europe is summarized and cited in Theodore S. Hamerow, *The Birth of a New Europe: State and Society in the Nineteenth Century* (Chapel Hill, N.C., 1983), pp. 121–148.

5. Paul A. David and Peter Solar, "A Bicentenary Contribution to the History of the Cost of Living in America," in Paul Uselding, ed., *Research in Economic History*, 2 vols. (Greenwich, Conn., 1977), 2:39; C. D. Long, *Wages and Earnings in the United States, 1860–1980* (Princeton, N.J., 1960), p. 61; Albert Rees, *Real Wages in Manufacturing, 1890–1914* (Princeton, N.J., 1961), p. 5.

6. Dorothy Brady, "Consumption and the Style of Life," in Lance Davis et al., *American Economic Growth* (New York, 1972), p. 83; Elizabeth Bacon, "The Growth of Household Conveniences in the United States, 1865–1900" (Ph.D. thesis, Radcliffe, 1942), p. 56; F. J. Warne, "The Rise in the Standard of Living," *Good Housekeeping* (October, 1910), 51:395; Elsa G. Herzfeld, *Family Monographs: The History of Twenty-Four Families Living in the Middle West Side of New York City* (New York, 1905), pp. 6, 12, 16–17, 124; Louise Bolard More, *Wage-Earners' Budgets: Study of Standards and Cost of Living in New York* (New York, 1907), pp. 139, 195; Thomas Jesse Jones, *Sociology of a New York City Block* (New York, 1904), p. 44.

7. Robert H. Bremner, *From the Depths: The Discovery of Poverty in the United States* (New York, 1972), pp. 125, 128–29. The book was first published in 1956. The emerging definition of the American standard of living is found in the numerous budget studies conducted by social workers, many of which are cited in Frank Streightoff, *The Standard of Living Among the Industrial People of America* (New York, 1911).

8. United States Bureau of Labor, *Fourth Annual Report of the Commissioner of Labor, 1888* (Washington, D.C., 1889), p. 20.

9. Pierre Emile Levasseur, *The American Workman* (Baltimore, 1900), p. 431; British Board of Trade, *Cost of Living*, p. lxix.

10. Wright's data were not culled from a random sample of workers and thus may be exaggerated. Nevertheless, Edgar W. Martin surmised that the wage-earning family at mid-century spent at least half of its income on food; *The Standard of Living in 1860: American Consumption Levels on the Eve of the Civil War* (Chicago, 1942), p. 398. Economic historians have conservatively estimated the portion of the budget devoted to food to have been 57.4 percent between 1851 and 1880 and then to have declined to 42.5 percent during the decade 1880–1890; David and Solar, in Uselding, *Research in Economic History*, p. 25.

11. New York State Bureau of Labor Statistics, *Twenty-Fifth Report, 1907* (New York, 1908), p. xxxviii; New York State Bureau of Statistics of Labor, *Tenth Annual Report, 1892* (New York, 1893), p. 315; More, *Wage-Earners' Budgets*, p. 55; Robert Coit Chapin, *Standard of Living Among Workingmen's Families in New York City* (New York, 1909), pp. 123, 137; Sue Ainslee Clark and Edith Wyatt,

1. Perspective of Abundance

Making Both Ends Meet: The Income and Outlay of New York Working Girls (New York, 1911), pp. 18, 20, 25–26, 50, 52.

12. United States Department of Commerce and Labor, *Bulletin of the Bureau of Labor* (July 1904), 9:705–706; "Food Cost of an Average Family," *World's Work* (April 1905), 9:6011.

13. British Board of Trade, *Cost of Living*, pp. xxxiii, lxxii–lxxiii, lxxxvi, lxxxviii; More, *Wage-Earners; Budgets*, p. 209.

14. Caroline Goodyear, "Household Budgets of the Poor," *Charities* (May 5, 1906), 16:194.

15. "Discussion on Standards of Living," *National Conference of Charities and Correction, Proceedings* (1906), pp. 516–517; S. E. Forman, "Conditions of Living Among the Poor," *Bulletin of the United States Bureau of Labor* (May 1906), 64:601.

16. David A. Wells, *Recent Economic Changes* (New York, 1889), p. 387.

17. George Katona, Burkhard Strumpel, and Ernest Zahn, *Aspirations and Affluence* (New York, 1971), pp. 41–73.

18. Alexis de Tocqueville, *Democracy in America*, Richard D. Heffner, ed. (New York, 1956), p. 171. Tocqueville's lucid interpretation of American society, based on a visit from May 1831 to February 1832, was first published in two parts, the first appearing in 1835 and the second in 1840.

19. Leonard W. Labaree, Ralph L. Ketcham, Helen C. Boatfield, and Helene H. Fineman, eds., *The Autobiography of Benjaman Franklin* (New Haven, 1974), p. 149. The first edition of the autobiography to be based directly on Franklin's original manuscript was published in 1868.

20. "Forty Years Ago, and Now," *Harper's Bazaar* (August 14, 1880), 13:514.

21. Bernard Bailyn, "Politics and Social Structure in Virginia," in Paul Goodman, ed., *Essays in American Colonial History* (New York, 1967), pp. 288–291.

22. Gunther Barth, *City People: The Rise of Modern City Culture in Nineteenth-Century America* (New York, 1982), pp. 30–31. The book was first published in 1980.

23. G. W. Steevens, *The Land of the Dollar* (New York, 1897), p. 24.

24. *New York Times*, January 26, 1880.

25. Massachusetts Commission on the Cost of Living, *Report of the Commission on the Cost of Living* (Boston, 1910), p. 256.

26. *Ladies' Home Journal* (April 1884), 1:4; Ellen H. Richards, *The Cost of Living as Modified by Sanitary Science* (New York, 1900), p. 13; E. T. Jackson, "Thrift in the Kitchen from the European Standpoint," *Journal of Home Economics* (April 1911), 3:127–128.

27. Thorstein Veblen, *The Theory of the Leisure Class* (New York, 1981), p. 103. Veblen's analysis first appeared in 1899.

28. Chapin, *Standard of Living in New York City*, p. 233; More, *Wage-Earners' Budgets*, pp. 16–21.

29. Walter E. Weyl, "The Italian Who Lived on Twenty-Six Cents a Day," *Outlook* (December 1909), 93:975.

30. In addition to the studies conducted by Chapin and More, see Elsa G.

1. Perspective of Abundance

Herzfeld, *Family Monographs: The History of Twenty-Four Families Living in the Middle West Side of New York City* (New York, 1905), p. 42.

31. Howard Brubaker, "The Penny Provident Fund," *University Settlement Studies* (1906), 2:62–63.

32. United States Department of Commerce, *Women in Gainful Occupations, 1870–1920* (Washington, D.C., 1929), p. 40.

33. *New York Herald*, August 19, 1894.

34. Richard Y. Giles, *Credit for the Millions* (New York, 1951), p. 74; Robert Bruce Davies, *Peacefully Working to Conquer the World: Singer Sewing Machines in Foreign Markets, 1854–1920* (New York, 1976), p. 20; Dorothy S. Brady, "Relative Prices in the Nineteenth Century," *Journal of Economic History* (June 1964), 24:181; *New York Herald*, January 1, 1876, January 1, 1880, and January 1, 1886, for advertisements of Biddle and Gordon and B. M. Cowperthwait; *New York Times*, January 1, 1900, for advertisement of Steck Co., January 1, 1910, for advertisements of Bloomingdale's and Steinway and Sons, January 1, 1915, for advertisement of Gimbels; More, *Wage-Earners' Budgets*, pp. 145–147.

35. Katherine Busbey, *Home Life in America* (London, 1910), p. 136.

36. William E. Harmon, "Investing Power of the Masses," *Academy of Political Science, Proceedings* (1911), 2:9.

37. "Cost of Living and the Money Market," *Nation* (December 23, 1909), 89:636; see also W. de Wagstaffe, "Cost of Living in New York," *Harper's Weekly* (May 23, 1908), 52:17; B. Squire, "Women and Money Spending," *Harper's Bazaar*, (November–December 1905), 39:1144; "What Every Grocer Knows," *McClure's* (September 1913), 41:126.

38. Edith Elmer Wood, "The Ideal and Practical Organization of a Home," *Cosmopolitan* (April 1899), 26:661.

39. Clarence Wycliffe Wassam, *Salary Loan Business in New York City* (New York, 1908), p. 20.

40. Provident Loan Society of New York, *Twenty-Fifth Annual Report* (New York, 1919), p. 1.

41. More, *Wage-Earners' Budgets*, p. 146.

42. Bayrd Still, *Mirror for Gotham: New York as Seen by Contemporaries from Dutch Days to the Present* (New York, 1956), p. 248.

43. Jacob A. Riis, *How the Other Half Lives* (New York, 1957), pp. 115–116. This classic exposé of life among the urban poor was originally published in 1890.

44. See Booker T. Washington's criticism of black consumers in the *New York Times*, March 6, 1905; see editorials in the *New York Age* during these years for the emphasis on sober economy.

45. Albert Einstein, *Ideas and Opinions* (New York, 1954), p. 5.

46. T. Roosevelt, "The High Cost of Living," *Outlook* (October 5, 1912), 102:247.

47. John A. Kouwenhoven, *The Beer Can by the Highway: Essays on What's American about America* (Garden City, N.Y., 1961), pp. 41–73.

2. The Immigrant as Consumer

2. From Scarcity to Abundance:
The Immigrant as Consumer

1. Louis Borgenicht, *The Happiest Man: The Life of Louis Borgenicht* (New York, 1942), p. 368.

2. British Board of Trade, *Report on the Cost of Living in American Towns* (London, 1911), pp. xxxix–xl.

3. Leonard Dinnerstein and David M. Reimers, *Ethnic Americans: A History of Immigration and Assimilation* (New York, 1975), pp. 164–165.

4. George E. Pozzeta, "The Italians of New York City, 1890–1914" (Ph.D. thesis, University of North Carolina, 1971), pp. 17–19, 177–179.

5. For a detailed description of conditions in Lithuania, see Peter Paul Jonitis, *The Acculturation of the Lithuanians of Chester, Pennsylvania* (New York, 1985), pp. 4–65. This book is a reprint of the author's Ph.D. thesis, University of Pennsylvania, 1951.

6. Carole Malkin, *The Journeys of David Toback* (New York, n.d.), pp. 213–214. The book was first published in 1981.

7. Morris R. Cohen, *A Dreamer's Journey* (Boston, 1949), pp. 17–19; Marcus E. Ravage, *An American in the Making* (New York, 1917), p. 82.

8. Joachim Schoenfeld, *Shtetl Memoirs: Jewish Life in Galicia Under the Austro-Hungarian Empire and in the Reborn Poland, 1898–1939* (Hoboken, N.J., 1985), p. 33.

9. New York *Jewish Daily News*, August 2, 1898. The *Jewish Daily News* was the English page of the *Yiddishes Tageblatt*. It appeared for about a decade after 1897 and was reinstituted in 1914. As an aid to the reader, this source will be identified by its English title throughout the book.

10. *Ibid.*, April 28, 1900.

11. Isaac M. Rubinow, *Economic Conditions of the Jews in Russia* (New York, 1975), p. 526. The book was first published in 1907.

12. Philip Cowen, *Memories of an American Jew* (New York, 1932), p. 231.

13. *Ibid.*

14. Quoted from Sidney Alexander, *Chagall* (New York, 1978), p. 42.

15. Benjamin L. Gordon, *Between Two Worlds: The Memoirs of a Physician* (New York, 1952), p. 12, for a specific recollection of the home of a petty grain merchant in Lithuania during the 1880s.

16. Mary Antin, *The Promised Land* (Boston, 1969), p. 100. This well-written account of the immigration of a Jewish family from Russia to America first appeared in 1912.

17. United States Immigration Commission, *Reports* (Washington, D.C., 1911), vol. 4, *Emigration Conditions in Europe*, p. 56.

18. Marcus Lee Hansen, *The Atlantic Migration 1607–1860* (New York, 1961), pp. 157–158. The book was first published in 1940; Maldwyn Allen Jones, *American Immigration* (Chicago, 1960), p. 100.

19. Hansen, *Atlantic Migration*, pp. 157–158.

2. The Immigrant as Consumer

20. United States Immigration Commission, *Emigration Conditions in Europe*, p. 57.

21. Ewa Morawska, " 'For Bread with Butter': Life-Worlds of Peasant Immigrants from East Central Europe, 1880–1914," *Journal of Social History* (Spring 1984), 17:388–389, 392. For an expanded version of this work, see Ewa Morawska, *'For Bread with Butter': Life-Worlds of East Central Europeans in Johnstown, Pennsylvania, 1890–1940* (New York, 1985). Robert Anthony Orsi, *The Madonna of 115th Street: Faith and Community in Italian Harlem, 1880–1950* (New Haven, 1985), pp. 156–162.

22. Salo W. Baron, *The Russian Jew Under Tsars and Soviets* (New York, 1976), pp. 68–69; Howard Morley Sachar, *The Course of Modern Jewish History* (New York, 1982), p. 188. The first editions of these standard texts of Jewish history in the modern era appeared in 1964 and 1958 respectively.

23. Hans Rogger, *Russia in the Age of Modernization and Revolution, 1881–1917* (New York, 1983), p. 199; Baron, *Russian Jew Under Tsars and Soviets*, pp. 43–62.

24. Bernard Weinryb, "Eastern European Immigration to the United States," *Jewish Quarterly Review* (April 1955), 45:501.

25. *New York Tribune*, July 11, 1880.

26. Leon Stein, Abraham P. Conan, and Lynn Davison, eds., *The Education of Abraham Cahan* (Philadelphia, 1969), p. 400.

27. *Encyclopedia Judaica* (Jerusalem, 1972), 2:337–339; 13:78–86; L. Jacobs, "Eating as an Act of Worship in Hasidic Thought," in Siegfried Stein and Raphael Loewe, *Studies in Jewish Religious and Intellectual History* (Tuscaloosa, Ala., 1979), 157–161. The verses evoking the aura of the divine banquet are from "Akdamut," a mystical poem composed in Aramaic by a European rabbi of the eleventh century. This version of the poem was described by a reporter for the *New York Tribune*, whose story on the celebration of Shavuoth by Jewish newcomers appeared on May 31, 1903.

28. Isaac Loeb Peretz, *Alle Verk* (Buenos Aires, 1944), 6:98–106.

29. Kate Simon, *Bronx Primitive* (New York, 1982), p. 18.

30. Humbert S. Nelli, *The Italians in Chicago* (New York, 1970), pp. 42–47.

31. C. Bezalel Sherman, *The Jew Within American Society* (Detroit, 1965), pp. 60–61.

32. Robert E. Park and Herbert A. Miller, *Old World Traits Transplanted* (New York, 1921), p. 101.

33. Mendele Moykher-Sforim, "The Travels of Benjamin the Third," in Joachim Neugroschel, ed., *The Shtetl* (New York, 1979), p. 182.

34. *New York Tribune*, March 29, 1903.

35. Miriam Blaustein, ed., *Memoirs of David Blaustein* (New York, 1913), p. 60.

36. *Harkavy's American Letter Writer and Speller, English and Yiddish* (New York, 1902).

37. Mordecai Soltes, *The Yiddish Press: An Americanizing Agency* (New York, 1925), p. 44.

2. The Immigrant as Consumer

38. Dorothee Schneider, " 'For Whom Are All the Good Things in Life?':
German-American Housewives Discuss Their Budgets," in Hartmut Keil and
John B. Jentz, eds., *German Workers in Industrial Chicago, 1850–1910* (DeKalb,
Ill., 1983), p. 152.

39. Nelli, *Italians in Chicago*, p. 119.

40. Abraham Cahan, *The Rise of David Levinsky* (New York, 1960), p. 95. The
book was first published in 1917.

41. Henry James, *The American Scene* (London, 1907), pp. 135–136.

42. The Lower East Side as a prototype of urban poverty appears in Anthony
Sutcliffe, ed., *Metropolis, 1890–1940* (Cambridge, 1984), p. 24, which draws on
the depiction of Irving Howe, *World of Our Fathers* (New York, 1976), p. 88. The
almost chronic tendency to preface the phrase "Jewish immigrants" with the
adjective "poor" can be observed in the symposium "A Reexamination of a Classic
Work in American Jewish History: Moses Rischin's The Promised City, Twenty
Years Later," *American Jewish History*, (December 1983), 73:141. Moses Rischin,
however, originally noticed the marked improvement in standards of consumption
on the Lower East Side, *The Promised City, New York's Jews, 1870–1914* (Cambridge, Mass. 1977), p. 92. The book was first published in 1962.

43. For a chronicle of change on the Lower East Side since the 1880s, see
New York *Yiddishes Tageblatt*, March 20, 1910.

44. *Tageblatt*, December 31, 1901.

45. Two vivid accounts of food on the Lower East Side are found in the *New
York Tribune*, August 20, 1899, and *Jewish Daily News*, February 11, 1900. A visit
of college students to the Lower East Side in 1904 is recalled by Philip Cowen,
founder and publisher of the *American Hebrew*, in *Memories of an American Jew*
(New York, 1932), p. 298. For the high opinion held by social workers of Jewish
tastes, see Charles Bernheimer, *Russian Jew in the United States* (Philadelphia,
1905), p. 35, and Mary Simkhovitch, *The City Worker's World in America* (New
York, 1917), pp. 12–13.

46. *Tageblatt*, July 4, 1902.

47. *Ibid.*

48. New York City Tenement House Department, *Seventh Report of the Tenement House Department of the City of New York* (New York, 1915), pp. 8–9.

49. Marie Jastrow, *A Time to Remember: Growing Up in New York Before the
Great War* (New York, 1979), p. 149.

50. *Jewish Daily News*, April 23, 1900.

51. New York *Forward*, December 1, 1904.

52. On Jewish economic advancement, see Thomas Kessner, *The Golden Door:
Italian and Jewish Immigrant Mobility in New York City, 1880–1915* (New York,
1977); see Moses Rischin, *The Promised City New York's Jews, 1870–1914* (Cambridge, Mass. 1977), pp 51–75, 92–93, 199–200 for discussions of activity in
business, real estate, and education; the theme of education as a means of advancement is addressed by Leonard Dinnerstein, "Education and the Advancement of
American Jews," in Bernard J. Weiss, *American Education and the European Immigrant, 1840–1940* (Urbana, Ill., 1982), pp. 44–60; good primary references to

2. The Immigrant as Consumer

Jewish investment in real estate are Isaac Markens, *The Hebrews in America* (New York, 1975), p. 157, first published in 1888; Riis, *How the Other Half Lives*, p. 94; Charles S. Bernheimer, ed., *Russian Jew in the United States* (Philadelphia, 1905), pp. 46, 354–55; *New York Tribune*, June 25, 1905; *Jewish Daily News*, January 1, 1906.

53. Jastrow, *A Time to Remember*, p. 147.

54. *Yiddishes Tageblatt*, January 1, 1889, for advertisement of H. Silberman and Son, January 18, 1892, for advertisement of Mt. Neboh Cemetery, and January 15, 1892 for advertisement of B. Zeller; Stein, et al., *Education of Abraham Cahan*, pp. 219, 261; Samuel Chotzinoff, *A Lost Paradise* (New York, 1955), p. 75.

55. Chotzinoff, *Lost Paradise*, p. 122, also pp. 113, 124.

56. Stein et al., *Education of Abraham Cahan*, p. 306.

57. Thomas B. Eyges, *Beyond the Horizon: The Story of a Radical Emigrant* (Boston, 1944), p. 140.

58. *Tageblatt*, July 3, 1914.

3. The Holy and the Mundane

1. Marcus E. Ravage, *An American in the Making* (New York, 1917), pp. 75–77.

2. *Ibid.*, p. 118.

3. Morris Raphael Cohen, *A Dreamer's Journey* (Boston, 1949), p. 25.

4. Rabbi Joseph H. Hertz, *The Authorized Daily Prayer Book* (New York, 1982), p. 11. This standard text was first printed in 1948.

5. Rabbi H. Freedman, trans. and ed., *Shabbath*, 2 vols. (London, 1938), 1:xiv; Aryeh Kaplan, *Sabbath: Day of Eternity* (New York, 1984), p. 13. Kaplan's compact commentary first appeared in 1974.

6. Abraham Joshua Heschel, *The Earth Is the Lord's and the Sabbath* (Philadelphia, 1963), pp. 22–23. The best sense of the place of the Sabbath in traditional Jewish life is obtained from a reading of the *Shulkhan Arukh (Set Table)*, the condensation of Jewish law published in 1555 by Joseph Karo, a talmudic scholar who was born in Spain and settled in Safed. The *Shulkhan Arukh* was quickly accepted by Jews throughout the diaspora as the authoritative code of Jewish law. See the revised English edition, Rabbi Solomon Ganzfried, ed., *Code of Jewish Law* (New York, 1963), part 2, chapters 71–96.

7. Abraham P. Bloch, *The Biblical and Historical Background of Jewish Customs and Ceremonies* (New York, 1980), pp. 113–125.

8. Leon Stein, Abraham P. Conan, and Lynn Davison, eds., *The Education of Abraham Cahan* (Philadelphia, 1969), 36.

9. Cohen, *Dreamer's Journey*, p. 18.

10. Sidney Alexander, *Chagall* (New York, 1978), p. 31.

11. Charles Patrick Daly, *The Jews of New York* (New York, 1883), p. 4.

12. Matthew Hale Smith, *Wonders of a Great City: Or the Sights, Secrets, and Sins*

of New York (Philadelphia, 1887), pp. 415. The book was originally published in 1877.

13. Moses Rischin, *The Promised City: New York's Jews, 1870–1914* (Cambridge, Mass., 1977), pp. 146–147. *The Promised City* first appeared in 1962.

14. Charles S. Liebman, "The Religion of American Jews," in Jacob Neusner, ed., *Understanding American Judaism: Toward the Description of a Modern Religion*, 2 vols. (New York, 1975), 1:35. Charles Liebman's thesis was originally stated in "Orthodoxy in American Jewish Life," *American Jewish Year Book* (1965), 66:27–30, and it was elaborated in the fine essay cited above.

15. Liebman, in Neusner, *Understanding American Judaism*, 1:36. The point about mikves is based on sparse evidence—a statement made in 1928 by an unidentified observer about life in New York City prior to World War I.

16. *New York Tribune*, December 7, 1884.

17. Richard Wheatley, "The Jews in New York," *Century Magazine* (January 1892), 43:338.

18. New York *Jewish Daily News (Yiddishes Tageblatt)*, January 8, 1899.

19. Sanborn Map Company, *Insurance Maps of the City of New York, Borough of Manhattan*, 1903, 1905.

20. Ray Stannard Baker, *The Spiritual Unrest* (New York, 1910), pp. 121–122. Baker's expressive portrait of the plight of religion in New York City was originally published in the *American Magazine* in 1908 and 1909.

21. Joachim Schoenfeld, *Shtetl Memoirs: Jewish Life in Galicia Under the Austro-Hungarian Empire and in the Reborn Poland, 1898–1939* (Hoboken, N.J., 1985), p. 7. The layout of a typical shtetl, including its mikve, is illustrated on page 2 of Diane K. Roskies and David G. Roskies, eds., *The Shtetl Book* (n.p., 1979), which focuses on Tishevits, a shtetl in the Lublin province of Poland.

22. Hutchins Hapgood, *The Spirit of the Ghetto* (New York, 1976), pp. 121–122. This lucid evocation of the varied experiences that made up life on the Lower East Side, which Hapgood toured with the help of Abraham Cahan, first appeared as a series of magazine articles between 1898 and 1902.

23. *Jewish Daily News*, December 13, 1901.

24. Bernard Weinryb, "Jewish Immigration and Accommodation to America," in Marshall Sklare, ed., *The Jews: Social Patterns of an American Group* (New York, 1967), p. 16. The book was issued originally in 1958.

25. Moses Rischin, "Responsa" to "A Re-examination of a Classic Work in American Jewish History: Moses Rischin's *The Promised City*, Twenty Years Later," *American Jewish History* (December 1983), 73:191.

26. *Jewish Daily News*, April 6, 1898.

27. Ravage, *American in the Making*, pp. 160–170; Baker, *Spiritual Unrest*, p. 117.

28. Sydelle Kramer and Jenny Masur, eds., *Jewish Grandmothers* (Boston, 1976), p. 42.

29. Baker, *Spiritual Unrest*, p. 119.

30. Moses Rischin, ed., *Grandma Never Lived in America: The New Journalism of Abraham Cahan* (Bloomington, Ind., 1985), pp. xxxi, 63–70.

3. The Holy and the Mundane

31. Steven J. Zipperstein, *The Jews of Odessa: A Cultural History, 1794–1881* (Stanford, Calif. 1985), pp. 151–154.

32. Beatrice C. Baskerville, *The Polish Jew: His Social and Economic Value* (New York, 1906), p. 303.

33. Ezra Mendelsohn, *The Jews of East Central Europe Between the World Wars* (Bloomington, Ind., 1983), p. 28; Moses A. Shulvass, *Between the Rhine and the Bosporus* (Chicago, 1924), p. 64; Jacob Lestchinsky, "Aspects of the Sociology of Polish Jewry," *Jewish Social Studies* (October 1966), 28:211; Isaac M. Rubinow, *Economic Conditions of the Jews in Russia* (New York, 1975), p. 543, the book first appeared in 1907; *Jewish Daily News*, May 5, 1898.

34. Lucy S. Dawidowicz, *On Equal Terms: Jews in America, 1881–1891* (New York, 1982), pp. 30–33; Oscar Handlin, *The Uprooted* (Boston, 1973), pp. 112–113, 126. Handlin's graceful interpretation of American immigration was originally published in 1951.

35. C. Bezalel Sherman, *The Jew Within American Society* (Detroit, 1965, p. 81; Nathan Glazer, *American Judaism* (Chicago, 1972), pp. 34, 70. Glazer's excellent survey was first published in 1957.

36. *Tribune*, August 16, 1903.

37. Quoted by Rischin, *Promised City*, p. 75.

38. Samuel Chotzinoff, *A Lost Paradise* (New York, 1955), p. 60.

39. New York *Forward*, October 3, 1903.

40. New York *Morgen Zhurnal*, October 6, 1909.

41. From an interview in the *Tribune*, August 16, 1903.

42. See the biographical summaries of New York City congregations and their presidents in the *Jewish Communal Register, 1917–1918* (frontispiece missing), pp. 145–285.

43. Abraham Cahan, *Bleter Fun Mayn Leben*, 5 vols. (New York, 1926–1931), 2:404–405.

44. Oscar Handlin evokes the animated world of the European peasant and its ruin in America in *The Uprooted*, pp. 86–89, 94–95.

45. *Jewish Communal Register*, p. 346.

46. Solomon Poll, *The Hasidic Community of Williamsburg*, (New York, 1969), p. 101. The book was first published in 1962.

47. The comparison to the sensibility of the Middle Ages was inspired by the opening pages of Johann Huizinga's *The Waning of the Middle Ages* (Garden City, N.Y., 1954), which originally appeared in 1924.

48. *New York Times*, April 3, 1905.

49. *Forward*, December 13, 1907.

50. See issues of the *Tageblatt* between January and june 190.

51. *Tageblatt*, April, 10, 1889.

52. This sort of promotion abounded in the Yiddish press. The Siegel-Cooper advertisement can be found in *Forward*, April 17, 1902; the Regal advertisement in *Tageblatt*, March 20, 1907.

53. *Forward*, April 10, 1906.

4. Luxuries, Holidays, Identity

54. *Tageblatt*, September 22, 1897, March 7, 1899; *Forward*, March 19, 1900, September 16, 1900.

55. *Forward*, January 3, 1914.

56. For example, see the advertisements in *Forward*, September 16, 1900.

57. See the advertisements for Regal Shoes in *Tageblatt*, April 7, 1914.

58. *Tageblatt*, January 2, 1913.

4. Luxuries, Holidays, and Jewish Identity

1. Deuteronomy 31:10–11.

2. This summary of Sukkot relies on Bloch, *Biblical and Historical Background of Jewish Customs*, pp. 181–191; Simon Greenberg, *A Jewish Philosophy and Pattern of Life* (New York, 1981), p. 354; Heszel Klepfisz, *Culture of Compassion: The Spirit of Polish Jewry from Hasidism to the Holocaust* (New York, 1983), p. 212.

3. New York *Yiddishes Tageblatt*, September 26, 1901.

4. New York *Forward*, September 30, 1909.

5. *New York Tribune*, September 24, 1899. Other accounts of the celebration of Sukkot in New York City can be found in *Tribune*, October 6, 1895, October 1, 1898, October 7, 1900, October 14, 1905; *New York Evening Post*, September 25, 1897. The article in the *Evening Post* appears in Allon Schoener ed., *Portal to America: The Lower East Side, 1870–1925* (New York, 1967), p. 111; Wheatley, "Jews in New York," *Century Magazine*, pp. 43, 338; Chotzinoff, *Lost Paradise*, p. 91.

6. *Tribune*, October 6, 1895.

7. *Tageblatt*, September 25, 1912.

8. *Ibid.*, September 23, 1904.

9. This summary of the events leading to the Maccabean rebellion and to the rededication of the Temple relies on Abraham Schalit, ed., *The World History of the Jewish People: The Hellenistic Age* (London, 1976), pp. 115–182, the volume was first published in 1961; Elias Bickerman, *The God of the Maccabees: Studies on the Meaning and Origin of the Maccabean Revolt* (Leiden, 1979), pp. 32–92, a fascinating analysis that originally appeared in 1937; Jonathan A. Goldstein, ed., *II Maccabees* (Garden City, 1983), pp. 84–123. This last book is volume 41a of the *Anchor Bible*.

10. New York *Morgen Zhurnal*, September 12, 1909.

11. *Tageblatt*, July 4, 1904.

12. Elizabeth G. Stern, *My Mother and I* (New York, 1917), pp. 108–109. The memoir first appeared one year earlier, in 1916.

13. James H. Barnett, *The American Christmas: A Study in National Culture* (New York, 1954), p. 3. See also the discussion of Christmas in Daniel J. Boorstin, *The Americans: The Democratic Experience* (New York, 1974), pp. 158–162, which is based in part on Barnett's work. Boorstin's book first appeared in 1973.

4. Luxuries, Holidays, Identity

14. Peter C. Marzio, *The Democratic Art: Pictures for a Nineteenth Century America: Chromolithography, 1840–1900* (Boston, 1979), p. 99.

15. Esther Paige, "Old Fashioned Thanksgivings," *Good Housekeeping* (November 24, 1888), 8:38.

16. *Tribune*, January 2, 1898,

17. *Tageblatt*, December 19, 1900.

18. The interview with Stern appeared in the *Tribune*, December 25, 1906. The *Jewish Daily News (Yiddishes Tageblatt)* noted the celebration of Christmas in the social settlements of the Lower East Side, in an article of December 24, 1903.

19. "Christmas and the Jews," letter to the editor, *Tribune*, December 26, 1906.

20. *Jewish Daily News*, January 11, 1899.

21. *Ibid.*, December 24, 1902.

22. *Ibid.*, December 21, 1897.

23. *Ibid.*, December 15, 1897.

24. Miriam Blaustein, ed., *Memoirs of David Blaustein* (New York, 1913), p. 17.

25. Bloch, *Biblical and Historical Background of Jewish Customs*, p. 277.

26. *Selected Stories of Sholom Aleichem* (New York, 1956), pp. 196–211.

27. *Jewish Daily News*, January 11, 1899.

28. *Ibid.*, February 2, 1900.

29. See the advertisement for Horn, Sachar, and Co., 86–88 Forsyth Street, in *Tageblatt*, November 29, 1900.

30. Marie Jastrow, *A Time to Remember: Growing Up in New York Before the Great War* (New York, 1979), p. 90.

31. *Tribune*, December 25, 1904.

32. *Forward*, December 25, 1904.

33. *Ibid.*, December 25, 1904.

34. *Tribune*, December 25, 1904.

35. See, for example, *Jewish Daily News*, December 20, 1897, December 21, 1904, January 8, 1905, December 19, 1905; *Tageblatt*, December 18, 1910; *Forward*, December 30, 1904.

36. *Jewish Daily News*, January 1, 1899.

37. *Tageblatt*, December 15, 1907.

38. *Ibid.*, December 11, 1906.

39. *Ibid.*, December 19, 1897.

40. *Ibid.*, December 14, 1911.

41. *The Complete Writings of Henry Wadsworth Longfellow*, 11 vols. (Boston, 1904), 4:325.

42. *Tribune*, December 30, 1900.

43. Observations of the neglect of the story of Chanukah are made in *Forward*, December 14, 1903 and *Tageblatt*, December 23, 1913.

44. *Tageblatt*, December 9, 1912.

45. Baruch M. Bokser, *The Origins of the Seder: The Passover Rite and Early Rabbinic Judaism* (Berkeley, Calif., 1984), pp. 1–4, 79, 99–100.

46. Bloch, *Biblical and Historical Background of Jewish Customs*, 213.

47. The thoroughness of the regulation of Passover can be observed in Ganzfried, *Code of Jewish Law*, part 3, chapters 107–117.

48. Ita Kalish, "Life in a Hassidic Court in Russian Poland Toward the End of the Nineteenth and the Early Twentieth Centuries," *YIVO Annual of Jewish Social Science* (1965), 13:268.

49. *Jewish Daily News*, April 12, 1906.

50. The spirit of the holiday is captured well in Benjamin L. Gordon, *Between Two Worlds: The Memoirs of a Physician* (New York, 1952), p. 23; Mary Antin, *The Promised Land* (Boston, 1969), p. 7, *The Promised Land* first appeared in 1912; Marcus E. Ravage, *An American in the Making* (New York, 1917), p. 121; Leon Stein, Abraham P. Conan, and Lynn Davison, eds., *The Education of Abraham Cahan* (Philadelphia, 1969), p. 13.

51. Abraham Cahan, *Bleter Fun Mayn Leben*, 5 vols. (New York, 1926–1931), 2:415. Cahan reiterated this point in the discussion of the Leo Frank case with which he chose to conclude his five volume autobiography. For a full discussion of that incident, see Leonard Dinnerstein, *The Leo Frank Case* (New York, 1968).

52. *Jewish Daily News*, April 6, 1898.

53. *Tageblatt*, April 19, 1900.

54. *Ibid.*, April 25, 1900.

55. *Forward*, April 20, 1905.

56. *Ibid.*, April 17, 1902.

57. *Tageblatt*, April 1, 1907.

58. *Ibid.*, April 1, 1910.

59. *Forward*, March 31, 1907.

60. *Ibid.*, April 7, 1904.

61. *Tageblatt*, March 25, 1904.

62. *Jewish Daily News*, March 30, 1900.

63. *Tribune*, March 18, 1906.

64. *Ibid.*, April 22, 1902.

65. *Jewish Daily News*, April 6, 1898.

66. *Tribune*, April 6, 1898.

67. *Ibid.*, April 5, 1896.

68. This popular view can be observed in a description of the Seder published in the *Tageblatt*, April 10, 1903.

69. *Forward*, April 6, 1906.

5. The Clothing of an American

1. New York *Forward*, May 6, 1902.

2. Gregory P. Stone, "Appearance and the Self" and Erving Goffman, "Identity Kits" in Mary Ellen Roach and Joanne Bubolz Eicher, eds., *Dress, Adornment, and the Social Order* (New York, 1965), pp. 230, 266–268.

5. The Clothing of an American

3. Mary Antin, *The Promised Land* (Boston, 1969), p. 187. This autobiography was originally published in 1912.

4. Abraham Cahan, *Yekl and the Imported Bridegroom and Other Stories of the New York Ghetto* (New York, 1970), pp. 34–40.

5. Abraham Cahan, *The Rise of David Levinsky* (New York, 1960), p. 101. Cahan's master work first appeared in 1917.

6. Claudia Kidwell and Margaret Christman, *Suiting Everyone: The Democratization of Clothing in America* (Washington, D.C., 1974), pp. 135–145; Margaret L. Brew, "American Clothing Consumption, 1879–1909" (Ph.D. thesis, University of Chicago, 1945), pp. 63–65; James R. McGovern, "The American Woman's Pre–World War I Freedom in Manners and Morals," *Journal of American History*, (September, 1968) 55:320; V. S. Clark, *History of Manufactures in the United States, 1607–1914*, 2 vols. (Washington, D.C., 1916–1928), 2:731–273; Jesse E. Pope, *The Clothing Industry in New York* (Columbia, Mo., 1905), p. 25.

7. Quoted from an extract of Giuseppe Giacosa's *Impressioni d'America*, which is reproduced in Oscar Handlin, *This Was America* (Cambridge, Mass. 1949), p. 398.

8. Quoted from Sandy Lydon, *Chinese Gold: The Chinese in the Monterey Bay Region* (Capitola, Calif., 1985), p. 135.

9. Manuel Gamio, *The Mexican Immigrant: His Life-Story* (New York, 1969), p. 262. Reissued by Arno Press as part of the American Immigration Collection, this book originally appeared in 1931.

10. Hasia R. Diner, *Erin's Daughters in America: Irish Immigrant Women in the Nineteenth Century* (Baltimore, 1983), pp. 141–142; Kerby A. Miller, *Emigrants and Exiles: Ireland and the Irish Exodus to North America* (New York, 1985), p. 508.

11. Margaret F. Byington, *Homestead: The Households of a Mill Town* (Pittsburgh, n.d.), p. 150. This volume is the fourth edition of a reprint done by the University of Pittsburgh in 1974. *Homestead* was originally published in 1910.

12. Ewa Morawska, " 'For Bread with Butter': Life Worlds of Peasant Immigrants from East Central Europe, 1880–1914," *Journal of Social History* (Spring 1984), 17:397; Jon Gjerde, *From Peasants to Farmers: The Migration from Balestrand, Norway, to the Upper Middle West* (Cambridge, 1985), pp. 222–225, 236.

13. Walter Weyl, "The Italian Who Lived on 26 Cents a Day," *Outlook* (December 1909), 93:972.

14. New York *Tribune*, August 26, 1900, in Allon Schoener, ed., *Portal to America: The Lower East Side, 1870–1925 (New York, 1967)*, p. 120.

15. Viola Paradise, "The Jewish Immigrant Girl in Chicago," *Survey* (September 6, 1913), 30:703–704.

16. New York *Tribune*, August 26, 1900, in Schoener, *Portal to America*, p. 121.

17. *Forward*, March 11, 1906, March 13, 1906.

18. *Ibid.*, December 26, 1911.

19. Samuel Joseph, *Jewish Immigration to the United States , From 1881–1910* (New York, 1914), pp. 177, 190.

20. Samuel Chotzinoff, *A Lost Paradise* (New York, 1955), p. 151.

5. The Clothing of an American

21. The diversity and the diversification of Jewish immigrant society in New York City are conveyed in chapter 4, "Urban Economic Frontiers," and in chapter 7, "Voices of Enlightenment," of Moses Rischin, *The Promised City: New York's Jews, 1870–1914* (Cambridge, Mass., 1977), which first appeared in 1962.

22. The egalitarian underpinnings of eastern European Jewish culture are emphasized by Theodore Bienenstok, "Social Life and Authority in the East European Shtetl Community," *Southwestern Journal of Anthropology* (Autumn 1950), 6:238–254.

23. United States Industrial Commission, *Reports of the Industrial Commission*, 19 vols. (Washington, D.C., 1900–1902), 15:351.

24. Robert Anthony Orsi, *The Madonna of 115th Street: Faith and Community in Italian Harlem, 1880–1950* (New Haven, 1985), p. 104.

25. W. I. Thomas and Florian Znaniecki, *The Polish Peasant in Europe and America*, 5 vols. (Chicago, 1918–1920), 1:162–164.

26. *Forward*, January 14, 1909.

27. "The Autobiography of a Shop Girl: Life Outside the Store," *Frank Leslie's Popular Monthly* (May 1903), 56:60.

28. Quoted by Bernard Weinryb, "Jewish Immigration and Accommodation to America," in Marshall Sklare, ed., *The Jews: Social Patterns of an American Group* (New York, 1967), p. 12. This collection of historical and sociological essays was originally published in 1958.

29. Elizabeth G. Stern, *My Mother and I* (New York, 1917), p. 34. This autobiography was first published in 1916.

30. Marcus E. Ravage, *An American in the Making* (New York, 1917), pp. 112–113; Cahan, *Rise of David Levinsky*, p. 228.

31. Marie Ganz, in collaboration with Nat J. Ferber, *Rebels Into Anarchy and Out Again* (New York, 1920), p. 17.

32. The significance of immigrant destinations is suggested by Caroline Golab, *Immigrant Destinations* (Philadelphia, 1977).

33. Jurgen Kocka, *White Collar Workers in America, 1890–1940: A Social-Political History in International Perspective* (Beverly Hills, 1980), pp. 44, 46.

34. *Thirteenth Census of the United States, 1910, Report by States, Supplement* (Washington, D.C., 1913), p. 746.

35. W. de Wagstaffe, "Cost of Living in New York," *Harper's Weekly* (May 23, 1908), 52:17.

36. New York State Factory Investigating Commission, *Fourth Report*, 5 vols. (New York, 1915), 4:1707.

37. John S. Steele, "General Storekeeping in New York," *Arena* (August 1899), 22:175.

38. *Tales of O. Henry* (Garden City, New York, 1969), p. 477.

39. Thomas Kessner, *The Golden Door: Italian and Jewish Immigrant Mobility in New York City, 1880–1915* (New York, 1977), pp. 59–65. See also, Simon Kuznets, "Economic Structure and Life of the Jews," in Louis Finkelstein, ed., *The Jews: Their History, Culture, and Religion*, 2 vols. (New York, 1960), 2:1635–1641. This comprehensive collection of essays first appeared in 1949.

5. The Clothing of an American

40. Marsha L. Rozenblit, *The Jews of Vienna, 1867–1914: Assimilation and Identity* (Albany, 1983), pp. 48–49.

41. New York *Jewish Daily News (Yiddishes Tageblatt)*, March 2, 1900; also May 18, 1900.

42. *Forward*, March 2, 1906; Bernard Weinstein, *Di Idishe Yunyons in Amerika* (New York, 1929), p. 500.

43. *Jewish Daily News*, January 13, 1902.

44. "Autobiography of a Shop Girl," *Frank Leslie's Popular Monthly* (May 1903), 56:60.

45. *Forward*, December 24, 1903.

46. Edward Alfred Steiner, "The Russian and Polish Jew in New York," *Outlook* (November 1, 1902), 72:537.

47. The depiction of Mose the Bowery Boy and Lizzie can be found in G. G. Foster, *New York by Gaslight: With Here and There a Streak of Sunshine* (New York, 1850), pp. 105–108.

48. Elizabeth E. Hoyt, *The Consumption of Wealth* (New York, 1928), p. 282. See also Louise Bolard More, *Wage-Earners' Budgets: Study of Standards and Cost of Living in New York* (New York, 1907), pp. 57, 60, and Robert Coit Chapin, *Standard of Living Among Workingmen's Families in New York City* (New York, 1909), p. 162.

49. Jane Addams, "The Subtle Problems of Charity," *Atlantic Monthly* (February 1899), 83:168–169.

50. *Forward*, June 15, 1904.

51. *Ibid.*, January 12, 1903. See also, *Forward*, November 21, 1911.

52. The term is borrowed from Mordecai Soltes, *The Yiddish Press: An Americanizing Agency* (New York, 1925).

6. Jewish Women and the Making of an American Home

1. New York *Jewish Daily News (Yiddishes Tageblatt)*, November 22, 1903.

2. Henry Roth, *Call It Sleep* (New York, 1964). The literary stature of this fascinating novel about the life of Jewish immigrants in urban America was overlooked when the book was first published in 1934.

3. Elizabeth Ewen, *Immigrant Women in the Land of Dollars: Life and Culture on the Lower East Side, 1890–1925* (New York, 1985), pp. 203, 264–269.

4. Some good examples are Leon Stein, Abraham P. Conan, and Lynn Davison, eds., *The Education of Abraham Cahan* (Philadelphia, 1969), p. 36; Morris Raphael Cohen, *A Dreamer's Journey* (Boston, 1949), pp. 18, 34; Miriam Blaustein, ed., *Memoirs of David Blaustein* (New York, 1913), pp. 6–8; Benjamin L. Gordon, *Between Two Worlds: The Memoirs of a Physician* (New York, 1952), pp. 31, 75; Miriam Zunser, *Yesterday* (New York, 1939), pp. 42–48; Samuel Chotzinoff, *A Lost Paradise* (New York, 1955), pp. 73–74.

6. Jewish Women and the American Home

5. Isaac M. Rubinow, *Economic Condition of the Jews in Russia* (New York, 1975), p. 560. Rubinow's fine report appeared in 1907.

6. Abraham Ain, "Swislocz: Portrait of a Shtetl," in Irving Howe and Eliezer Greenberg, *Voices from the Yiddish* (Ann Arbor, 1972), p. 102; Schoenfeld, *Shtetl Memoirs*, p. 25.

7. *Jewish Daily News*, May 23, 1898.

8. Marc Lee Raphael, *Jews and Judaism in a Mid-Western Community, Columbus, Ohio, 1840–1975* (Columbus, 1979), p. 166; *Jewish Daily News*, July 18, 1898.

9. United States Immigration Commission, *Reports*, 41 vols. (Washington, D.C., 1911), vol. 1, *Immigrants in Cities*, pp. 229–230, 232, 198; Paula E. Hyman, "Culture and Gender: Women in the Immigrant Jewish Community," in David Berger ed., *The Legacy of Jewish Migration: 1881 and its Impact* (New York, 1983), pp. 161–62.

10. Hasia R. Diner, *Erin's Daughters in America: Irish Immigrant Women in the Nineteenth Century* (Baltimore, 1983), pp. 26–27, 67–69.

11. Virginia Yans-McLaughlin, *Family and Community: Italian Immigrants in Buffalo, 1880–1930* (Ithaca, 1977), pp. 203–206.

12. Dorothee Schneider, " 'For Whom Are All the Good Things in Life?': German-American Housewives Discuss Their Budgets," in Harmut Keil and John B. Jentz, eds., *German Workers in Industrial Chicago, 1850–1910* (DeKalb, Ill., 1983), pp. 148–149; also see the table of income of women from different ethnic groups in Elizabeth H. Pleck, "A Mother's Wages: Income-Earning among Married Italian and Black Women," in Michael Gordon, ed., *The American Family in Social-Historical Perspective* (New York, 1978), p. 496.

13. Charles S. Bernheimer, *Russian Jew in the United States* (Philadelphia, 1905), p. 35.

14. Thomas Kessner, *The Golden Door: Italian and Jewish Immigrant Mobility in New York City, 1880–1915* (New York, 1977), pp. 59–64, 109–110.

15. Robert K. Foerster, *The Italian Emigration of Our Times* (Cambridge, Massachusetts, 1919), p. 381.

16. Mencken's views on the status of American women and men are elaborated in the ironically titled book *In Defense of Women* (New York, 1918).

17. Christine Frederick, "How Advertising Looks to a Consumer," *Advertising and Selling* (June 30, 1914), 24:15; Louise B. More, "The Cost of Living for a Wage-Earner's Family in New York City," *Annals of the American Academy of Political and Social Science* (July 1913), 48:104; Louise Bolard More, *Wage-Earners' Budgets: Studies of Standards and Cost of Living in New York* (New York, 1907), p. 3.

18. Ellen H. Richards, *The Cost of Living as Modified by Sanitary Science* (New York, 1900), p. 103.

19. Excerpted in the *Jewish Daily News*, February 11, 1900.

20. United States Agricultural Economics Bureau, *Push Cart Markets in New York City* (Washington, D.C., 1925), p. 30.

21. Alexis de Tocqueville, *Democracy in America*, Richard D. Heffner, ed., (New York, 1956), p. 170. Tocqueville's classic interpretation of American soci-

ety, based on a visit from May 1831 to February 1832, was first published in two parts, in 1835 and 1840.

22. New York *Times*, May 14, 1899; a good illustration of the passion for bargain hunting is given in the story "Priscilla Goes Shopping." *Ladies' Home Journal* (August 1906), 23:7.

23. Robert W. Twyman, *History of Marshall Field and Company, 1852–1906* (Philadelphia, 1954), pp. 112–114; "Bargain-Counters," *Printer's Ink* (February 3, 1897), 18:43; Ralph Hower, *The History of Macy's of New York, 1853–1919* (Cambridge, Mass., 1943), p. 381.

24. *Yiddishes Tageblatt*, March 8, 1899.

25. *Jewish Daily News*, February 19, 1899.

26. *Tageblatt*, March 20, 1910.

27. *Ibid.*, March 26, 1896, for advertisement of Geiger and Braverman, a major furniture company of the Lower East Side, and New York *Forward*, March 24, 1900, for advertisement of the New York Furniture and Carpet Store.

28. Gunther Barth, *City People: The Rise of Modern City Culture in Nineteenth-Century America* (New York, 1982), pp. 123–124, 129–130, 136–137, 140–147, the book appeared first in 1980; Sheila M. Rothman, *Woman's Proper Place: A History of Changing Ideals and Practices, 1870 to the Present* (New York, 1978), pp. 19–21.

29. *New York Tribune*, November 3, 1895.

30. *Forward*, March 15, 1906.

31. *Tageblatt*, October 27, 1902.

32. *Ibid.*, April 8, 1910.

33. *Forward*, February 2, 1914.

34. *Ibid.*, September 15, 1905.

35. Quoted from Rudolf Glanz, *The Jewish Woman in America: Two Female Immigrant Generations, 1820–1929*, 2 vols. (New York, 1976), 2:61.

36. *Jewish Daily News*, August 14, 1898, May 10, 1898.

37. *Forward*, February 21, 1903.

38. Elizabeth G. Stern, *My Mother and I* (New York, 1917), p. 98. This evocative account of growing up in the New York City home of Jewish immigrants first appeared one year earlier, in 1916.

7. Urban Leisure and the Vacation

1. Both of these classic works are available in more recent editions: Werner Sombart, *Luxury and Capitalism* (Ann Arbor, 1967) and Thorstein Veblen, *The Theory of the Leisure Class* (New York, 1981).

2. Edgar W. Martin, *The Standard of Living in 1860: American Consumption Levels on the Eve of the Civil War* (Chicago, 1942), p. 391; Robert Toll, *The Entertainment Machine* (New York, 1982), pp. 5–6; Gunther Barth, *City People: The Rise of Modern City Culture in Nineteenth-Century America*, pp. 213–214, 222–223; Kathy Peiss, *Cheap Amusements: Working Women and Leisure in Turn-of-the-*

7. Urban Leisure and the Vacation

Century New York (Philadelphia, 1986), p. 93; Lewis A. Erenberg, *Steppin' Out: New York Nightlife and the Transformation of American Culture* (Westport, Conn., 1981), pp. 65–77; John F. Kasson, *Amusing the Million: Coney Island at the Turn of the Century* (New York, 1978); Larry May, *Screening Out the Past: The Birth of Mass Culture and the Motion Picture Industry, 1896–1929* (New York, 1980).

3. New York City Bureau of Standards, *Report on the Cost of Living for an Unskilled Laborer's Family in New York City* (New York, 1915), p. 16.

4. Miriam Blaustein, ed., *Memoirs of David Blaustein* (New York, 1913), p. 161.

5. Rev. Dr. Joseph H. Hertz, Chief Rabbi of the British Empire, ed., *Sayings of the Fathers* (New York, 1945), pp. 59, 53.

6. The importance of *tachlis* is recognized by Moses Kligsberg, "Jewish Immigrants in Business: A Sociological Study," *American Jewish Historical Quarterly* (March 1967), 56:283–318.

7. New York *Forward*, March 14, 1905.

8. Stanley Nadel, "Jewish Race and German Soul in Nineteenth-Century America," *American Jewish History* (September 1987), 77:13–18.

9. Michael M. Davis, *The Exploitation of Pleasure: A Study of Commercial Recreations in New York City* (New York, 1911), pp. 7–8.

10. Moses Rischin, *The Promised City: New York's Jews, 1870–1914* (Cambridge, Mass., 1977), p. 133, first published in 1962; Henry L. Feingold, *A Midrash on American Jewish History* (Albany, 1982), p. 92.

11. Paul Klapper, "The Yiddish Music Hall," *University Settlement Studies* (1906), 2:19; see also Rischin, *The Promised City*, p. 136.

12. Barth, *City People*, pp. 220–221.

13. Peiss, *Cheap Amusements*, pp. 148, 150, 152; Thomas C. O'Guinn, Ronald J. Faber, and Marshall Rice, "Popular Film and Television as Consumer Acculturation Agents: America, 1900 to the Present," in Chin Tiong Tan and Jagdish N. Sheth, eds., *Historical Perspective in Consumer Research: National and International Perspectives* (Singapore, 1985), pp. 298–299. See also the article by Elizabeth Ewen, "City Lights: Immigrant Women and the Rise of the Movies," *Signs* (Spring 1980), 5 (supplement):45–65, and the chapter on moviegoing in Roy Rosenzweig, *Eight Hours for What We Will: Workers and Leisure in an Industrial City, 1870–1920* (Cambridge, 1983), pp. 191–221.

14. Abraham Cahan, *Yekl and the Imported Bridegroom and Other Stories of the New York Ghetto* (New York, 1970), p. 15. *Yekl* first appeared in 1896.

15. Jacob A. Riis, *How the Other Half Lives* (New York, 1957), p. 82. Riis's investigation was originally published in 1890.

16. Annie Marion MacLean, *Wage-Earning Women* (New York, 1910), p. 52.

17. Thomas Jesse Jones, *Sociology of a New York City Block* (New York, 1904), p. 82.

18. *New York Tribune*, February 9, 1902.

19. New York *Jewish Daily News, (Yiddishes Tageblatt)*, January 5, 1903.

20. Marcus E. Ravage, *An American in the Making* (New York, 1917), p. 98.

21. Stephen Graham, *With Poor Immigrants to America* (London, 1914), p. 48.

22. *New York Tribune*, September 24, 1900.

7. Urban Leisure and the Vacation

23. *Yiddishes Tageblatt*, February 1, 1888.

24. Other aspects of treating are discussed by Peiss, *Cheap Amusements*, pp. 51–55, 107–114.

25. Edwin E. Slosson, "The Amusement Business," *Independent* (July 21, 1904), 57:139.

26. *Tribune*, September 30, 1900.

27. *Jewish Daily News*, March 9, 1900.

28. *Forward*, March 11, 1906.

29. Katherine Busbey, *Home Life in America* (London, 1910), pp. 89–90.

30. Cahan, *Yekl*, p. 201. "A Sweatshop Romance" first appeared in 1898.

31. *Tageblatt*, January 14, 1903.

32. *Ibid.*, August 13, 1911.

33. Sholom Aleichem, *Marienbad* (New York, 1982).

34. Neil Harris, "On Vacation," in Alf Evers, et al., *Resorts of the Catskills* (New York, 1979), p. 103.

35. *New York Times*, April 4, 1889.

36. Rischin, *The Promised City*, p. 261. The Seligman affair is discussed in the context of social discrimination against Jews by John Higham, *Send These to Me: Immigrants in Urban America* (Baltimore, 1984), pp. 127–128; on resorts as a focal point of anti-Semitism, see Alice Hyneman Rhine, "Race Prejudice at Summer Resorts," *Forum* (July 1887), 3:523–531.

37. The statistics of vacationers are given by Betsy Blackmar, "Going to the Mountains: A Social History," in Evers et al., *Resorts of the Catskills*, p. 79, but the original sources are not cited.

38. Abraham Cahan, *The Rise of David Levinsky* (New York, 1960), pp. 403–441. Cahan's incisive novel of American Jewish life originally appeared in 1917.

39. *Tageblatt*, September 3, 1897.

40. *Jewish Daily News*, July 21, 1902, August 8, 1902.

41. New York *Arbeter Tsaytung*, March 20, 1891.

42. *New York Tribune*, July 9, 1903.

43. "The Ghetto and the Summer Resorts," *American Israelite* (August 20, 1903), 50:8.

44. *Forward*, January 6, 1914.

45. New York *Morgen Zhurnal*, July 22, 1906; May 14, 1906; July 18, 1906.

46. *Ibid.*, May 23, 1906.

47. *Ibid.*, July 22, 1906; May 19, 1908.

48. *Ibid.*, July 19, 1908; August 15, 1906.

49. *Ibid.*, July 18, 1906; July 18, 1907.

50. *Ibid.*, May 9, 1907.

51. *Tageblatt*, August 19, 1908.

52. *Ibid.*, April 7, 1907.

53. *Morgen Zhurnal*, August 9, 1907.

54. *Jewish Daily News*, June 20, 1899.

55. *Ibid.*, July 25, 1900.

56. *Ibid.*, July 30, 1900.

8. The Parlor and the Piano

57. *Morgen Zhurnal*, July 9, 1908, August 1, 1906.
58. Cahan, *Rise of David Levinsky*, p. 406.
59. Robert Wooster Stallman, ed., *Stephen Crane: Stories and Tales* (New York, 1959), p. 167. Crane's report on Asbury Park originally appeared in the *New York Tribune*, August 21, 1892.
60. *Tageblatt*, August 12, 1902.

8. The Parlor and the Piano

1. A reproduction of "East Side Interior," which the author viewed at an exhibition of pen-and-ink drawings, appears in Gail Levin, *Edward Hopper: The Art and the Artist* (New York, 1980), p. 36.
2. On the introduction of the Singer sewing machine in Russia, see Robert Bruce Davies, *Peacefully Working to Conquer the World: Singer Sewing Machines in Foreign Markets, 1854–1920* (New York, 1976).
3. Louis Borgenicht, *The Happiest Man: The Life of Louis Borgenicht* (New York, 1942), p. 236.
4. Marie Jastrow, *A Time to Remember: Growing Up in New York Before the Great War* (New York, 1979), p. 70; see also Marcus E. Ravage, *An American in the Making* (New York, 1917), p. 71, and Morris Raphael Cohen, *A Dreamer's Journey* (Boston, 1949), p. 67.
5. New York *Yiddishes Tageblatt*, February 23, 1898, March 24, 1899.
6. Kevin M. Sweeney, "Furniture and the Domestic Environment in Wethersfield, Connecticut, 1639–1800," in Robert Blair St. George, ed., *Material Life in America, 1600–1860* (Boston, 1988), p. 264. Readers should also consult Katherine C. Grier, *Culture and Comfort: People, Parlors, and Upholstery, 1850–1930* (Amherst, Mass., 1988), which was not available to the author before this book went to press.
7. Frederik A. Fernald, "Household Arts at the World's Fair," *Popular Science Monthly* (October 1893), 43:803–804.
8. A. F. Sanborn, "Anatomy of a Tenement Street," *Forum* (January 1895), 18:555. See also Katherine Anthony, "Mothers Who Must Earn," a monograph published with separate pagination as part of Pauline Goldmark, ed., *West Side Studies* (New York, 1914), pp. 141–142, 147–148.
9. G. W. Steevens, *The Land of the Dollar* (New York, 1897), pp. 22–23.
10. Donna Gabaccia discusses the influence of old world conditions on the desire of Sicilian immigrants for a *salotto*, or parlor in America; see *From Sicily to Elizabeth Street: Housing and Social Change among Italian Immigrants, 1880–1930* (Albany, 1984), pp. xx, 21, 51.
11. Ravage, *American in the Making*, p. 72.
12. *Jewish Daily News (Yiddishes Tageblatt)*, November 11, 1905. Anatole Leroy-Beaulieu was inspired by the Jews of the Lower East Side to give a fuller description of their world in *Les Immigrants Juifs et al Judaïsme aux Etats-Unis* (Paris, 1905).

8. The Parlor and the Piano

13. Leon Stein, Abraham P. Conan, and Lynn Davison, eds., *The Education of Abraham Cahan* (Philadelphia, 1969), p. 242.

14. Abraham Cahan, *Yekl and the Imported Bridegroom and Other Stories of the New York Ghetto* (New York, 1970), p. 197. "A Sweatshop Romance" first appeared in 1898.

15. *Jewish Daily News*, November 5, 1897.

16. Elizabeth G. Stern, *My Mother and I* (New York, 1917), p. 98.

17. John Lee Mahin, "The Trademark and Its Relation to Business," in A. P. Johnson, ed., *Library of Advertising*, 2 vols. (Chicago, 1911), 2:102.

18. William Steinway, "American Musical Instruments," in Chauncey M. Depew, ed., *1795–1895, One Hundred Years of American Commerce*, 2 vols. (New York, 1895), 2:509–515.

19. Jeffrey G. Williamson, "Consumer Behavior in the Nineteenth Century: Carroll D. Wright's Massachusetts Workers in 1875," *Explorations in Entrepreneurial History*, second series (Winter 1967), 4:108.

20. Arthur L. Loesser, *Men, Women, and Pianos* (New York, 1954), p. 549.

21. Edward S. Babcox, "Milestones in Advertising," *Advertising and Selling* (October 1912), 22:26.

22. Louise Bolard More, *Wage-Earners' Budgets: Study of Standards and Cost of Living in New York* (New York, 1907), p. 139.

23. *Ibid.*, p. 195. See also Elsa G. Herzfeld, *Family Monographs: The History of Twenty-Four Families Living in the Middle West Side of New York City* (New York, 1905), p. 12.

24. Herzfeld, *Family Monographs*, pp. 12, 16–17, 124.

25. Emily Greene Balch, *Our Slavic Fellow Citizens* (New York, 1910), p. 373.

26. *New York Tribune*, March 27, 1899.

27. *Tageblatt*, September 25, 1912. See the New York *Forward*, March 12, 1910, for the advertisement of a distributor of Wissner pianos in Manhattan and Brooklyn, which gives a good sense of the variety of brands and prices available.

28. New York *Morgen Zhurnal*, March 26, 1909.

29. See the advertisements of Perlman and Rozansky in *Tageblatt*, February 12, 1904, and of the Wise Piano Company in *Tageblatt*, March 20, 1910.

30. J. E. T. Eldridge, ed., *Max Weber: The Interpretation of Social Reality* (New York, 1980), pp. 237–240.

31. Christine Harzig, "Chicago's German North Side, 1880–1900: The Structure of a Gilded Age Ethnic Neighborhood," in Hartmut Keil and John B. Jentz, eds., *German Workers in Industrial Chicago, 1850–1910* (DeKalb, Ill., 1983), p. 141.

32. Charles S. Bernheimer, *Russian Jew in the United States* (Philadelphia, 1905), p. 35.

33. Henry Collins Brown, *In the Golden Nineties* (Hastings-on-Hudson, N.Y., 1928), p. 166.

34. Mark Slobin, *Tenement Songs: The Popular Music of the Jewish Immigrants* (Urbana, Ill., 1982), pp. 123, 176.

35. This is Slobin's fascinating thesis in *Tenement Songs*.

9. Advertising in the Yiddish Press

36. On this subject, see Kenneth Aaron Kanter, *The Jews on Tin Pan Alley: The Jewish Contribution to American Popular Music, 1830–1940* (Cincinnati, 1982).

37. Slobin, *Tenement Songs*, pp. 124–181.

38. Samuel Chotzinoff, *A Lost Paradise* (New York, 1955), p. 287.

39. Stern, *Mother and I*, p. 75.

40. Marc D. Angel, *La América: The Sephardic Experience in the United States* (Philadelphia, 1982), p. 91.

41. *Forward*, February 3, 1914.

42. *Forward*, March 4, 1907.

43. Kate Simon remembers the event as it happened to her family in the 1920s, *Bronx Primitive* (New York, 1982), p. 170.

44. The symbolic value of the organ is explored by Kenneth A. Ames, "Material Culture as Non-Verbal Communication: A Historical Case Study," *Journal of American Culture* (Winter 1980), 3:619–641.

45. *Forward*, March 31, 1910.

9. American Advertising in the Yiddish Press

1. G. W. Steevens, *The Land of the Dollar* (New York, 1897), pp. 13–14.

2. The Mayor's Billboard Advertising Commission of the City of New York, *Report* (New York, 1913), p. 13.

3. *Ibid.*, pp. 19–20, 65–67, 76–80; New York City Accounts Commissioner, *A Report on an Investigation of Billboard Advertising in the City of New York* (New York, 1912), p. 10.

4. Benjamin L. Gordon, *Between Two Worlds: The Memoirs of a Physician* (New York, 1952), p. 142.

5. Marcus E. Ravage, *An American in the Making* (New York, 1917), p. 103.

6. H. L. Mencken, *The American Language: An Inquiry into the Development of English in the United States* (New York, 1921), pp. 405–408.

7. Robert E. Park, *The Immigrant Press and Its Control* (New York, 1922), pp. 73–74.

8. *Ibid.*, p. 89.

9. Mordecai Soltes, *The Yiddish Press: An Americanizing Agency* (New York, 1925), pp. 15, 21.

10. Moses Rischin, *The Promised City: New York's Jews, 1870–1914* (Cambridge, Mass., 1977), pp. 118–127, originally published in 1962; Soltes, *The Yiddish Press*, p. 24.

11. United States Department of Commerce, Bureau of the Census, *Historical Statistics of the United States: Colonial Times to 1957* (Washington, D.C., 1961), p. 526.

12. Gunther Barth, *City People: The Rise of Modern City Culture in Nineteenth-Century America* (New York, 1982), pp. 74–75, 106–109. The book was published originally in 1980.

9. Advertising in the Yiddish Press

13. Edward Bok, *The Americanization of Edward Bok: The Autobiography of a Dutch Boy Fifty Years Later* (New York, 1921), pp. 166–180. The autobiography was first published a year earlier. A good example of Bok's intimate style is found in the column "At Home with the Editor," *Ladies' Home Journal*, (December 1892), 10:16. See also Frank Luther Mott, *A History of American Magazines*, 5 vols. (Cambridge, Mass., 1938–1968), 4:545.

14. New York *Jewish Daily News (Yiddishes Tageblatt)*, April 5, 1898.

15. *Ibid.*, January 16, 1905; Victor R. Greene, *American Immigrant Leaders, 1800–1910: Marginality and Identity* (Baltimore, 1987), pp. 93–94.

16. Isaac Metzker, ed., *A Bintel Brief: Sixty Years of Letters from the Lower East Side to the Jewish Daily Forward* (New York, 1977), p. 8. This volume originally appeared in 1971.

17. Rischin, *The Promised City*, pp. 124–126. The breadth and quality of Cahan's journalism is the theme of Moses Rischin's *Grandma Never Lived in America: The New Journalism of Abraham Cahan* (Bloomington, Ind., 1985).

18. New York *Forward*, September 7, 1905.

19. Joseph H. Appel, *Growing Up with Advertising* (New York, 1940), p. 42.

20. *The 1902 Edition of the Sears, Roebuck Catalogue* (New York, 1969), p. 3. Examples of Sears' emphasis on the personal touch may be found in a good company history by Boris Emmet and John E. Jeuck, *Catalogues and Counters: A History of Sears, Roebuck and Company* (Chicago, 1950), pp. 39–40, 43–45, 83–84, 171–172.

21. John E. Sawyer, "The Entrepreneur and the Social Order: France and the United States," in William Miller, ed., *Men in Business* (New York, 1962), p. 18.

22. The comparison is based on the following newspapers of London, Paris, and Frankfort during selected months of 1885, 1895, and 1905: *Times, Pall Mall Gazette, Daily Telegraph, Daily News, Le Petit Parisien*, and *Frankfurter Zeitung und Handelsblatt*.

23. C. A. Kupferberg, "Advertising American Products in Germany," *Advertising and Selling* (November 1913), 23:50.

24. *Yiddishes Tageblatt*, October 8, 1889.

25. *Jewish Daily News*, March 19, 1900.

26. *Printer's Ink* (August 8, 1900), 32:30–31.

27. *Tageblatt*, October 10, 1888.

28. *Ibid.*, March 5, 1899. See advertisements for Shulman and Son in *Forward*, September 16, 1900, and for M. Yachnin in *Tageblatt*, December 24, 1900.

29. Mark Sullivan, *Our Times: The United States, 1900–1925*, 6 vols. (New York, 1926–1935), 1:194.

30. *Tageblatt*, September 25, 1912.

31. *Forward*, September 18, 1908, April 15, 1910.

32. *Tageblatt*, September 7, 1904.

33. Sullivan, *Our Times*, 1:15.

34. *Tageblatt*, September 22, 1911.

35. *Forward*, October 2, 1900. A good sample of Minsky's advertising can be seen in the *Forward* throughout 1900.

10. "American Bluff"

36. See advertisements for Crisco and Camels in *Tageblatt*, December 12, 1911, December 22, 1911, and December 1–4, 1914.

37. Park, *The Immigrant Press*, 353.

10. "American Bluff":
The Exaltation of American Products

1. New York *Yiddishes Tageblatt*, September 26, 1910.

2. Curt Leviant, trans., *Stories and Satires by Sholom Aleichem* (New York, 1959), pp. 230–232.

3. David M. Potter, *People of Plenty: Economic Abundance and the American Character* (Chicago, 1966), pp. 166–188. *People of Plenty* first appeared in 1954.

4. David E. Novack and Matthew Simon, "Commercial Responses to the American Export Invasion, 1871–1914: An Essay in Attitudinal History," *Explorations in Entrepreneurial History*, (1966), 3:131–132.

5. F. A. MacKenzie, *The American Invaders* (London, 1902), pp. 142–143.

6. William Dean Howells, *A Hazard of New Fortunes* (London, 1965), p. 196. The novel was originally published in serial form in 1889.

7. Christine Frederick, "How Advertising Looks to a Consumer," *Advertising and Selling* (June 30, 1914), 24:15.

8. T. Coleman DuPont, "The Inter-Racial Counsel—What It Is and Hopes to Do," *Advertising and Selling* (July 5, 1919), 29:2.

9. William Cahn, *Out of the Cracker Barrel: The Nabisco Story from Animal Crackers to ZuZus* (New York, 1969), p. 92.

10. George E. Mowry, *The Era of Theodore Roosevelt and the Birth of Modern America* (New York, 1962), p. 7. The book was first published in 1958.

11. Cahn, *Out of the Cracker Barrel*, pp. 70–72, 82–86, 144.

12. *Tageblatt*, March 15, 1899.

13. *Tageblatt*, January 16, 1899.

14. New York *Forward*, September 18, 1900. See also the reference by the East Side Observer in *Jewish Daily News (Yiddishes Tageblatt)*, March 19, 1900.

15. *New York World*, March 10, 1899.

16. *New York Times*, August 27, 1876; John Maass, *The Glorious Enterprise: The Centennial Exposition of 1876 and H. J. Schwarzmann, Architect in Chief* (Watkins Glen, N.Y., 1973). p. 108.

17. James E. Nichols, "The Grocery Trade," in Chauncey M. Depew, ed., *1795–1895: One Hundred Years of American Commerce*, 2 vols. (New York, 1895), 2:595.

18. *Printer's Ink* (August 15, 1900), 32:30.

19. Frank Presbrey, *The History and Development of Advertising* (Garden City, N.Y., 1929), p. 409.

20. *Jewish Daily News*, March 6, 1903.

21. Elizabeth G. Stern, *My Mother and I* (New York, 1917), p. 89. Stern's memoir appeared originally in 1916.

22. "Fifty Years," *Printer's Ink* (July 28, 1938), 184:129.

23. Interview with Anna Kuthan, cited in Elizabeth Ewen, *Immigrant Women in the Land of Dollars: Life and Culture on the Lower East Side, 1890–1925* (New York, 1985), p. 66.

24. *Jewish Communal Register, 1917–1918* (frontispiece missing), p. 733.

25. *Ibid.*, p. 731.

26. Edward A. Ross, *The Old World in the New* (New York, 1914), p. 158.

27. *Jewish Daily News*, February 15, 1900.

28. The opinion of the insurance agent is cited in Marquis James, *The Metropolitan Life: A Study in Business Growth* (New York, 1947), p. 82. For background on the poor reputation of the insurance industry, see Walter C. Wright, "Life Insurance in the United States," *American Statistical Association Publications* (December 1888), 1:141–142 and James, *Metropolitan Life*, pp. 37, 123–124.

29. Daniel Andrew Pope, "The Development of National Advertising, 1865–1920" (Ph.D. thesis, Columbia University, 1973), p. 158.

30. James, *Metropolitan Life*, pp. 183–189.

31. *Tageblatt*, March 20, 1910.

32. Alexis de Tocqueville, *Democracy in America*, Richard D. Heffner, ed. (New York, 1956), 172. Tocqueville's analysis was originally published in two parts, the first appearing in 1835 and the second in 1840.

33. Quoted by Nathan Rosenberg, "Technological Change," in Lance Davis et al., *American Economic Growth: An Economist's History of the United States* (New York, 1972), p. 248.

34. Albert S. Bolles, *Industrial History of the United States* (Norwich, Conn., 1889), p. 365, first issued in 1879; George Sweet Gibb, *The Whitesmiths of Taunton: A History of Reed and Barton, 1824–1943* (Cambridge, Mass., 1943), p. 59, 199–200.

35. Quoted by Charles W. Moore, *Timing a Century: History of the Waltham Watch Company* (Cambridge, Mass., 1945), p. 74. Historical background on the mass-marketing of clocks is provided by John J. Murphy, "Entrepreneurship in the Establishment of the American Clock Industry," *Journal of Economic History* (June 1966), 26:183.

36. *Forward*, March 24, 1900; March 26, 1900.

37. *Forward*, February 9, 1903.

38. Mitchell Okun, "Fair Play in the Marketplace: The Origins of Consumerism, 1865–1908," (Ph.D. thesis, City University of New York, 1982), pp. 2–3.

39. Oscar E. Anderson, *The Health of a Nation: Harvey W. Wiley and the Fight for Pure Food* (Chicago, 1958), pp. 129–130.

40. "The Experiences of a Tooth Powder Advertiser," *Printer's Ink* (February 8, 1893), 8:212.

41. Claude C. Hopkins, *My Life in Advertising* (New York, 1927), p. 80.

42. New York *Commercial Advertiser*, July 14, 1900.

43. Quoted from the translation of Jonathan D. Sarna, *People Walk on Their Heads: Moses Weinberger's Jews and Judaism in New York* (New York, 1982), p. 50.

11. Jewish Commerce, American Culture

44. *Jewish Daily News,* July 18, 1898, April 25, 1899, March 14, 1900; Marcus E. Ravage, *An American in the Making* (New York, 1917), p. 126. For an overview, see Harold P. Gastwirt, *Fraud, Corruption, and Holiness: The Controversy Over the Supervision of Jewish Dietary Practice in New York City, 1881–1940* (Port Washington, N.Y., 1974).

45. *Tageblatt,* March 12, 1899.

46. *Ibid.,* March 29, 1906.

47. *Ibid.,* September 22, 1901; January 6, 1911; September 12, 1912; March 5, 1912.

48. *Ibid.,* December 12, 1911; September 23, 1912.

49. *Ibid.,* March 20, 1910.

11. Jewish Commerce and American Culture

1. Cecil Roth, *The Jewish Contribution to Civilisation* (London, 1938), pp. 251, 254.

2. Alfred D. Chandler, Jr., "The Beginnings of 'Big Business' in American History," *Business History Review* (Spring 1959), 33:30–31; Alfred D. Chandler, Jr., *The Visible Hand: The Managerial Revolution in American Business* (Cambridge, Mass., 1977), p. 414; Glenn Porter and Harold C. Livesay, *Merchants and Manufacturers: Studies in the Changing Structure of Nineteenth-Century Marketing* (Baltimore, 1983), pp. 154–155.

3. Israel M. Kirzner, *Discovery and the Capitalist Process* (Chicago, 1985), pp. 165–168.

4. Murray Sices, *Seventh Avenue* (New York, 1953), pp. 24–30, 85–95.

5. Gunther Barth, *City People: The Rise of Modern City Culture in Nineteenth-Century America* (New York, 1982), pp. 123–129. The book was first published in 1980.

6. Naomi W. Cohen, *Encounter with Emancipation: The German Jews in the United States, 1830–1914* (Philadelphia, 1984), p. 30.

7. Some details of Jewish activity in the extension of the American department store are contained in Leon Harris, *Merchant Princes: An Intimate History of Jewish Families Who Built Great Department Stores* (New York, 1979).

8. Carl Wittke, *We Who Built America: The Saga of the Immigrant* (n.p., Press of Western Reserve University, 1964), pp. 195, 208–214, 393–396, a revision of the original 1939 edition; Peter C. Marzio, ed., *A Nation of Nations: The People Who Came to America as Seen Through Objects and Documents Exhibited at the Smithsonian Institution* (New York, 1976), pp. 218–222. A sense of the German impact on the development of Milwaukee can be gained from Kathleen Neils Conzen, *Immigrant Milwaukee, 1836–1860: Accommodation and Community in a Frontier City* (Cambridge, Mass., 1976). The rise of a major marketer of beer out of Milwaukee's German community is charted in Thomas C. Cochran, *The Pabst Brewing Company: The History of an American Business* (New York, 1948).

9. Roth, *Jewish Contribution to Civilisation*, pp. 221–224; Nachum Gross, ed., *Economic History of the Jews* (New York, 1975), pp. 64–66, 158–160, 189–190, 206–207, 275–276.

10. Samuel Joseph, *Jewish Immigration to the United States, from 1881–1910* (New York, 1914), pp. 43, 46, 49–52; Jacob Lestchinsky, "Aspects of the Sociology of Polish Jewry," *Jewish Social Studies* (October 1966) 28:198–200; Salo W. Baron, *The Russian Jew Under Tsars and Soviets* (New York, 1976), pp. 63–68.

11. I. J. Singer, *Of a World That Is No More* (New York, 1970), p. 90. Singer's reminiscence of Polish life at the turn of the century first appeared in Yiddish in 1946.

12. New York *Yiddishes Tageblatt*, August 14, 1892.

13. Matthew Hale Smith, *Wonders of a Great City: Or the Sights, Secrets, and Sins of New York* (Philadelphia, 1887), p. 234. This chronicle was originally published in 1877.

14. *New York Tribune*, August 5, 1883.

15. *Ibid.*, December 16, 1906.

16. Isaac Markens, *The Hebrews in America* (New York, 1975), pp. 151–156. The volume is a reprint of the 1888 edition.

17. *Trow Business Directory of New York City, 1892* (New York, 1892).

18. Jacob A. Riis, *How the Other Half Lives* (New York, 1957), p. 44. The book originally appeared in 1890.

19. Philip Cowen, *Memories of an American Jew* (New York, 1932), pp. 23–24; Judah D. Eisenstein, "Successful Russo-Jewish Immigrants," a paper delivered to the American Jewish Historical Society in New York City on March 21, 1904, printed in the *Jewish Daily News (Yiddishes Tageblatt)*, April 12, 1904.

20. The quotation comes from an article on the Lower East Side in *Furniture World*, October 22, 1898, which was reprinted in the *Jewish Daily News*, December 27, 1898.

21. Eugene F. Sofer, *From Pale to Pampa: A Social History of the Jews of Buenos Aires* (New York, 1982), pp. 104, 107–108.

22. Lloyd P. Gartner, *The Jewish Immigrant in England, 1870–1914* (London, 1973), pp. 6, 279–280. The first edition of the work appeared in 1960.

23. Thomas C. Cochran, "Cultural Factors in Economic Growth," *Journal of Economic History* (December 1960), 20:518–521; Sigmund Diamond, *The Reputation of the American Businessman* (Cambridge, Mass., 1955), pp. 50, 178; John E. Sawyer, "The Entrepreneur and the Social Order: France and the United States," in William Miller, ed., *Men in Business* (New York, 1962), p. 22.

24. *Tageblatt*, December 3, 1912.

25. Quoted by the *New York Tribune*, September 10, 1904.

26. Louis Borgenicht, *The Happiest Man: The Life of Louis Borgenicht* (New York, 1942), p. 370.

12. Jewish Street Merchants

12. Anonymous Entrepreneurs: Jewish Street Merchants

1. New York *Yiddishes Tageblatt*, January 9, 1902.
2. *Ibid.*, March 23 and 24, 1903.
3. See the discussion in E. Tcherikower, ed., *Geshikhte fun der Yidisher Arbeter-Bavegung in di Fareynikte Shtatn*, 2 vols. (New York, 1943–1945), 1:235–253. An abridged translation is provided by Aaron Antonovsky, *The Early Jewish Labor Movement in the United States* (New York, 1961), pp. 142–146.
4. Bernard Weinstein, *Di Idishe Yunyons in Amerika* (New York, 1929), pp. 42–43.
5. New York City Pushcart Commission, *Report of the Mayor's Pushcart Commission* (New York, 1906), p. 54.
6. E. E. Sterns, "The Street Vendors of New York," *Scribner's Monthly* (December 1870) 1:115.
7. New York *Times*, October 8, 1882, May 10, 1883, July 25, 1883; William H. Riding, "How New York is Fed," *Scribner's Monthly*, (October 1877), 14:738–739; George Filipetti, "The Wholesale Markets," in *Regional Survey of New York and Its Environs*, 8 vols. (New York, 1924–1928), 1-b:31, 36–37.
8. New York City Pushcart Commission, *Report of the Mayor's Pushcart Commission*, pp. 138–139.
9. United States Agricultural Economics Bureau, *Push Cart Markets in New York City* (Washington, D. C., 1925), p. 2.
10. New York City Pushcart Commission, *Report of the Mayor's Pushcart Commission*, pp. 39, 85; Agricultural Economics Bureau, *Push Cart Markets*, pp. 35–36.
11. New York City Pushcarts and Markets Committee (Gaynor Commission), "Report and Recommendations," *New York City, City Record* (April 1913), 41:3763.
12. *New York Times*, October 5, 1884.
13. Maria Parloa, "A Practical Family Provider, Chapter 7: A Morning Visit to the Market Stalls," *Good Housekeeping* (July 1893), 17:1.
14. Agricultural Economics Bureau, *Push Cart Markets*, p. 42.
15. Godfrey M. Lebhar, *Chain Stores in America, 1859–1962* (New York, 1963), p. 31; Einar Bjorklund and James L. Palmer, *A Study of the Prices of Chain and Independent Grocers in Chicago* (Chicago, 1930), pp. vli, 54–55 (published as vol. 1, no. 4 of the University of Chicago Studies in Business Administration); Clyde Lyndon King, "Can the Cost of Distributing Food Products Be Reduced?" *Annals of the American Academy of Political and Social Science* (July 1913), 48:210; Community Service Society Papers, Columbia University Libraries, Rare Books and Manuscripts Collections, "The Food Investigation: Some Reasons and Results" (October, 1913), pp. 4–9; Agricultural Economics Bureau, *Push Cart Markets*, p. 12.
16. *New York Tribune*, August 5, 1900.

12. Jewish Street Merchants

17. Archibald A. Hill, "The Pushcart Peddlers of New York," *Independent* (October 18, 1906), 61:920–921.

18. Agricultural Economics Bureau, *Push Cart Markets*, pp. 35–36.

19. Louis Borgenicht, *The Happiest Man: The Life of Louis Borgenicht* (New York, 1942), p. 197.

20. *New York Tribune*, September 15, 1898, reprinted in Allon Schoener, ed., *Portal to America: The Lower East Side, 1870–1925* (New York, 1967), pp. 58–59.

21. Rudolph Glanz, *Studies in Judaica Americana* (New York, 1970), pp. 105, 120–121; Richardson Wright, *Hawkers and Walkers in Early America* (New York, 1965), p. 93, originally published in 1927.

22. Thomas Sowell, *Markets and Minorities* (New York, 1981), p. 81.

23. See ch. 62, "Concerning Commerce," in Rabbi Solomon Ganzfried, ed., *Code of Jewish Law* (New York, 1963), part 2, pp. 36–37.

24. Joseph, *Jewish Immigration*, pp. 45–46; Leo Errera, *The Russian Jews: Extermination or Emancipation?* (London, 1894), p. 173.

25. Isaac M. Rubinow, *Economic Condition of the Jews in Russia* (New York, 1975), p. 561. This volume is a reprint of the 1907 edition.

26. *Yiddishes Tageblatt*, March 20, 1910.

27. New York *Forward*, March 2, 1906, September 9, 1909.

28. Frank Moss, *American Metropolis: The New York City Life*, 3 vols. (New York, 1897) 3:200–201.

29. Bureau of Agricultural Economics, *Push Cart Markets*, p. 16; New York City Pushcart Commission, *Report of the Mayor's Pushcart Commission*, pp. 115–116; *Jewish Daily News (Yiddishes Tageblatt)*, March 20, 1904.

30. New York City Pushcart Commission, *Report of the Mayor's Pushcart Commission*, pp. 227–228.

31. Hill, "Pushcart Peddlers of New York," p. 915.

32. "Merchandising on Wheels in New York's 'Little Italy,' " *Hardware Age* (June 11, 1914), 93:60.

33. See the advertisement for Horn, Sachar, and Co., 86–88 Forsyth Street, in the *Yiddishes Tageblatt*, November 29, 1900.

34. *Ibid.*, February 2, 1900.

35. Marie Jastrow, *A Time to Remember: Growing Up in New York Before the Great War* (New York, 1979), p. 90.

36. "Merchandising on Wheels," *Hardware Age* (June 11, 1914), 93:58.

37. *Yiddishes Tageblatt*, December 9, 1903.

13. A Jewish Monument to the Masses: Marketing the American Film

1. Charles Garrett, *The LaGuardia Years: Machine and Reform Politics in New York City* (New Brunswick, N. J., 1961), 182.

2. Joseph P. Kennedy, ed., *The Story of the Films* (New York, 1927), p. x.

3. Robert C. Allen, "Motion Picture Exhibition in Manhattan, 1906–1912:

Beyond the Nickleodeon," in John L. Fell, ed., *Film Before Griffith* (Berkeley, 1983), pp. 165–168.

4. An account of the Bingham incident is given by Arthur A. Goren, *New York Jews and the Quest for Community: The Kehillah Experiment, 1908–1922* (New York, 1970), pp. 25–37.

5. Patricia Erens, *The Jew in American Cinema* (Bloomington, Indiana, 1984), pp. 30–32.

6. New York *Yiddishes Tageblatt*, September 1, 1907.

7. *Upton Sinclair Presents William Fox* (Los Angeles, 1933), p. 36; Bosley Crowther, *The Lion's Share* (New York, 1985), pp. 30–31, part of the Cinema Classics series, this volume is a reprint of the original 1957 edition; Will Irwin, *The House That Shadows Built: The Story of Adolph Zukor and His Circle* (Garden City, N.Y., 1928), p. 5.

8. Carrie Balaban, *Continuous Performance: The Story of A. J. Balaban* (New York, 1942), p. 33.

9. Benjamin B. Hampton, *A History of the Movies* (New York, 1931), pp. 64–82.

10. *Ibid.*, pp. 105–106; Lewis Jacobs, *The Rise of the American Film: A Critical History* (New York, 1939), pp. 115–116; Kemp R. Niver, *The First Twenty Years: A Segment of Film History* (Los Angeles, 1968), p. 163.

11. Adolph Zukor (with Dale Kramer), *The Public Is Never Wrong* (New York, 1953), p. 42.

12. The article is reproduced in Joseph Csida and June Bundy Csida, *American Entertainment: A Unique History of Popular Show Business* (New York, 1978), p. 193.

13. W. Stephen Bush, "The Prisoner of Zenda: Remarkable Four Part Production by the Famous Players' Film Company," *Moving Picture World* (March 1, 1913), 15:871.

14. Gorham Kindem, "Hollywood's Movie Star System: A Historical Overview," in Gorham Kindem, ed., *The American Movie Industry* (Carbondale, Ill., 1982), pp. 80–81; John Drinkwater, *The Life and Adventures of Carl Laemmle* (New York, 1931), pp. 139–142.

15. Jacobs, *Rise of the American Film*, p. 162.

16. See the advertisement in *Moving Picture World* (July 15, 1916), 29: 363–365.

17. Zukor, *Public is Never Wrong*, pp. 39–40.

18. Marcus Loew, "The Motion Picture and Vaudeville," in Kennedy, *Story of Films*, p. 288.

19. Robert Grau, *The Theatre of Science* (n.p., 1914), p. 19.

20. *Upton Sinclair Presents William Fox*, p. 46.

21. "Dewey Theatre," *Variety* (December 19, 1908), 13:13.

22. *New York Times*, January 14, 1936; Glendon Allvine, *The Greatest Fox of Them All* (New York, 1969), pp. 108–109.

23. Samuel L. Rothapfel, "Dignity of the Exhibitor's Profession," *Moving Picture World* (February 26, 1910), 6:289.

13. Marketing the American Film

3. Marketing the American Film

24. James S. McQuade, "The Belasco of Motion Picture Presentations," *ibid.* (December 9, 1911), 10:796.

25. James S. McQuade, "Staging the Passion Play," *ibid.* (December 30, 1911), p. 1055.

26. David Naylor, *American Picture Palaces: The Architecture of Fantasy* (New York, 1981), p. 40.

27. W. Stephen Bush, "The Theatre of Realization," *Moving Picture World* (November 15, 1913), 18:714.

28. W. Stephen Bush, "Opening of the Strand," *ibid.* (April 25, 1914), 20:502.

29. The description of the Strand's design is based on "A Theatre with Four Million Patrons a Year," *Photoplay Magazine* (April, 1915), 7:84.

30. W. Stephen Bush, "Opening of the Strand," *Moving Picture World* (April 18, 1914), 20:371.

31. James S. McQuade, "The Spoilers," *ibid.* (April 3, 1914), p. 186, reproduced in Kalton C. Lahue, ed., *Motion Picture Pioneer: The Selig Polyscope Company* (New York, 1973), p. 191.

32. Bush, "Opening the Strand," *Moving Picture World* (April 25, 1914), p. 502.

Bibliographical Essay

There are many sources that shed light on Jewish life in the American city and on American patterns of consumption, but the following essay does not aim to list them. In this discussion of documents and texts, I will simply indicate the lines of research that I found most useful in exploring how eastern European Jews responded to the prospect of American abundance. Readers are encouraged to look at the chapter notes for a larger listing of the primary sources and the scholarly literature that have enriched my understanding of the topic.

Journalism

The Yiddish press provided the coverage of daily life in New York City without which a study on consumption among Jews could not have been undertaken. During the first decade and a half of the twentieth century, the competition between Abraham Cahan's *Forward* and Kasriel Sarasohn's *Yiddishes Tageblatt* produced a good number of feature articles on the ways of Jewish consumers, particularly the pursuit of the vogue, that enabled readers to muse over the zealousness with which they identified themselves as urban Americans.

Newspaper stories written in English enlarged the documentary base of this study. Between 1897 and 1907, the *Tageblatt* published an English page, the *Jewish Daily News*, containing valuable feature articles and commentaries on Jewish life in the city. The "East Side Observer" columns on the *Jewish Daily News* page were particularly useful. Of the metropolitan dailies, the *New York Tribune* proved to be a consistent, thorough, and usually sympathetic reporter on the city's booming population of Jewish immigrants. A good index makes this newspaper enjoyable to use. Two excellent anthologies of articles on Jewish New York, taken from the metropolitan press, are Allon Schoener, ed., *Portal to America: The Lower East Side, 1870–1925* (New York, 1967) and Moses Rischin, ed., *Grandma Never Lived in America: The New Journalism of Abraham Cahan* (Bloomington, Ind., 1985).

Three intimate accounts of the Jewish Lower East Side by leading journalists provided a valuable background for my inquiry into the causes and consequences of modern consumption among the immigrants: the abrupt but informative report of Jacob A. Riis, *How the Other Half Lives* (New York, 1957), which was first published in 1890; the poetic overview of Hutchins Hapgood, *The Spirit of the Ghetto* (Cambridge, Mass., 1967), which appeared originally as a series of magazine articles between 1898 and 1902; and the compelling chapter on the disintegration of traditional Judaism in Ray Stannard Baker, *The Spiritual Unrest* (New York, 1910), which was first published in the *American Magazine* during 1908 and 1909.

In addition to these journalistic accounts, the collection of reports on Jewish life in major American cities edited by Philadelphia social worker Charles S. Bernheimer, *Russian Jew in the United States* (Philadelphia, 1905), contains valuable information about domestic consumption.

Reminiscences

A handful of published autobiographies and recollections of life in New York City around the turn of the century helped me to understand the emotional and psychological impact of American habits of consumption upon eastern European Jews. Marcus Ravage, *An American in the Making* (New York, 1917), a lucid account of the journey of a Rumanian Jew into middle America, first inspired me to think that American abundance played a primary role in the psychic drama of Jewish immigration. Elizabeth G. Stern, *My Mother and I* (New York, 1916) expanded my understanding of the role of Jewish women as managers of consumption in their households. The lure of luxuries, including that greatest luxury, a piano, in a struggling Jewish household, is depicted in the recollections of Samuel Chotzinoff, *A Lost Paradise* (New York, 1955). Louis Borgenicht, *The Happiest Man: The Life of Louis Borgenicht* (New York, 1942) manifested the connection between the lush environment of consumption in the American city and the trading impulse that motivated so many Jewish immigrants.

Translated and edited by Leon Stein, Abraham P. Conan, and Lynn Davison under the title *The Education of Abraham Cahan* (Philadelphia, 1969), the first two volumes of Abraham Cahan's five-volume Yiddish autobiography, *Bleter Fun Mayn Leben, (Leaves from My Life)* (New York, 1926–1931) are rich in insights about Jewish adjustment to America that shed light on the prevailing attitude toward the American standard of living. In his fiction, Abraham Cahan created

Bibliographical Essay

for the English-speaking public a mosaic of American Jewish life around the turn of the century. Between the novella and short stories contained in *Yekl and the Imported Bridegroom and Other Stories of the New York Ghetto* (New York, 1970) and the seminal novel *The Rise of David Levinsky* (New York, 1960), few activities of Jewish newcomers as consumers are overlooked. The short stories originally appeared in 1896 and 1898, and *David Levinsky* was published in 1917.

Other valuable reminiscences shedding light on the relation between the material and spiritual worlds of the eastern European Jews include: Mary Antin, *The Promised Land* (Boston, 1969), first published in 1912; Miriam Blaustein, ed., *Memoirs of David Blaustein* (New York, 1913); Benjamin L. Gordon, *Between Two Worlds: The Memoirs of a Physician* (New York, 1952); Philip Cowen, *Memories of an American Jew* (New York, 1932); Marie Jastrow, *A Time to Remember: Growing Up in New York Before the Great War* (New York, 1979); Joachim Schoenfeld, *Shtetl Memoirs: Jewish Life in Galicia Under the Austro-Hungarian Empire and in the Reborn Poland, 1898–1939* (Hoboken, N.J., 1985).

Household Budget Studies

A range of evidence about urban Americans in general had to be explored in order to evaluate the social context into which eastern European Jews were placing themselves. The two most coherent bodies of information about urban consumption were studies of household budgets and magazine articles about the cost of living.

Our potential for understanding daily life during the late nineteenth and early twentieth centuries has been enlarged by the professional studies of the budgets of wage-earning families that began to appear after the 1870s. The government reports comprising the bulk of this literature have been cited by historian Jeffrey Williamson as the richest "quantitative legacy in American history." Williamson provides a good survey and bibliography in "Consumer Behavior in the Nineteenth Century: Carroll D. Wright's Massachusetts Workers in 1875," *Explorations in Entrepreneurial History*, 2d ser. (Winter 1967), 4:98–135.

The most illuminating studies of this kind are those that enrich the statistical evidence with commentary on the attitudes of city people toward the spending of hard-earned money. Social workers in New York City left an excellent literature on wage earners as consumers during the first decade of the new century. I found Louise Bolard More, *Wage-Earners' Budgets: Study of Standards and Cost of Living in New York* (New York, 1907) to be, by far, the most valuable of these studies. Striking a rich balance between raw data and careful interpretation, this comprehensive analysis of two hundred households on the lower West Side conveys the rhythm of getting and spending in a fairly representative population of urban people.

Robert Coit Chapin, *The Standard of Living Among Workingmen's Families in New York City* (New York, 1909) is also a useful survey of a large sample of New Yorkers, although the method of obtaining budgets left the households under review without any cohesive principle, such as that of More's West Side neighborhood, within which to evaluate the individual cases. Readers should be aware, as well, that Chapin's judgment on the adequacy of the urban diet is skewed by outdated information on nutrition that exaggerated the daily requirement for protein.

The geographical scope and the insightful commentary on American conditions and habits make the *Report on the Cost of Living in American Towns* (London, 1911) authorized by the British Board of Trade, an important study. The volume contains a multifaceted comparison of diets and food prices between American and English workers, among American ethnic groups, and among various cities in the United States.

A good synopsis of the contemporary literature and additional commentary is furnished by the *Report on the Cost of Living for an Unskilled Laborer's Family in New York City* (New York, 1915), prepared by the city's Bureau of Standards in conjunction with the Bureau of Municipal Research. I also profited from an examination of the household budgets of manual laborers in New York City that are contained in the collection of Community Service Society Papers, kept with the Rare Books and Manuscripts Collections at Columbia University.

Students of urban consumption should consult the valuable *Civic Bibliography for Greater New York* (New York, 1911), which was sponsored by the Russell Sage Foundation and edited by James Bronson Reynolds.

Articles on the Cost and Standard of Living

In the early stages of this study, I wandered through what seemed a wilderness of magazine articles on the cost of living in America between 1890 and 1914. Led by the *Readers Guide to Periodical Literature*, I was impressed not only by the number of articles on consumption that appeared after the depression of the 1890s, but, more significantly, by the pressure toward a more affluent lifestyle that helped to inflate prices for some products and that led people to see the comparatively modest inflation of the time as an urgent social problem.

As a glance at the categories "Cost of Living" and "Standard of Living" in the *Readers Guide* will indicate, many magazines considered the economic, social, and moral sides of urban consumption during the Progressive Era. Symposia on the cost of living were held during the spring and summer of 1910 in *Cosmopolitan*, *Independent*, and *Journal of Political Economy*, and in July 1913 in the *Annals of the American Academy of Political and Social Science*. I found the collection of articles in *Charities* (1906–1908) and that in the *American Magazine* (1907–1910) to be illustrative of how different groups of urban consumers thought and acted. The inevitable monotony of research would have been alleviated if there had been more satires like Finley Peter Dunne's "Mr. Dooley on the Cost of Living," which appeared in the January 1910 issue of *American Magazine*.

The sudden increase in the price of kosher meat in May 1902 sparked a newsmaking boycott on the part of Jewish women in New York City. Although this event, and similar demonstrations that occurred in the following years in New York and other cities, were not treated in this study, they may be examined within the larger context of popular anxiety about the standard of living at the time. Accounts of the boycotts are cited by Paula E. Hyman, "Immigrant Women and Consumer Protest: The New York City Kosher Meat Boycott of 1902," *American Jewish History* (September 1980), vol. 52.

Two statistical studies focusing on the standard of living around the turn of the century are Peter Shergold, *Working Class Life: The "American Standard" in Comparative Perspective, 1899–1913* (Pittsburgh, 1982) and F. H. Early, "French Canadian Economy and Standard of Living in Lowell," *Journal of Family History* (Summer 1982), 7:180–199.

Advertising

Without a sense of the prevailing trends in American advertising, I would have had difficulty interpreting the advertisements that leapt out of the pages of the major Yiddish newspapers. Having already been impressed by the colloquial style that seemed to permeate the advertisements I had seen in American newspapers and magazines, and in the early editions of the Sears, Roebuck catalogue, I set out to gain a better understanding of "salesmanship in print" by turning to the trade journals *Printer's Ink*, which began in 1888, and *Advertising and Selling*, which developed out of *Profitable Advertising*, founded in 1891. These periodicals were full of details about the modern approach to marketing.

My awareness of the distinctive style of American advertising sharpened as I read through the chronicles left behind by a trailblazing generation of advertising agents. Frank Presbrey, *The History and Development of Advertising* (Garden City, N.Y., 1929), Joseph H. Appel, *Growing Up with Advertising* (New York, 1940), and Claude C. Hopkins, *My Life in Advertising* (New York, 1927) were particularly helpful.

Histories of companies that pioneered in the development of modern advertising conveyed the element of personal dynamism that infused the most successful promotional campaigns. Insight into the marketing strategies that made the Uneeda Biscuit, Ivory Soap and Crisco, Quaker Oats, and Metropolitan Life household words in Yiddish—as well as English—can be gained from William Cahn, *Out of the Cracker Barrel: The Nabisco Story from Animal Crackers to ZuZus* (New York, 1969), William G. Panschar, *Baking in America* (Evanston, Ill., 1956), Alfred Lief, *It Floats: The Story of Procter and Gamble* (New York, 1958), Harrison John Thornton, *The History of the Quaker Oats Company* (Chicago, 1933), Richard Ellsworth Day, *Breakfast Table Autocrat: The Life Story of Henry Parsons Crowell* (Chicago, 1946), Gerald Carson, *Cornflake Crusade* (New York, 1957), and Marquis James, *The Metropolitan Life: A Study in Business Growth* (New York, 1947). Although not exhaustive, this list includes some fine examples of business history, a field that has not received as much attention in recent decades as it deserves.

Two indispensable guides to sources in the history of American marketing are

Bibliographical Essay

Henrietta M. Larson, *Guide to Business History* (Cambridge, Mass., 1948) and John N. Ingham, ed., *Biographical Dictionary of American Business Leaders*, 5 vols. (Westport, Conn., 1983).

Stimulating interpretations of the distinctive qualities of American advertising can be found within the pages of David M. Potter, *People of Plenty: Economic Abundance and the American Character* (Chicago, 1966), first published in 1954, and Daniel J. Boorstin, *The Image: A Guide to Pseudo-Events in America* (New York, 1972). Scholarly treatments of the economic and institutional dimension of American advertising prior to World War I are Ralph M. Hower, *The History of an Advertising Agency: N. W. Ayer and Son at Work, 1869–1949* (Cambridge, Mass., 1949) and Daniel Pope, *The Making of Modern Advertising* (New York, 1983).

Street Marketing and Movie Showing

Although the involvement of Jews in the development of street marketing and in the evolution of the modern American film was decisive, the amount of literature in the two areas varies to an extreme. Two official studies of street marketing in New York City form a large part of the foundation on which my analysis rests. The *Report of the Mayor's Pushcart Commission* (New York, 1906) and the federal study of *Push Cart Markets in New York City* (Washington, D.C., 1925) undertaken by the Agricultural Economics Bureau provide vital statistics and commentary on the nature and progress of the occupation. Some early sources on Jewish street peddlers are cited and discussed in E. Tcherikower, ed., *Geshikhte fun der Yidisher Arbeter-Bavegung in di Fareynikte Shtatn*, 2 vols. (New York, 1943–1945), pp. 235–253. In addition, the study by George Filipetti on the wholesale markets of the city, which is part of volume 1B of the *Regional Survey of New York and Its Environs*, 8 vols. (New York, 1924–1928), furnished important geographical and historical information.

Whereas street marketing has often been overlooked by historians, the moving picture industry has been honored with many volumes. Yet, considering the outstanding role of Jews in the business, the dearth of scholarship on the founding fathers of the leading American studios is surprising.

I found Adolph Zukor's autobiography, *The Public Is Never Wrong*, written with Dale Kramer (New York, 1953) to be a good starting point, particularly when followed up with newspaperman Will Irwin's *The House That Shadows Built: The Story of Adolph Zukor and His Circle* (Garden City, N.Y. 1928), the first interpretive work to recognize the unique role of Jewish entrepreneurs in the creation of "the first universal language of mankind" (p. 243). Bosley Crowther gives what appears to be a well-researched chronicle of the rise of several Jewish film magnates in *The Lion's Share* (New York, 1985), first published in 1957, which is one of the few reliable sources on the career of Marcus Loew as an exhibitor before World War I. Insight into the social and psychological background of the Jewish role in creating the picture palace may be obtained from the memoirs of

Bibliographical Essay

A. J. Balaban, which were faithfully and well rendered by his wife Carrie Balaban, *Continuous Performance: The Story of A. J. Balaban* (New York, 1942).

Six Jewish movie men—Adolph Zukor, Jesse Lasky, William Fox, Marcus Loew, Samuel Katz, and Harry Warner—explained some of the approach to marketing, and ultimately producing, film that distinguished the group as a whole in a symposium held at the Harvard Business School in March and April 1926. Their talks were published in Joseph P. Kennedy, ed., *The Story of The Films* (New York, 1927).

A sense of the personalities of most of the Jewish movie magnates is provided by Neal Gabler, *An Empire of Their Own: How the Jews Invented Hollywood* (New York, 1988), Norman Zierold, *The Moguls* (New York, 1969), and Philip French, *The Movie Moguls* (Chicago, 1969). Lary L. May and Elaine Tyler May consider some explanations for the superlative success of the Jewish film pioneers in "Why Jewish Movie Moguls: An Exploration in American Culture," *American Jewish History* (September 1982), 72:7–25.

Two scholarly histories focusing on the content of films in relationship to Jews are Lester D. Friedman, *Hollywood's Image of the Jew* (New York, 1982) and Patricia Erens, *The Jew in American Cinema* (Bloomington, Ind., 1984).

Indispensable background for the American movie business during the first two decades of its existence has been provided by three substantial histories: Terry Ramsaye, *A Million and One Nights: A History of the Motion Picture*, 2 vols. (New York, 1926), Benjamin B. Hampton, *A History of the Movies* (New York, 1931), and Louis Jacobs, *The Rise of the American Film: A Critical History* (New York, 1939).

A gold mine of references to the periodical literature on the early moving picture industry exists in the form of *The Film Index: A Bibliography*, 3 vols. (vol. 1, New York, 1941; vols. 2–3, White Plains, N.Y. 1985), which was largely compiled between 1935 and 1940 by workers in the writers' program of the Works Progress Administration. *The Film as Industry*, vol. 2, referred me to many important articles on the Jewish film entrepreneurs. I also made extensive use of George Rehrauer, ed., *The Macmillan Film Bibliography*, 2 vols. (New York, 1982).

General Works of History and Theory

A number of historians have established the foundation of knowledge that supported my inquiry into the relationship of Jewish immigration and mass consumption in the United States.

David Potter's bold effort to link material abundance to the American national character, *People of Plenty*, cited above, made a large and lasting impression upon me. Potter's analysis of *Freedom and Its Limitations in American Life* (Stanford, Calif., 1976), published posthumously under the editorship of Don E. Fehrenbacher, enriched my understanding of how a remarkably diverse people attained a remarkable degree of conformity in the sphere of consumption. Potter's cultural interpretations hark back to the outstanding commentary on America written by Alexis de Tocqueville, *Democracy in America* (published in two parts, 1835 and 1840), a volume that anchored my sense of the overwhelming impact that democratic aspirations have had upon the development of American urban culture.

My specific interest in linking mass consumption to Jewish immigration led me continually back to two authoritative works of American history. The painstaking research and balanced perspective of Moses Rischin, *The Promised City: New York's Jews, 1870–1914* (Cambridge, Mass., 1962) have made this book an essential guide to students of the eastern European immigration. The scholarly breadth and conceptual rigor of Gunther Barth, *City People: The Rise of Modern City Culture in Nineteenth-Century America* (New York, 1980) have paved the way for anyone interested in assessing American urban culture, particularly with an eye to mass consumption, during the late nineteenth century.

Other valuable sources of information on the topic of urban consumption in this period are Chauncey M. Depew, ed., *1795–1895, One Hundred Years of American Commerce*, 2 vols. (New York, 1895), Arthur Meier Schlesinger, *The Rise of the City, 1878–1898* (New York, 1933), Daniel J. Boorstin, *The Americans: The Democratic Experience* (New York, 1974), Claudia Kidwell and Margaret Christman, *Suiting Everyone: The Democratization of Clothing in America* (Washington, D. C., 1974), Margaret L. Brew, "American Clothing Consumption, 1879–1909," (Ph.D. thesis, University of Chicago, 1945), and Elizabeth Bacon, "The Growth of Household Conveniences in the United States, 1865–1900" (Ph.D. thesis, Radcliffe, 1942).

A fine synthesis and interpretation of the scholarly literature on American material culture has been made by Thomas J. Schlereth in the introduction to Thomas J. Schlereth, ed., *Material Culture Studies in America* (Nashville, 1982), 1–75.

Despite its focus on Europe, Fernand Braudel's *Capitalism and Material Life, 1400–1800* (New York, n.d.) has inspired students of American material life. That study originally appeared in 1967 as *Civilisation Matérielle et Capitalisme* and became available in English in the mid-1970s.

Although I did not attempt to digest the wide-ranging theoretical literature of the social sciences on the topic of consumption, a number of general studies helped me to see how the discipline of history compared with the distinctive perspectives of anthropology, sociology, and economics.

Grant McCracken, *Culture and Consumption: New Approaches to the Symbolic Character of Consumer Goods and Activities* (Bloomington, Ind., 1988) contains sophisticated summaries of research in the field of consumer studies, fresh insights into consumer behavior, and a very good though not exhaustive bibliography. Daniel Miller, *Material Culture and Mass Consumption* (Oxford, 1987) offers a thoughtful reappraisal of the conventional criticisms of mass consumption. Though not comprehensive, its bibliography covers most of the pertinent Marxist writings on the topic. W. T. Tucker, *Foundations for a Theory of Consumer Behavior* (New York, 1967) is now dated, but it may provide the newcomer to the field with a basic sense of the psychological, anthropological, sociological, and economic approaches to consumption.

Several studies by anthropologists have highlighted the connection between consumption and culture. A starting point is provided by Arjun Appadurai, ed., *The Social Life of Things: Commodities in Cultural Perspective* (Cambridge, 1986). Theodor H. Gaster, *The Holy and the Profane: Evolution of Jewish Folkways* (New York, 1980), first published in 1955, stresses the dynamic change in Jewish custom over time, in contrast to Mary Douglas, *Purity and Danger: An Analysis of Concepts of Pollution and Taboo* (New York, 1966), which offers a structuralist interpretation of the Jewish dietary code. Mary Douglas and Baron Isherwood, *The World of Goods* (New York, 1979) is an ambitious theoretical overview focusing on the centrality of consumption to the creation of culture in both traditional and modern societies. Margaret Mead, *And Keep Your Powder Dry: An Anthropologist Looks at America* (New York, 1942) examines American society in a way that permits reflection on the general attitude of Americans as consumers.

Sociologists have pinpointed some of the pitfalls of interpreting consumption hastily, in addition to making cogent observations on the relationship between social position and the conduct of consumers. Michael E. Sobel, *Lifestyle and Social Structure* (New York, 1981) concisely summarizes the prevailing sociological assessments of the relationship between consumption and social class and contributes his own insights on that theme for the post–World War II period. Herbert Gans, *Popular Culture and High Culture: An Analysis and Examination of Taste* (New York, 1974) constructs a fine critique of the trends in contemporary criticism of "mass culture," and develops a more subtle analysis of the relationship between socioeconomic position and consumer behavior than has usually been attempted. I was attracted also by the perspective of symbolic interactionism, with its emphasis on change and its sharp understanding of how social behavior is guided by people's subjective sense of their social position. See Herbert Blumer, "Society as Symbolic Interaction," in Jerome G. Manis and Bernard N. Meltzer, eds., *Symbolic Interaction: A Reader in Social Psychology* (Boston, 1967) and the rich introductory discussion in W. I. Thomas and Florian Znaniecki, *The Polish Peasant in Europe and America,* 5 vols. (Chicago, 1918–1920).

I was impressed by the effort of economists to go beyond old-fashioned models in which the consumer stands outside of culture. A fine summary of economic theories of consumption is given by Elizabeth W. Gilboy, *Economics of Consumption* (New York, 1968). A more recent bibliography of economists' writings on the topic of consumption is included in Peter Earl's critique of the orthodox model of the "rational" consumer, *Lifestyle Economics: Consumer Behaviour in a Turbulent World* (n.p., Great Britain, 1986). George Katona, Burkhard Strumpel, and Ernest Zahn, *Aspirations and Affluence* (New York, 1971) helped me to place the behavior of American consumers in comparative perspective.

My reflections on the nature of entrepreneurship were sharpened by the intelligent summary of dominant theories rendered by Mark Casson, *The Entrepreneur: An Economic Theory* (London, 1982), which also contains a good bibliography of scholarly writings on the subject.

Bibliographical Essay

In spite of its flaws, Thorstein Veblen, *The Theory of the Leisure Class* (1899) remains a fascinating theoretical critique of consumption in modern society. Veblen's concept of "conspicuous consumption" is analyzed by Roger S. Mason, *Conspicuous Consumption: A Study of Exceptional Consumer Behavior* (New York, 1981).

Index

Index

Index

Index

Index

Index